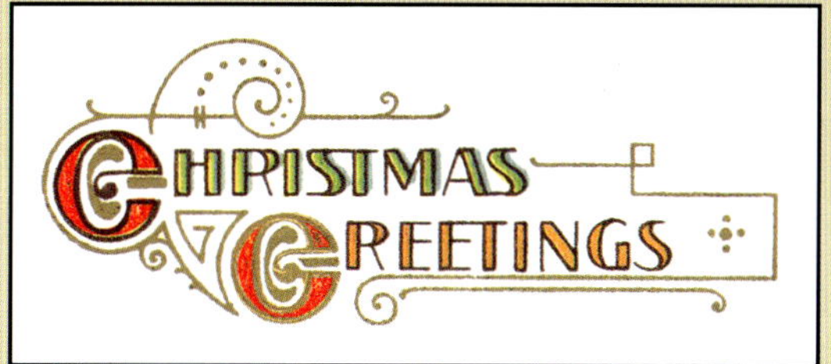
Christmas Greetings

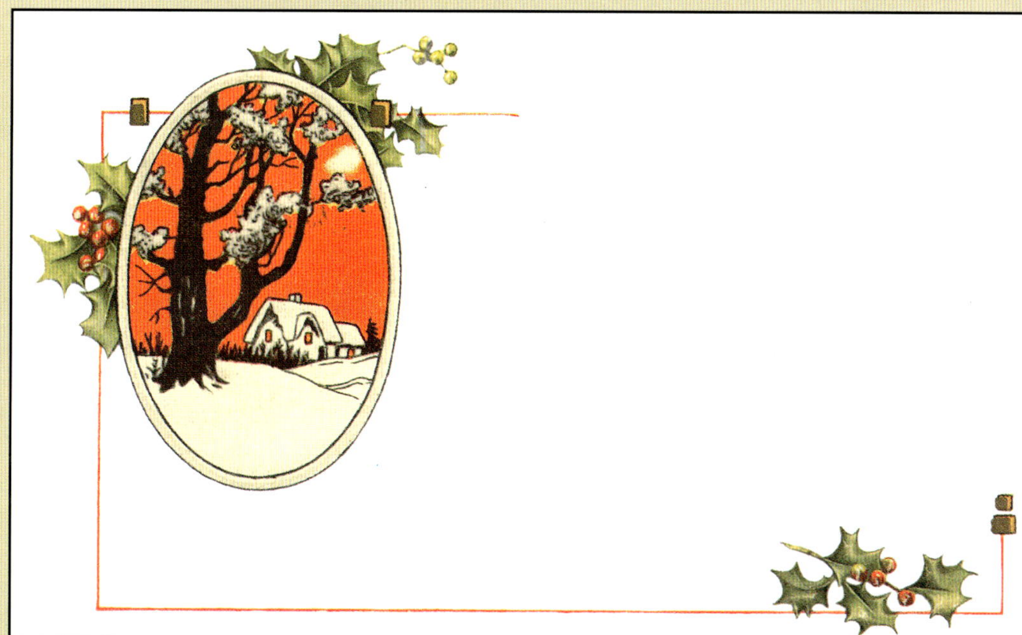

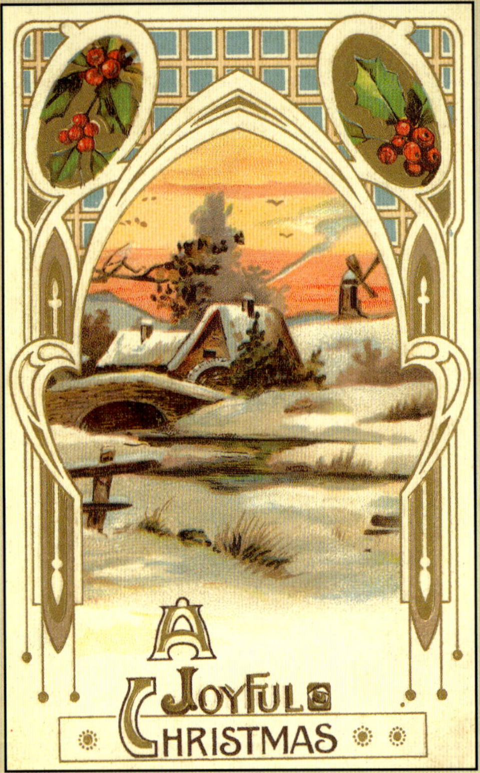
A Joyful
Christmas

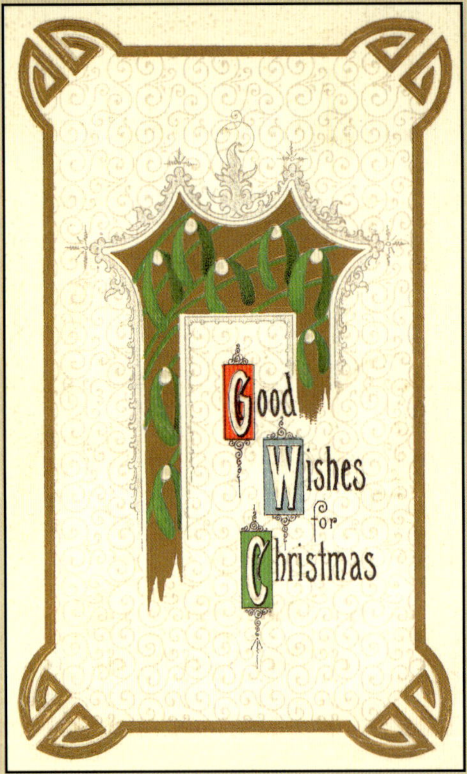
Good
Wishes
for
Christmas

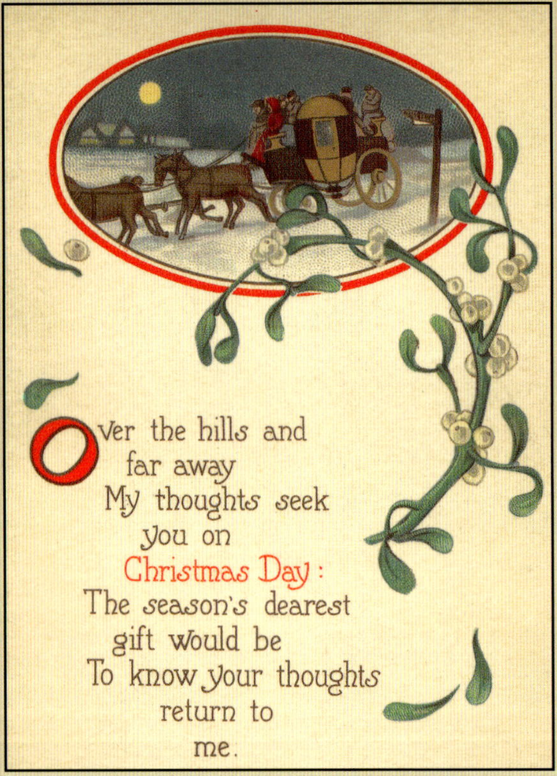
Over the hills and
far away
My thoughts seek
you on
Christmas Day:
The season's dearest
gift would be
To know your thoughts
return to
me.

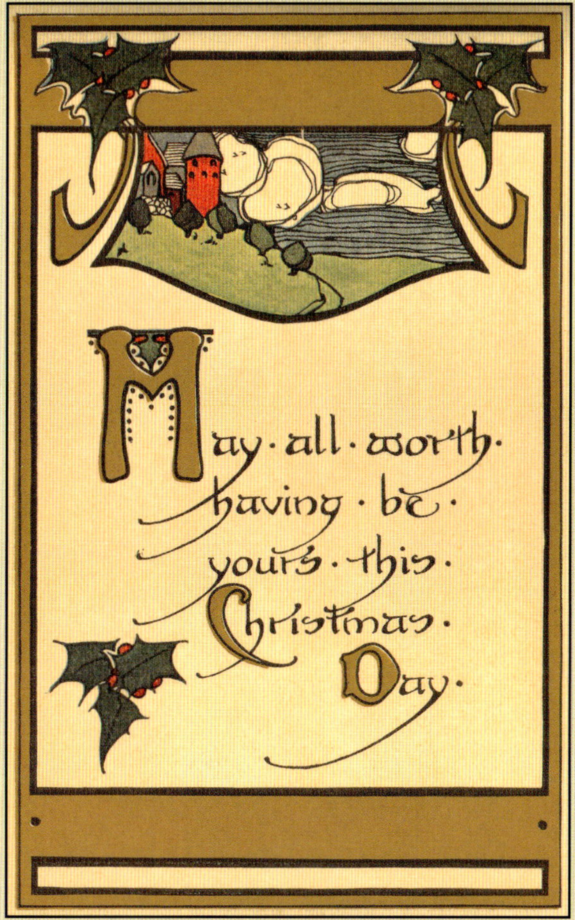
May · all · worth ·
having · be ·
yours · this ·
Christmas ·
Day ·

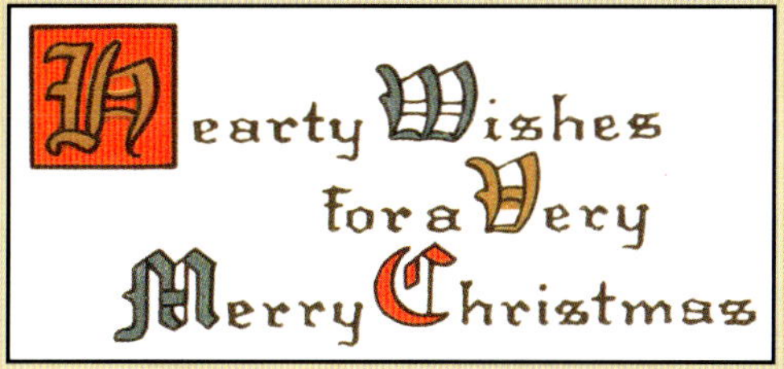
Hearty Wishes
for a Very
Merry Christmas

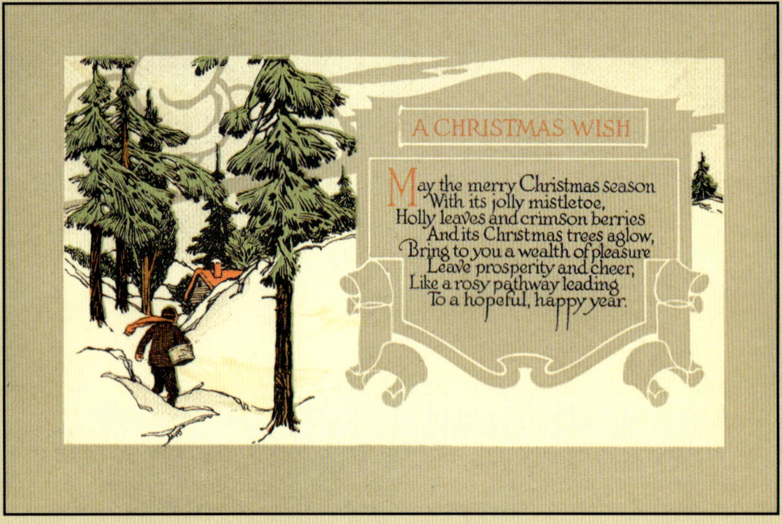
A CHRISTMAS WISH
May the merry Christmas season
With its jolly mistletoe,
Holly leaves and crimson berries
And its Christmas trees aglow,
Bring to you a wealth of pleasure
Leave prosperity and cheer,
Like a rosy pathway leading
To a hopeful, happy year.

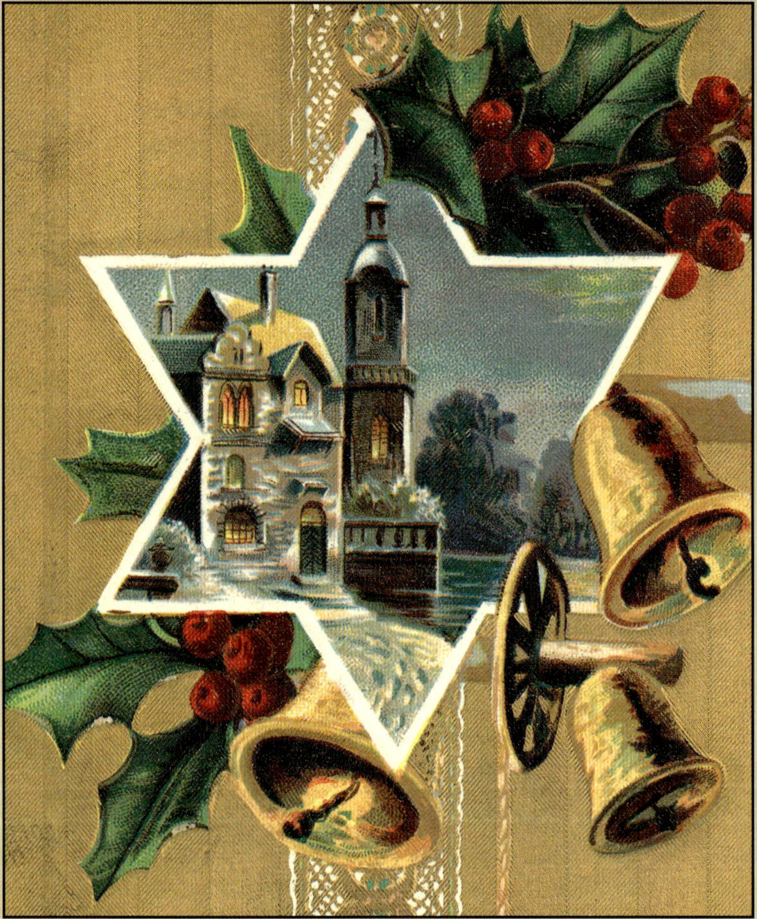

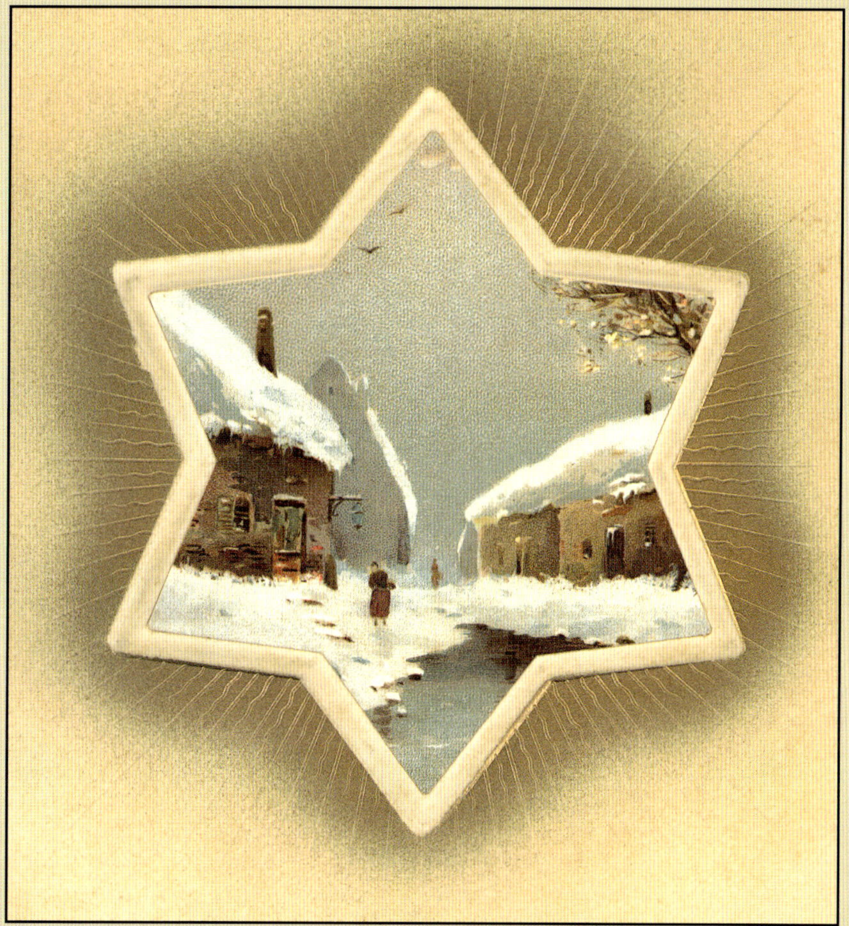

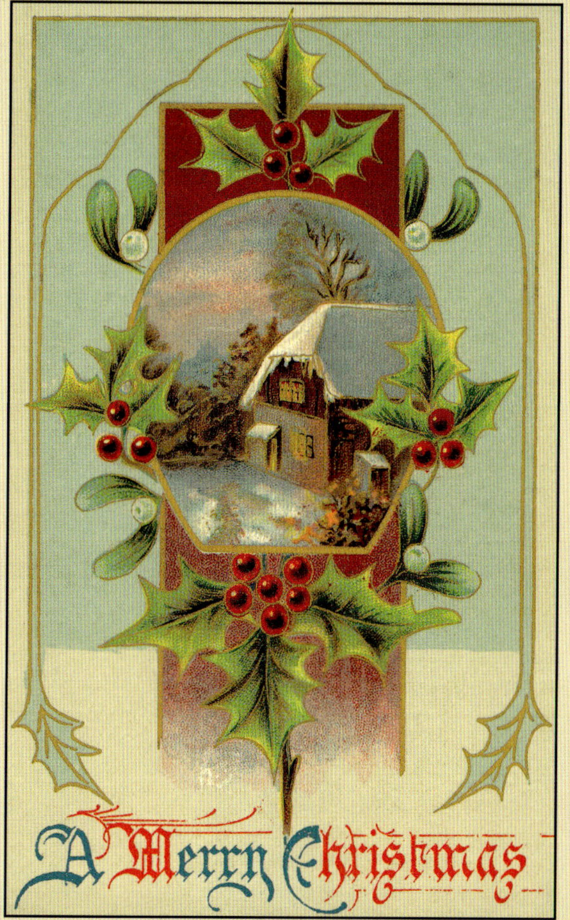
A Merry Christmas

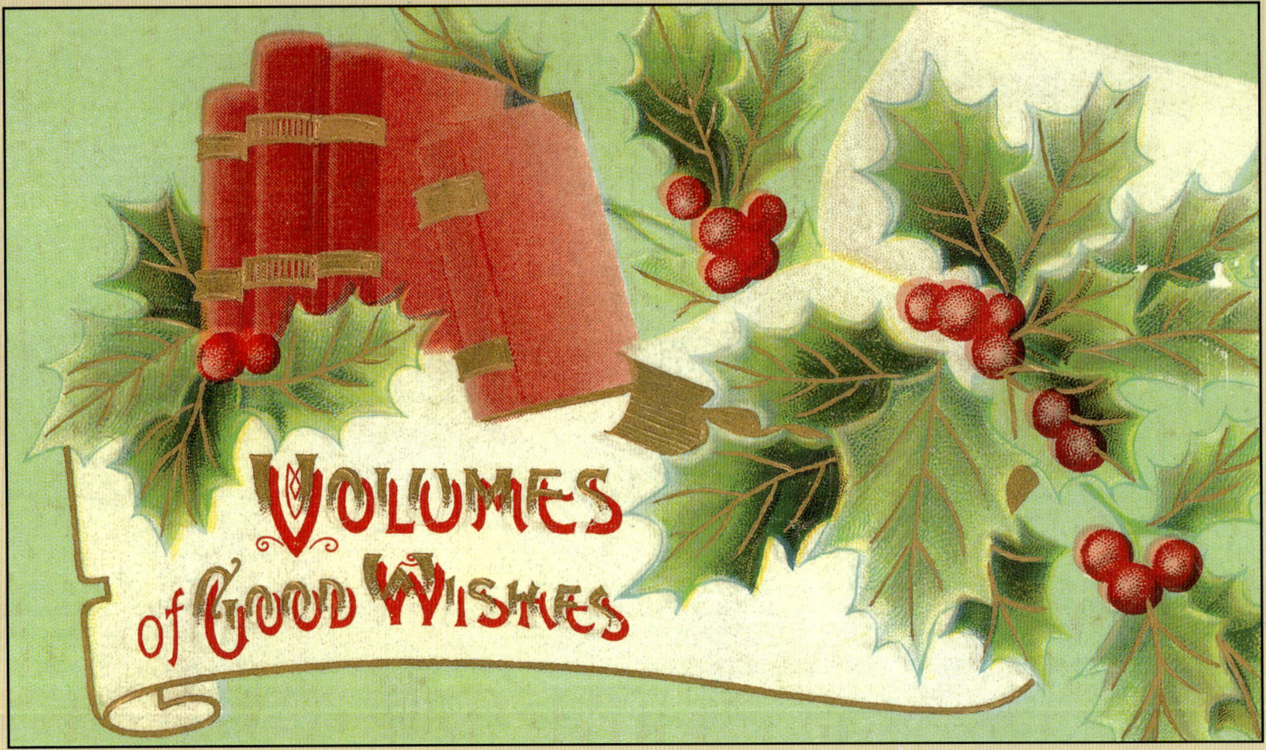
Volumes
of Good Wishes

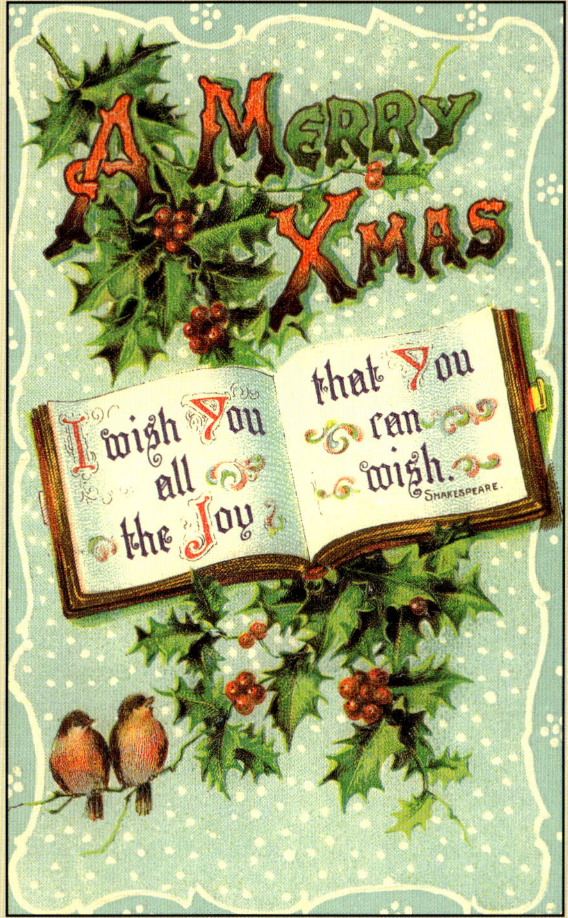
A Merry Xmas
I wish You all the Joy that You can wish.
Shakespeare.

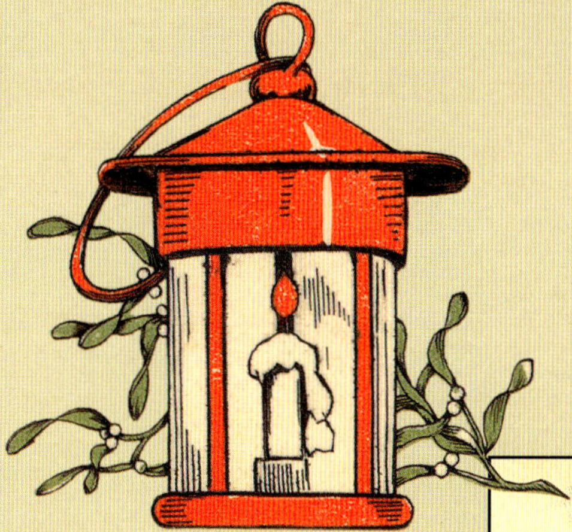

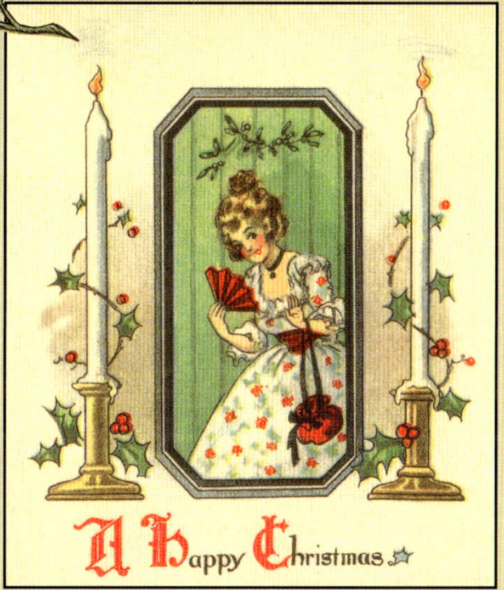
A Happy Christmas

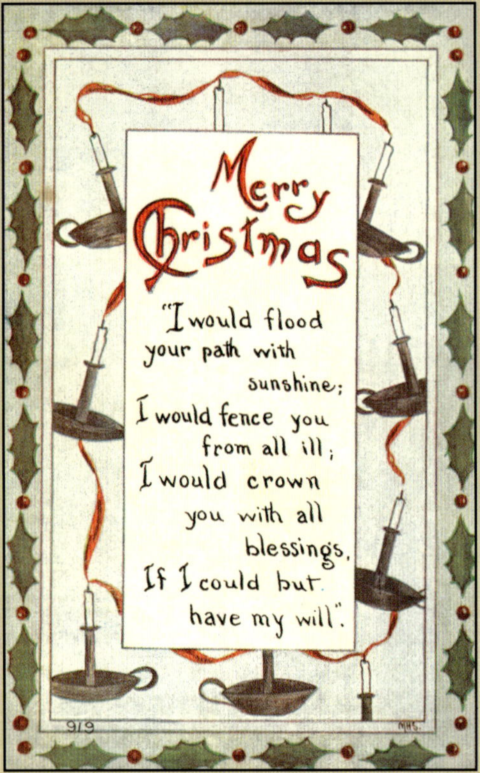
Merry Christmas
"I would flood your path with sunshine;
I would fence you from all ill;
I would crown you with all blessings,
If I could but have my will".
919
MHS.

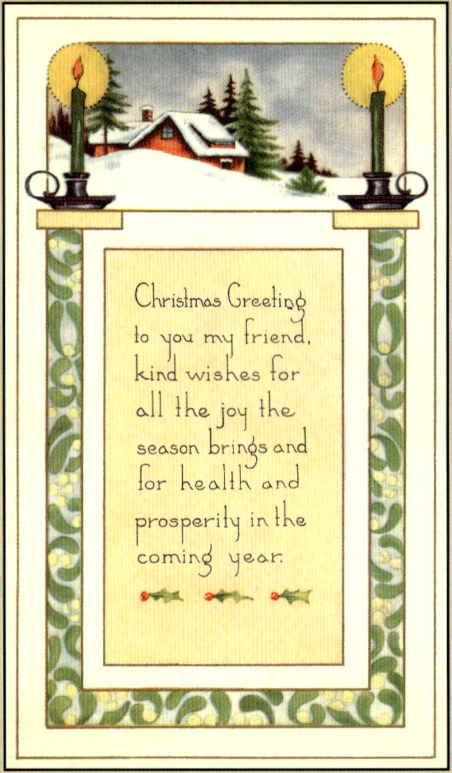
Christmas Greeting to you my friend, kind wishes for all the joy the season brings and for health and prosperity in the coming year.

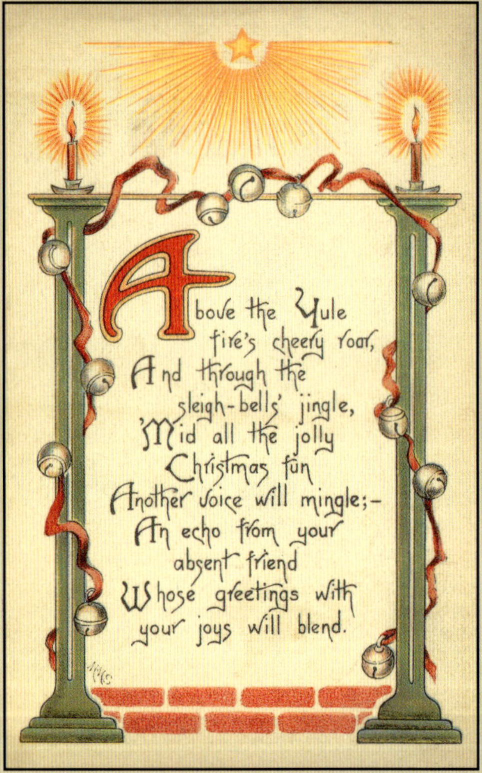
Above the Yule fire's cheery roar,
And through the sleigh-bells' jingle,
'Mid all the jolly Christmas fun
Another voice will mingle;-
An echo from your absent friend
Whose greetings with your joys will blend.

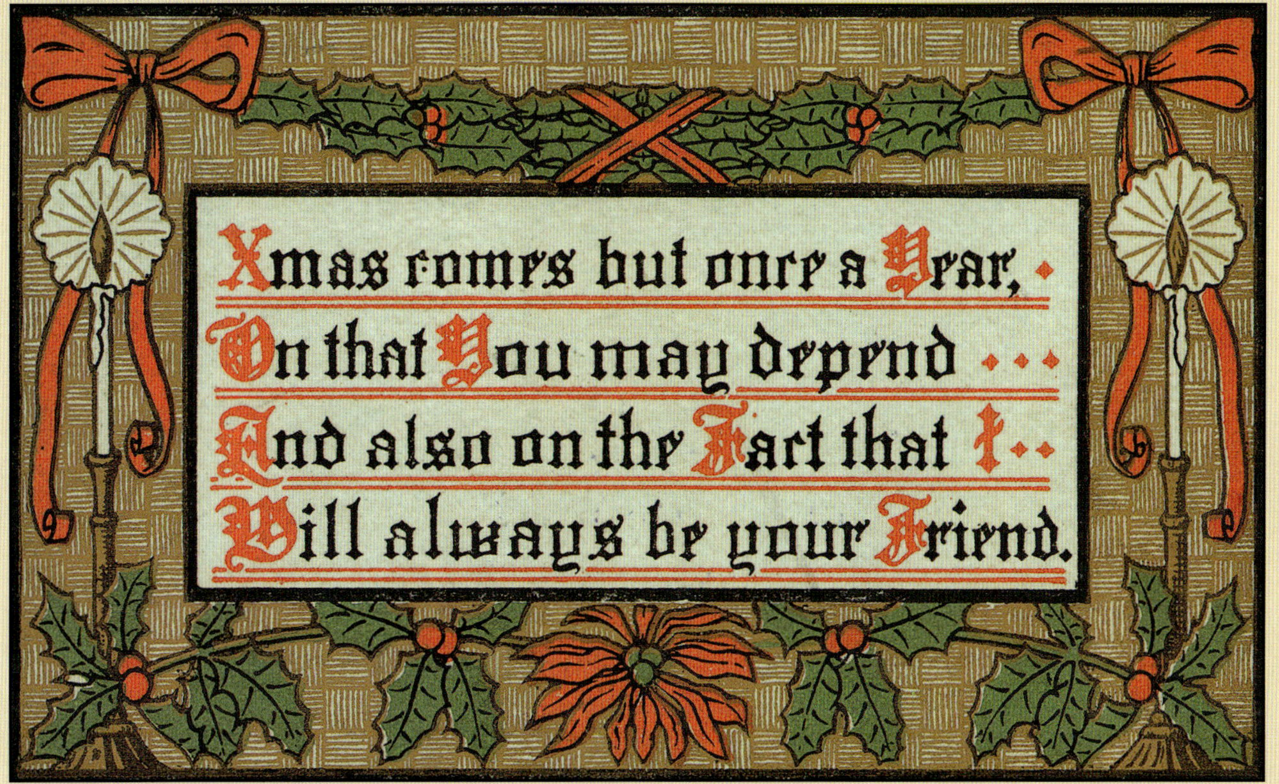
Xmas comes but once a Year,
On that You may depend
And also on the Fact that I
Will always be your Friend.

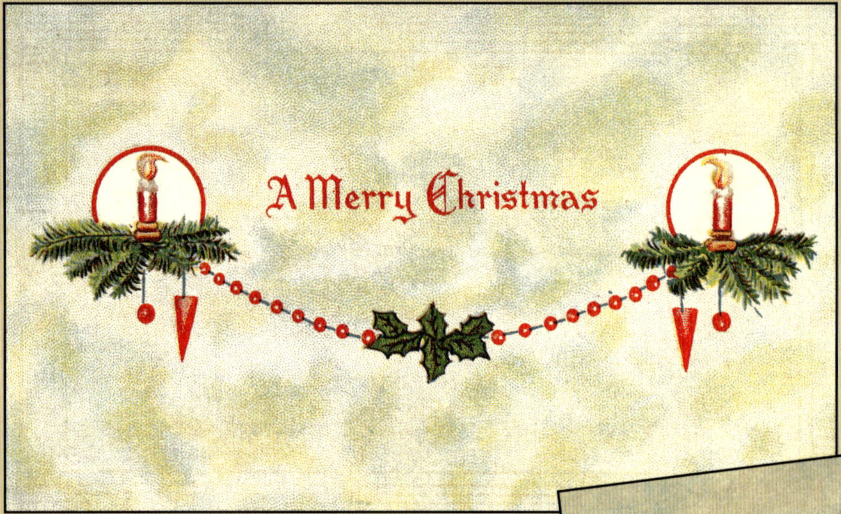
A Merry Christmas

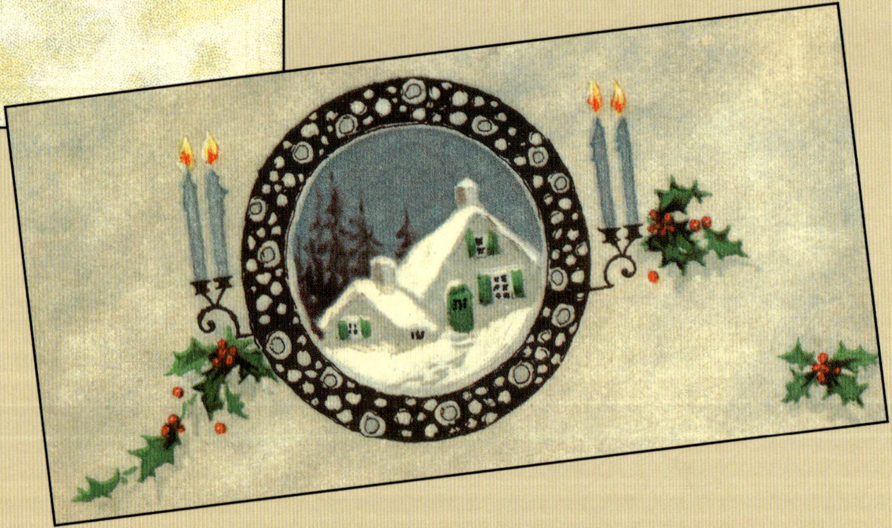

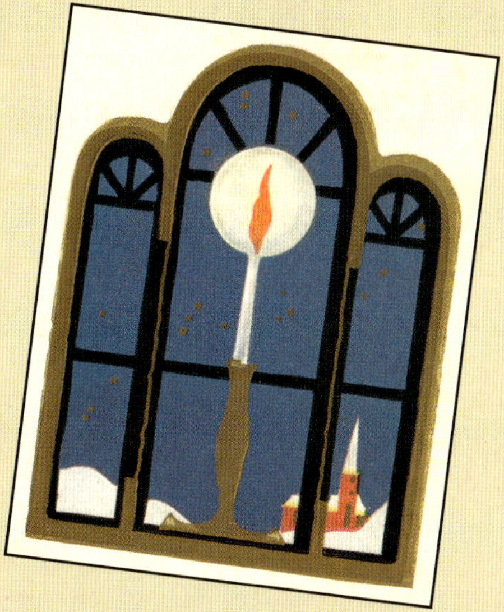

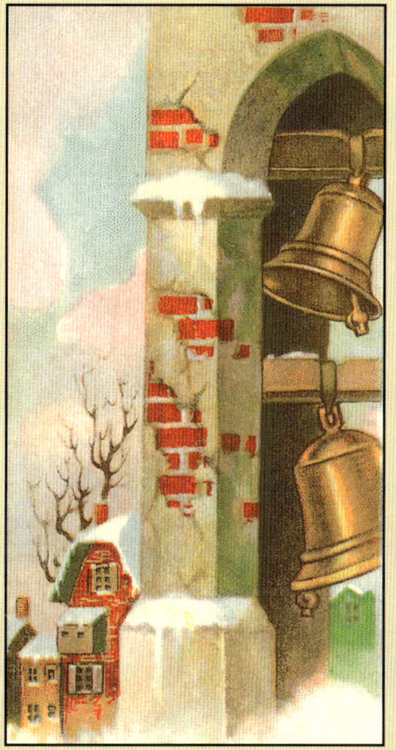

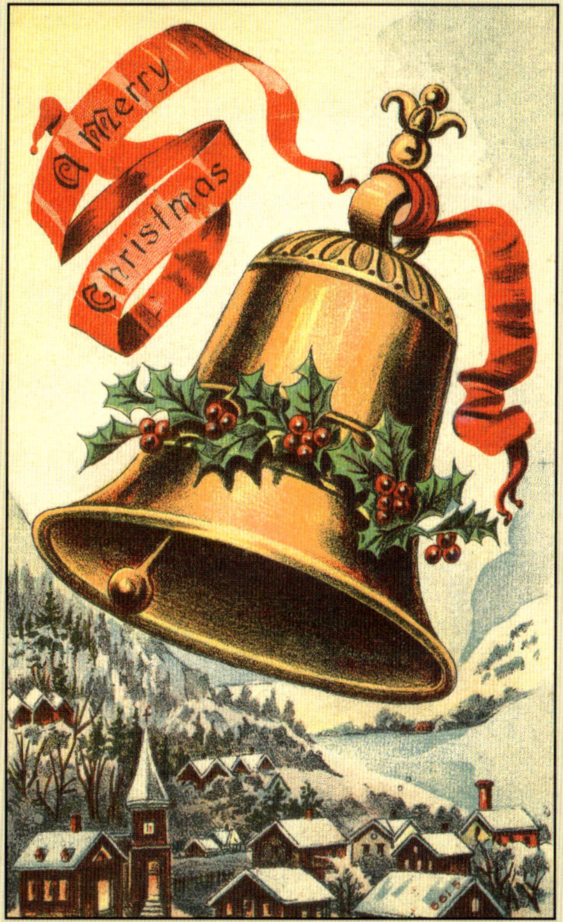
A Merry
Christmas

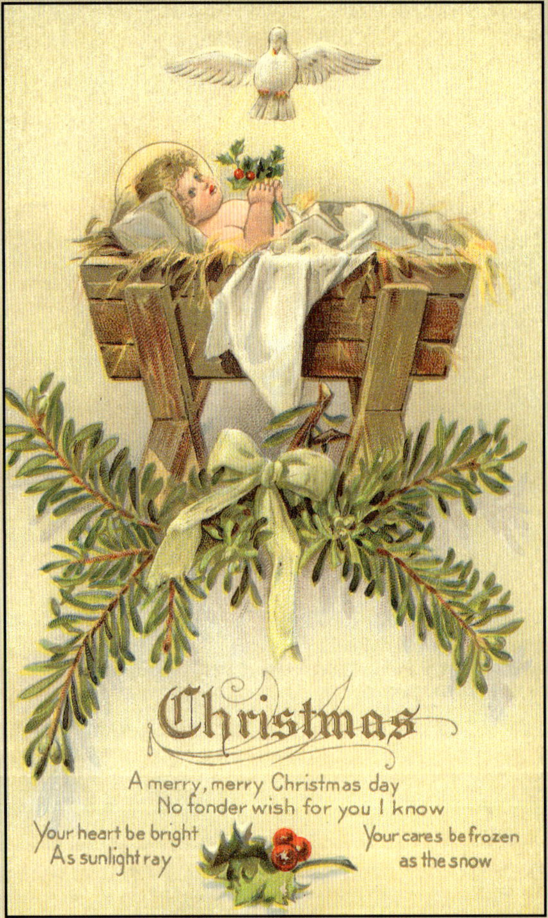
Christmas
A merry, merry Christmas day
No fonder wish for you I know
Your heart be bright
As sunlight ray
Your cares be frozen
as the snow

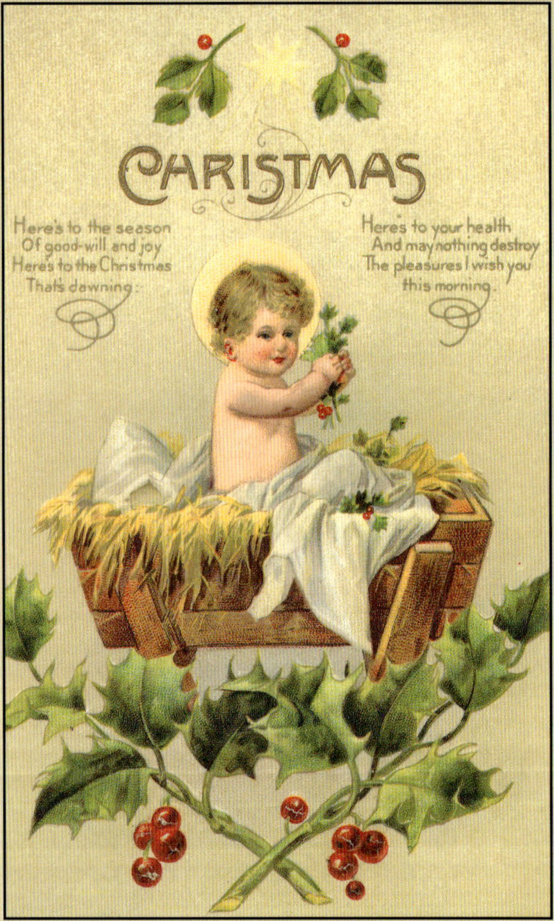
CHRISTMAS
Here's to the season
Of good-will and joy
Here's to the Christmas
That's dawning:
Here's to your health
And may nothing destroy
The pleasures I wish you
this morning.

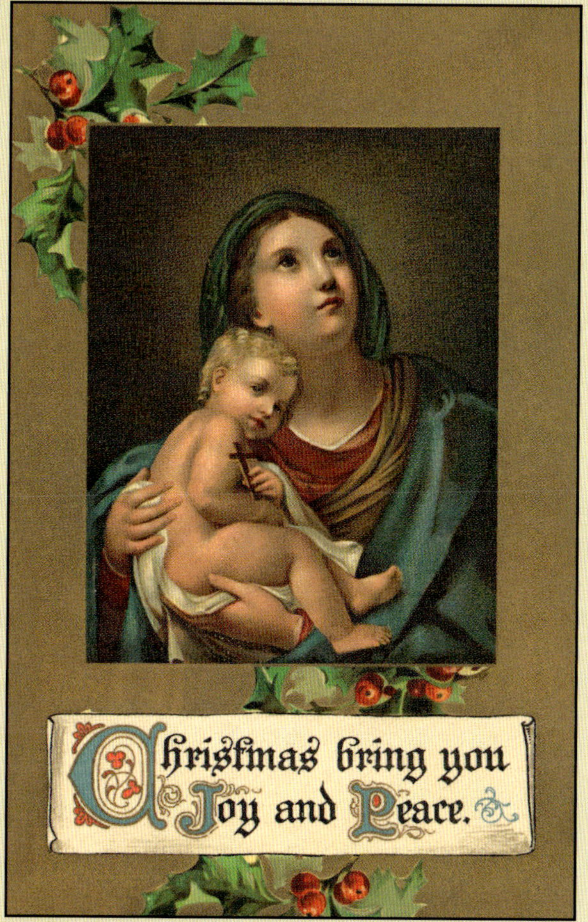
Christmas bring you
Joy and Peace.

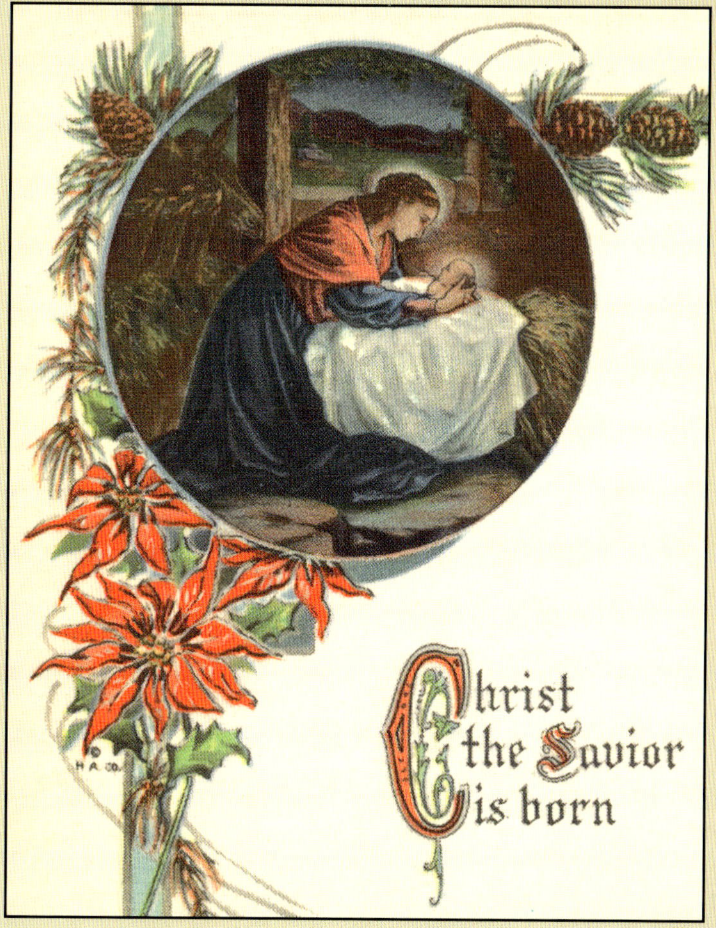
Christ
the Savior
is born

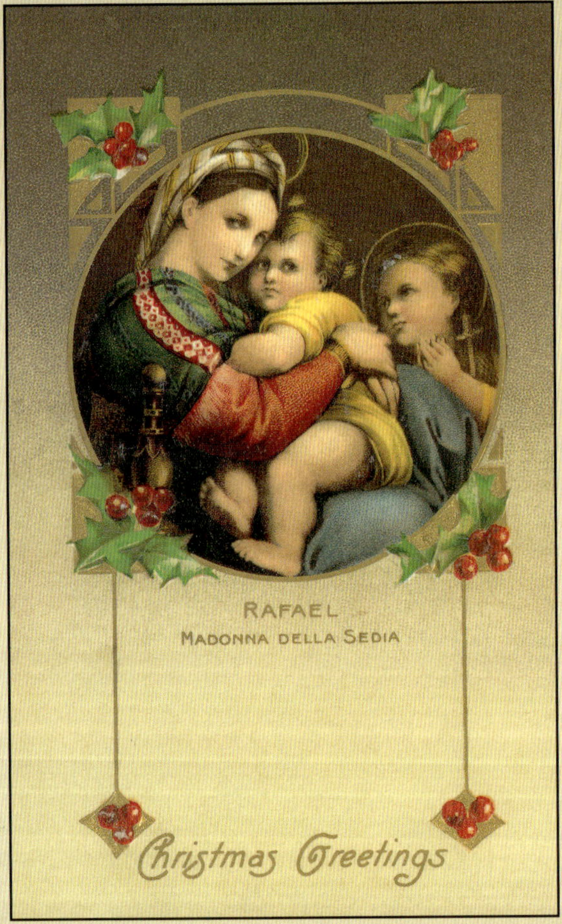
RAFAEL
MADONNA DELLA SEDIA
Christmas Greetings

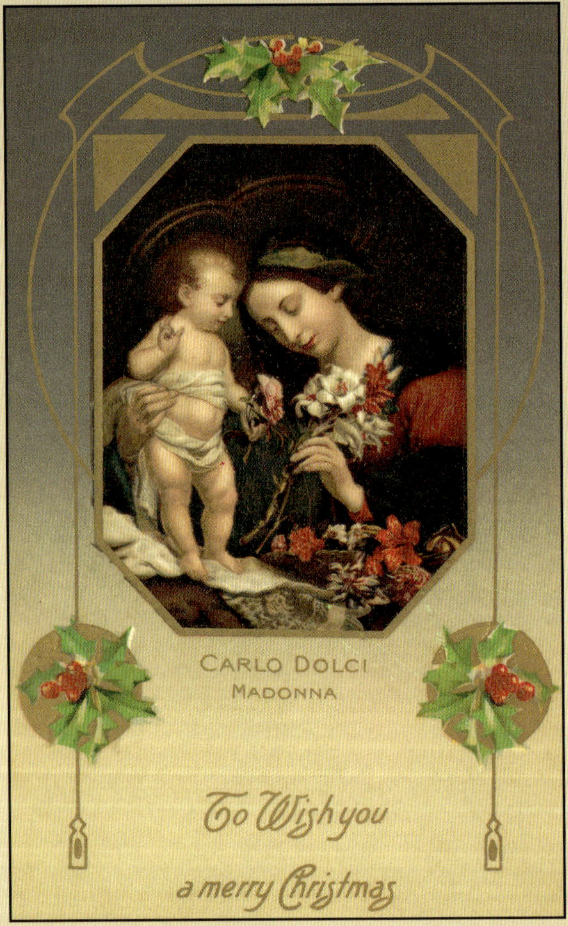
CARLO DOLCI
MADONNA
To Wish you
a merry Christmas

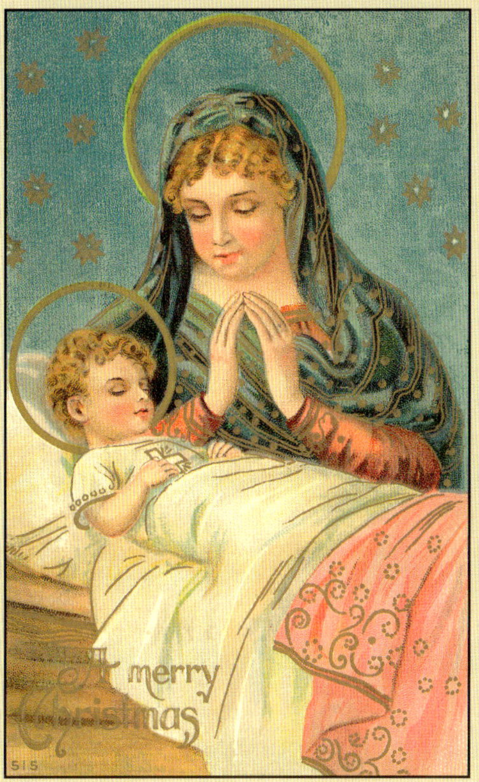
A merry
Christmas
515

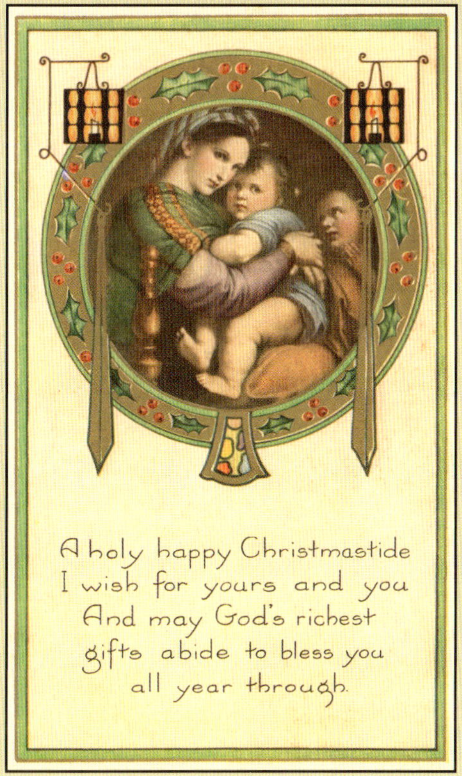
A holy happy Christmastide
I wish for yours and you
And may God's richest
gifts abide to bless you
all year through.

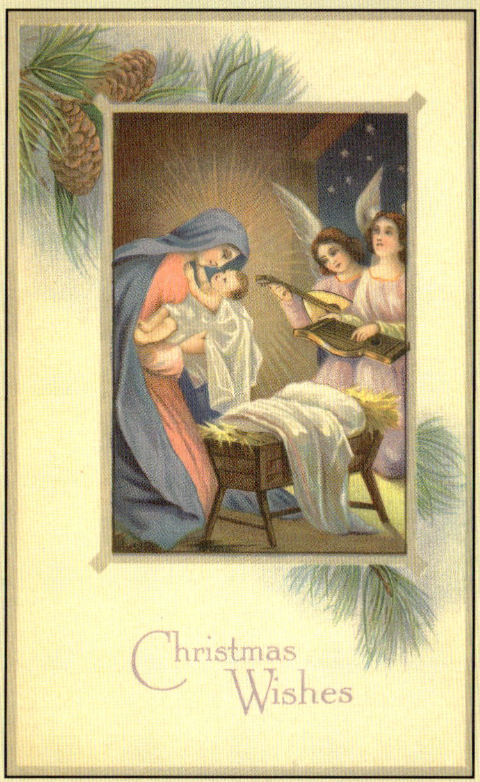
Christmas
Wishes

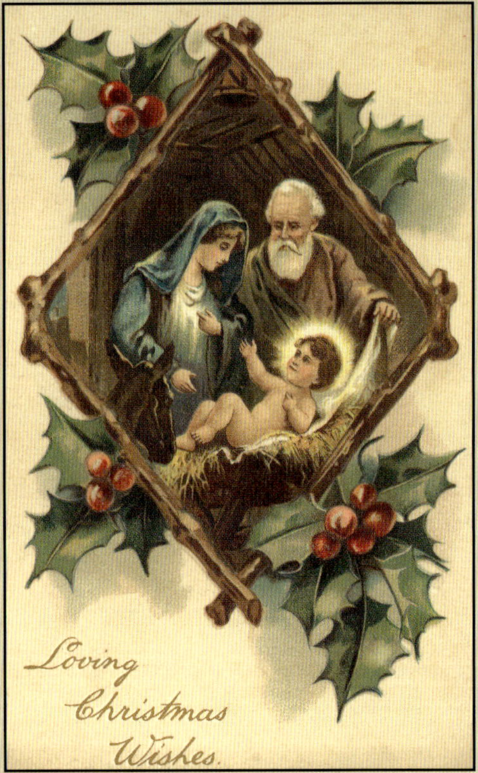
Loving
Christmas
Wishes.

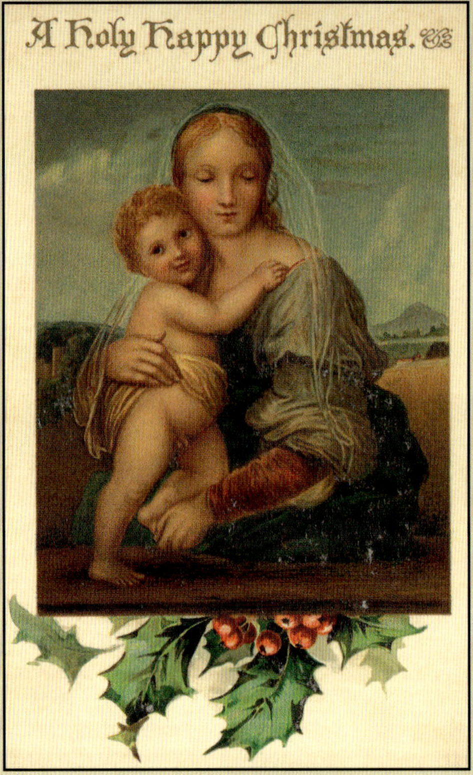
A Holy Happy Christmas.

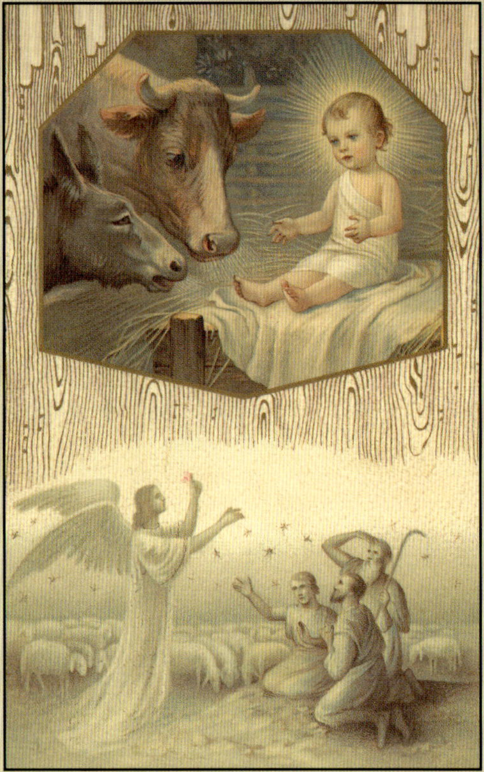

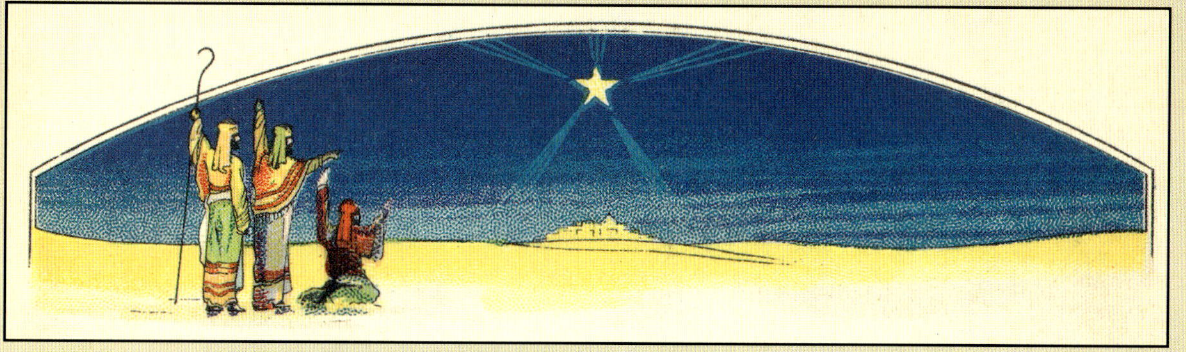

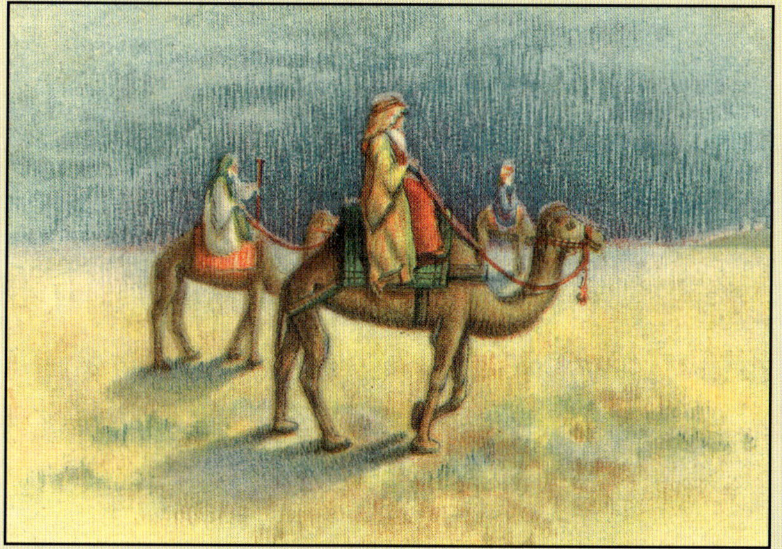

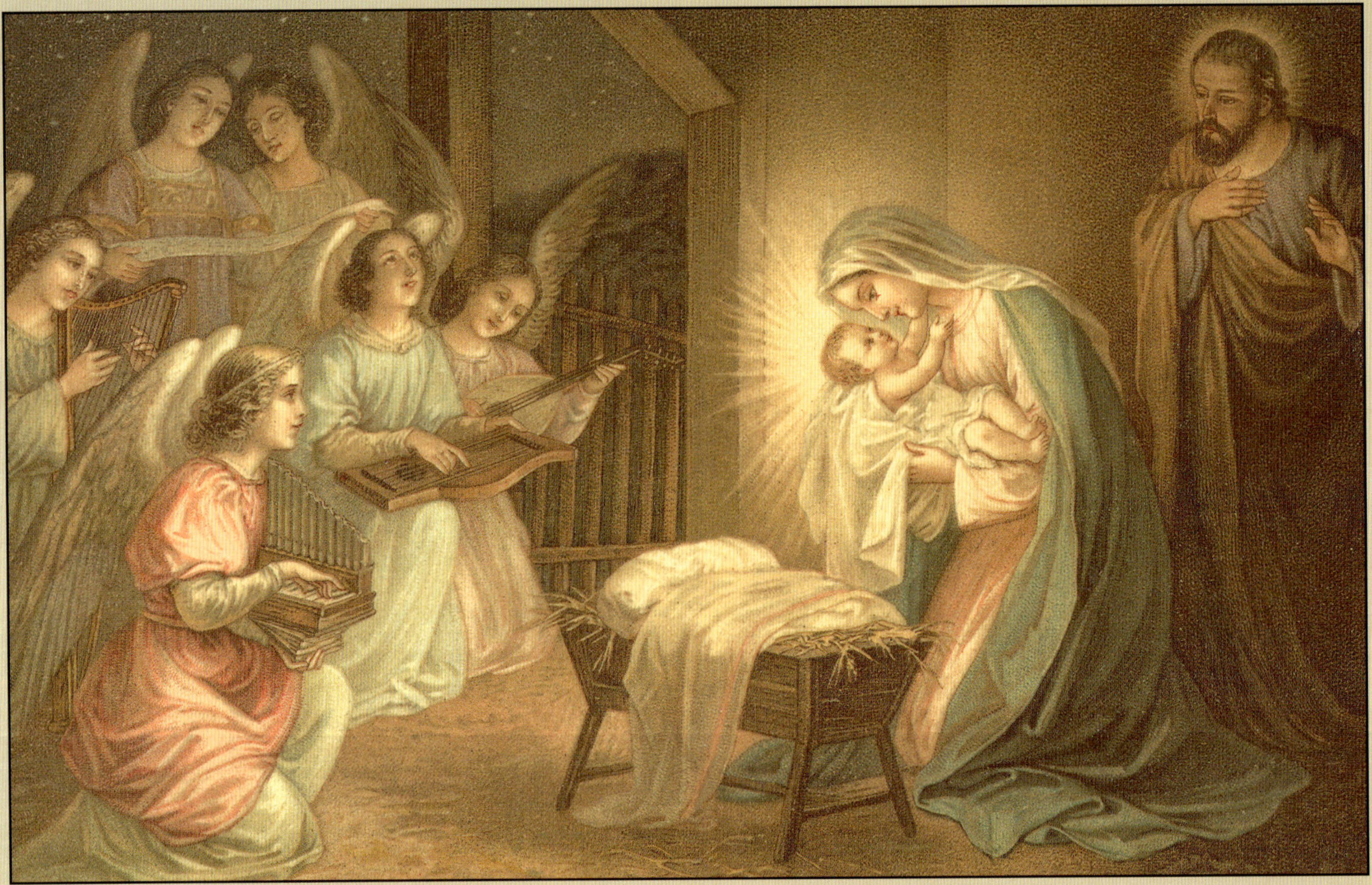

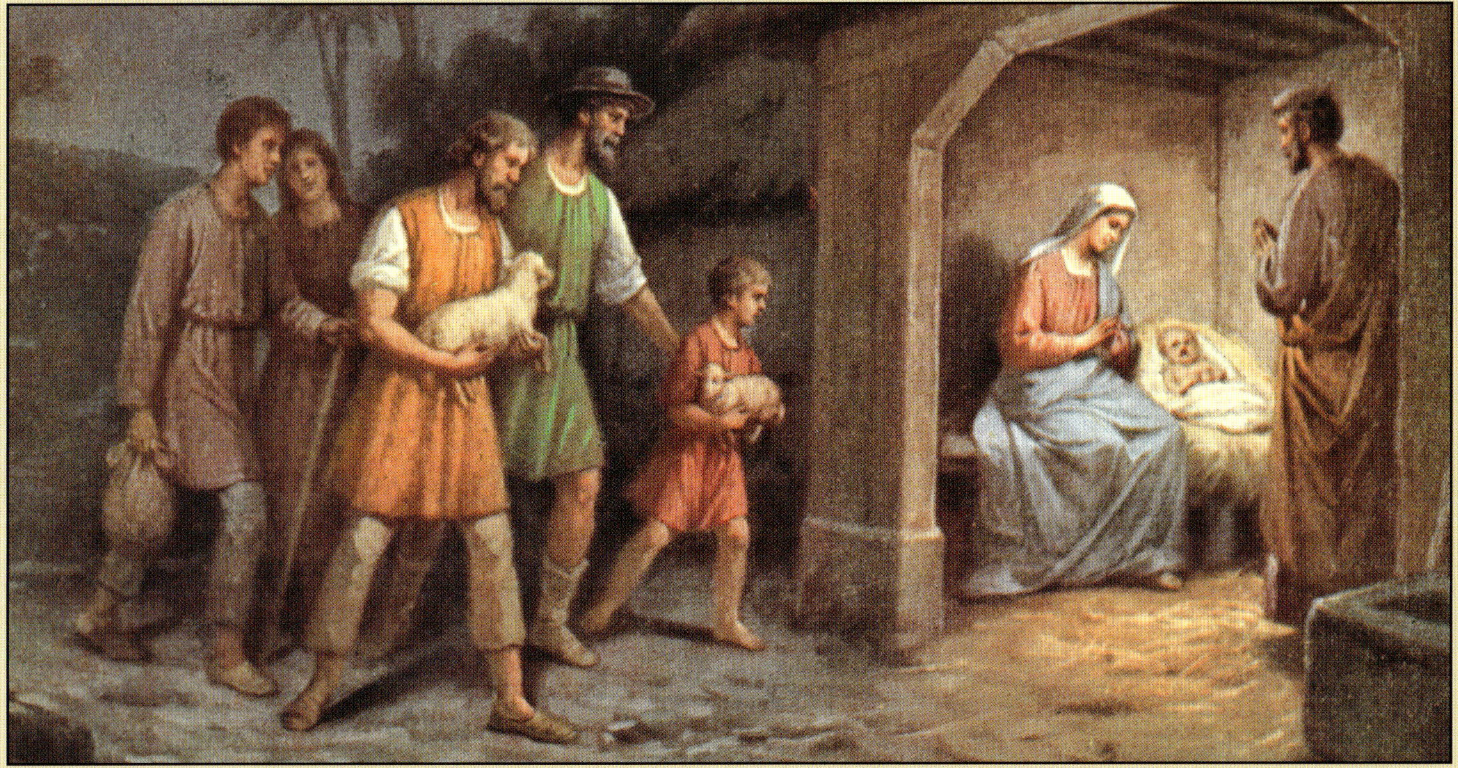

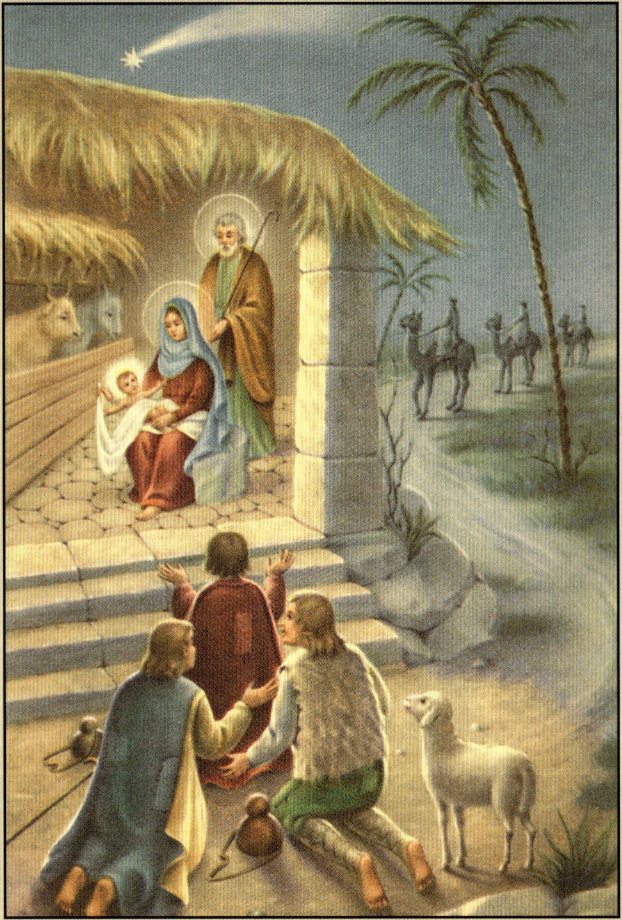

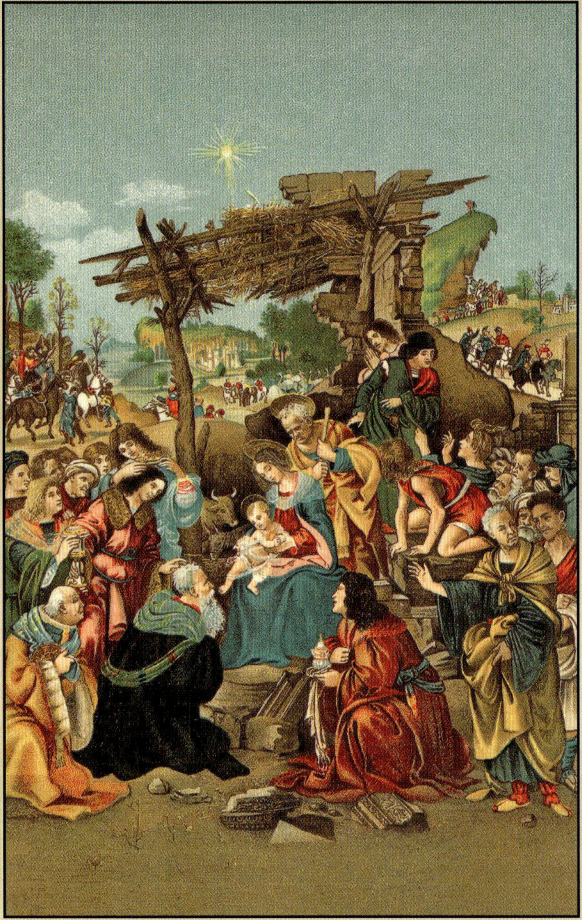

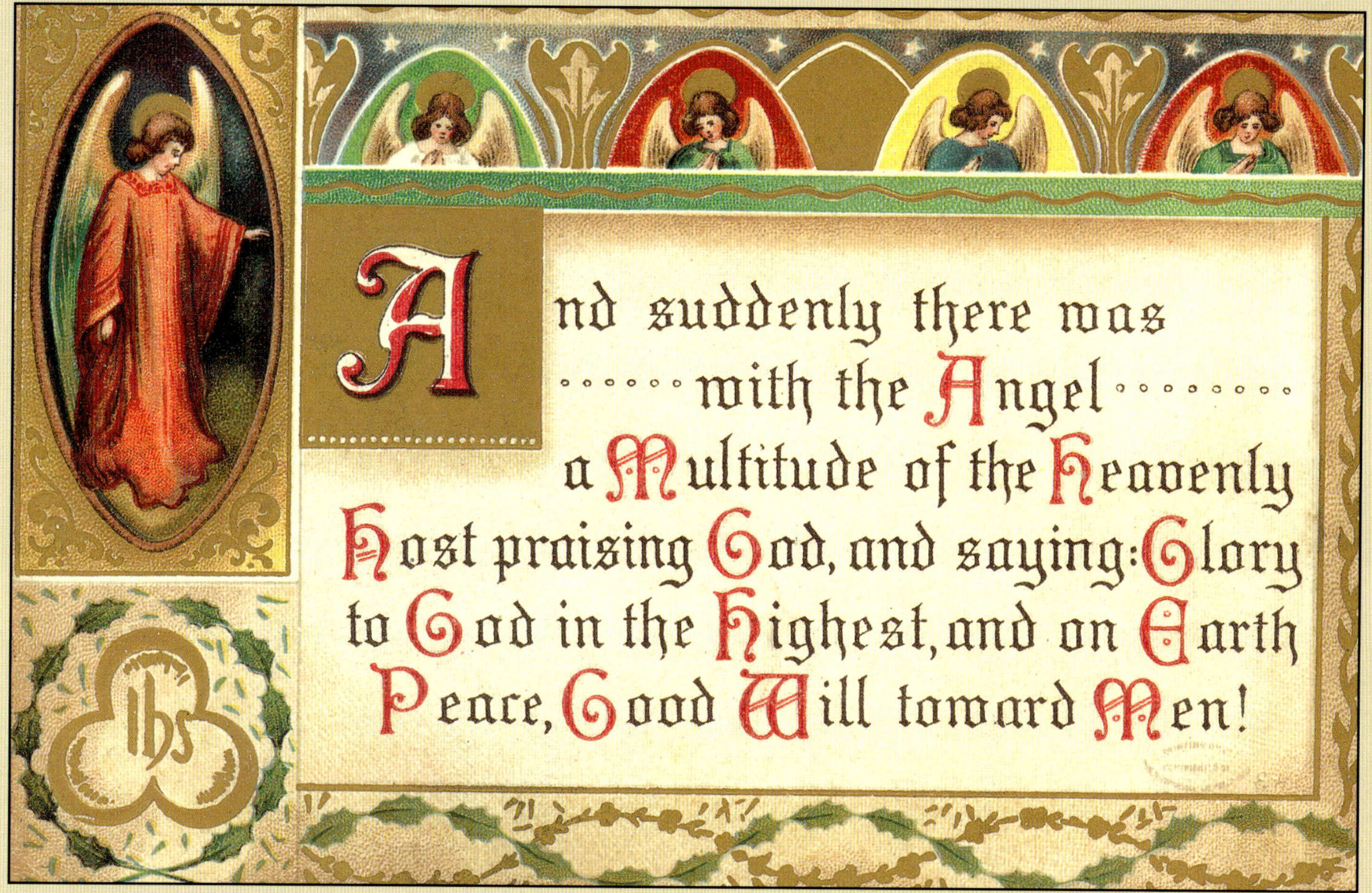
And suddenly there was
with the Angel
a Multitude of the Heavenly
Host praising God, and saying: Glory
to God in the Highest, and on Earth
Peace, Good Will toward Men!
Ihs

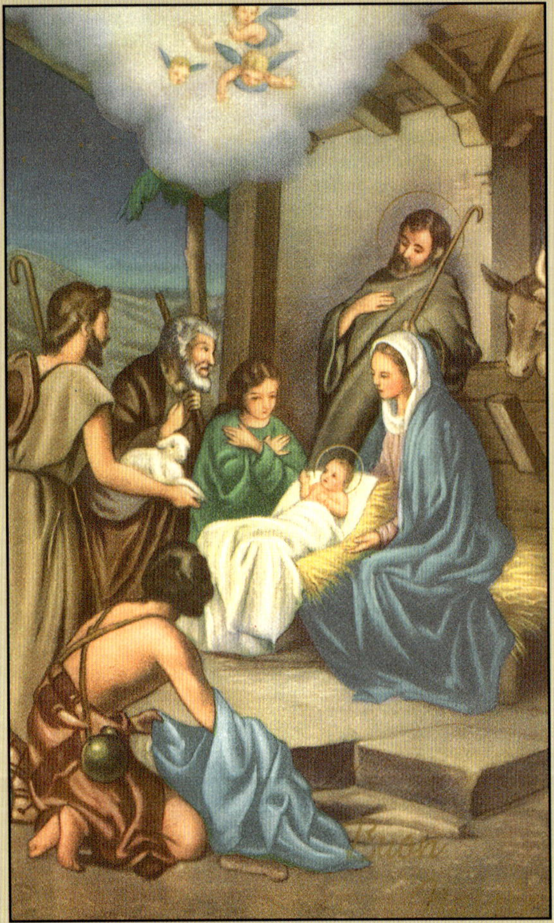

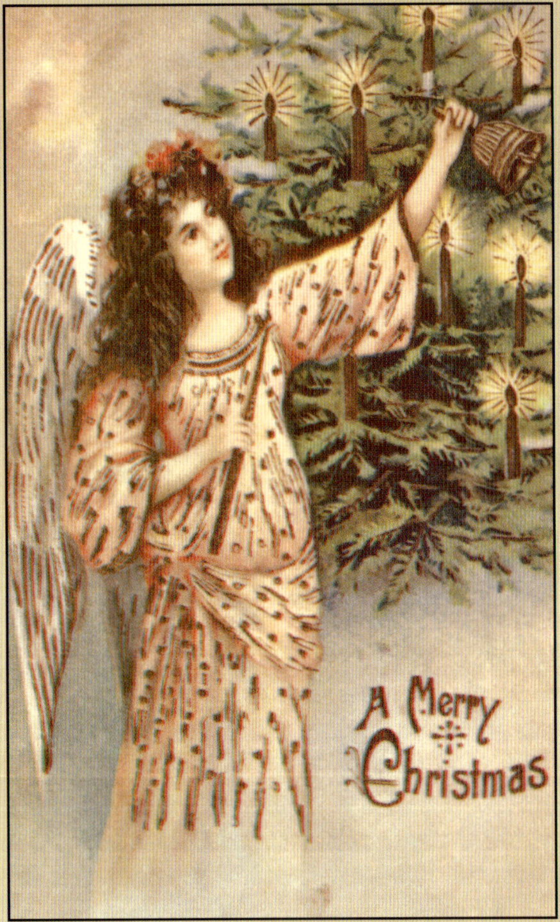
A Merry
Christmas

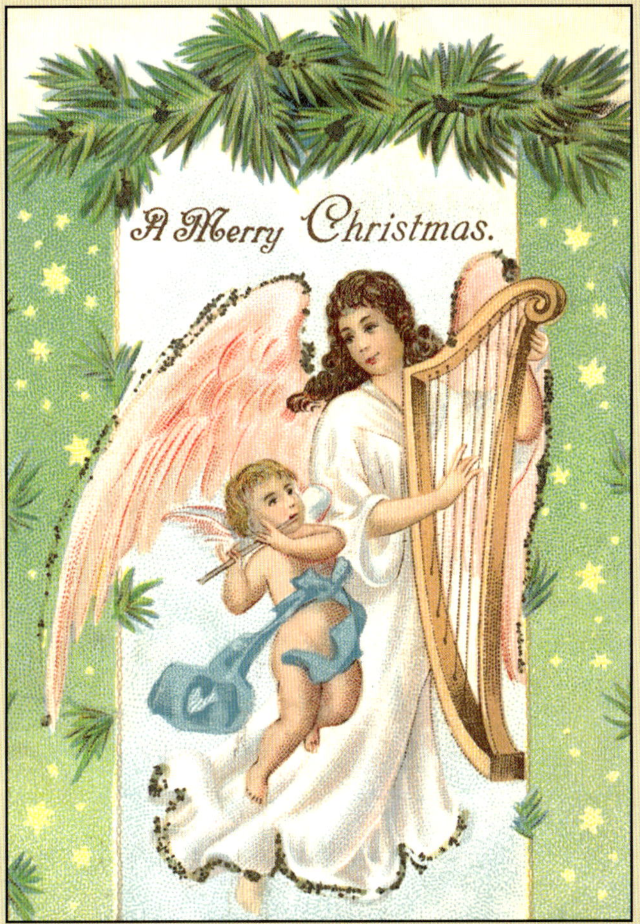
A Merry Christmas.

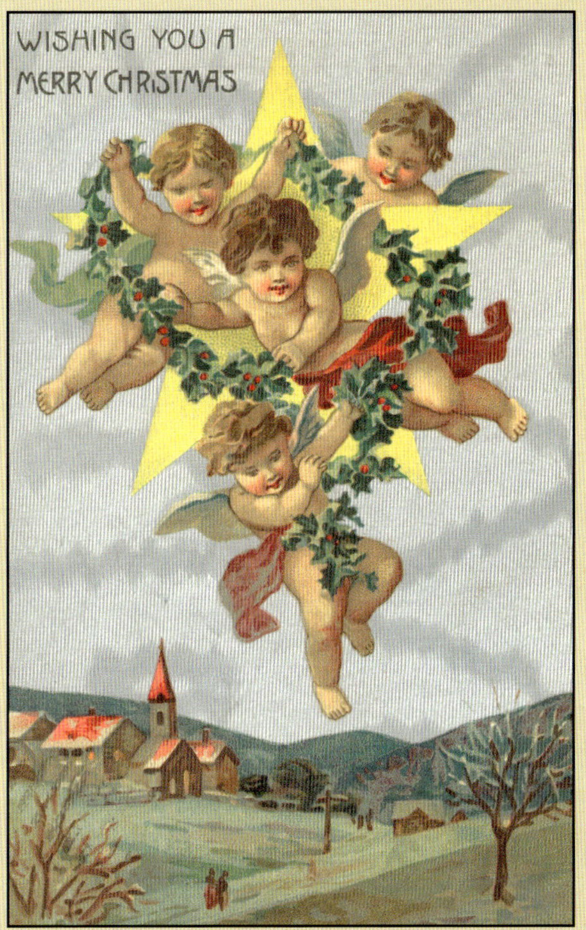
WISHING YOU A
MERRY CHRISTMAS

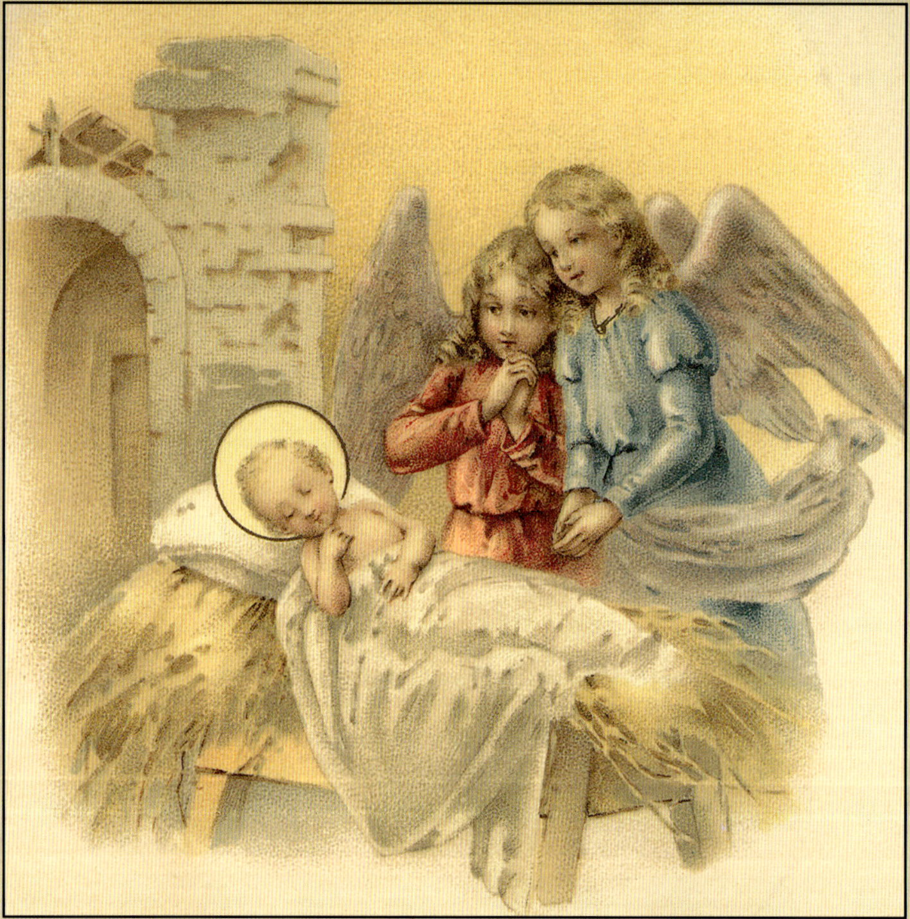

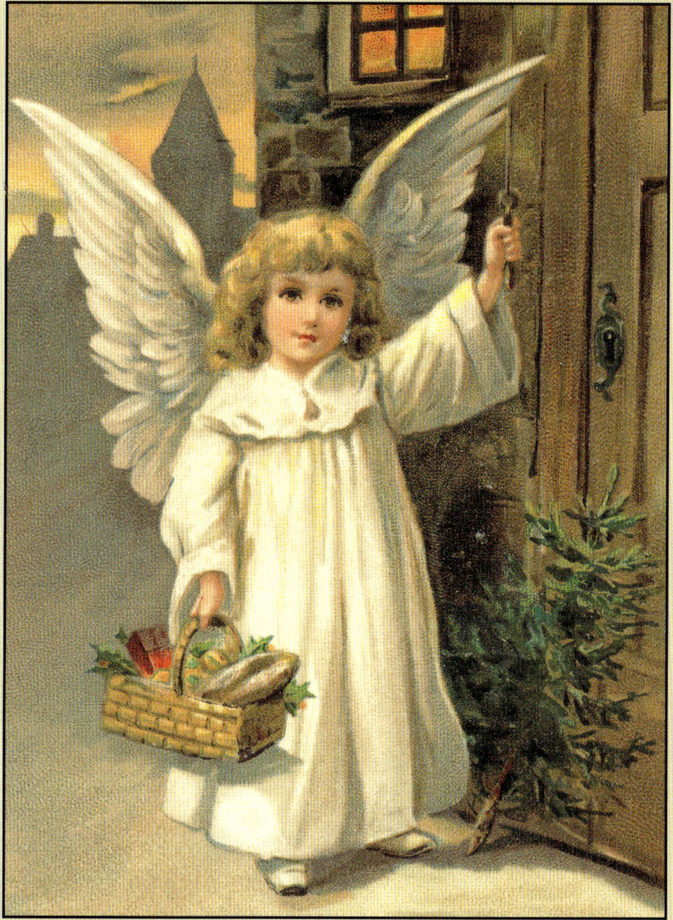

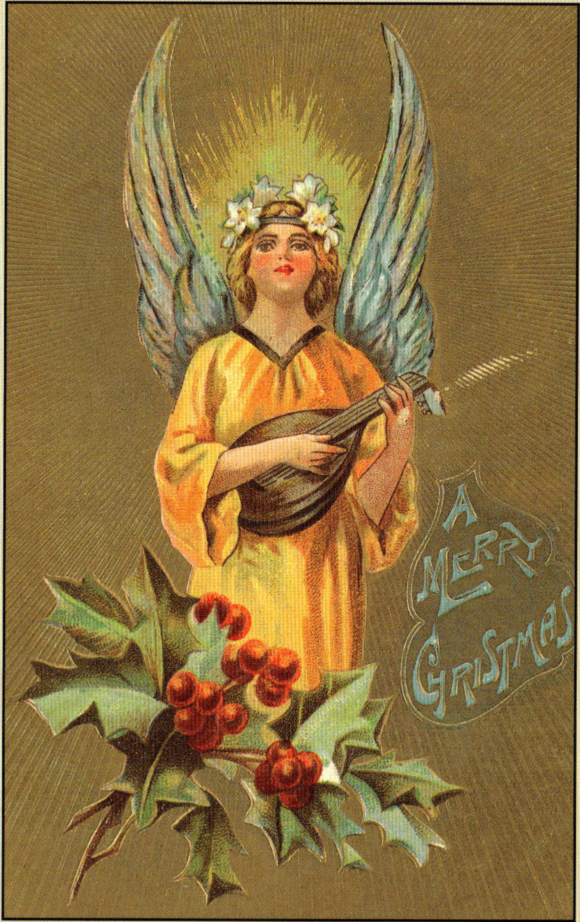
A MERRY CHRISTMAS

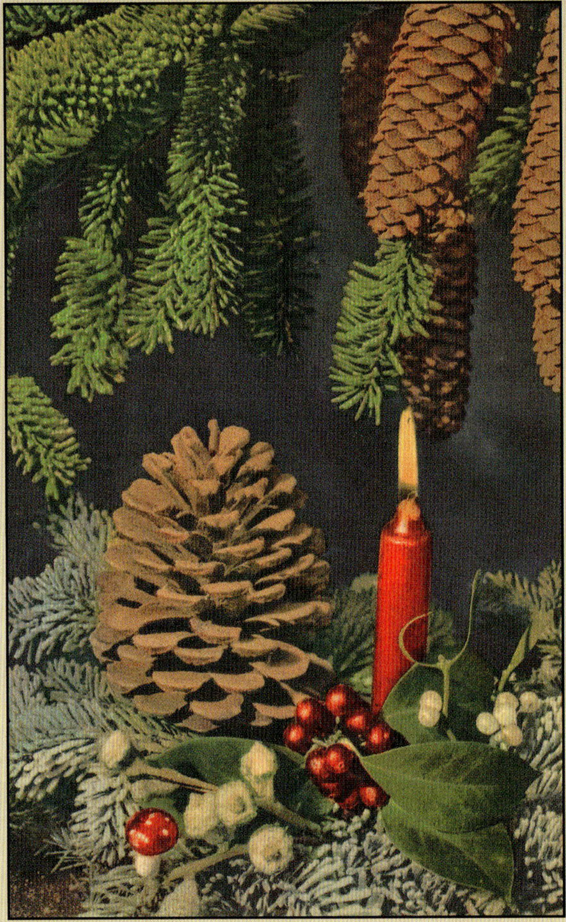

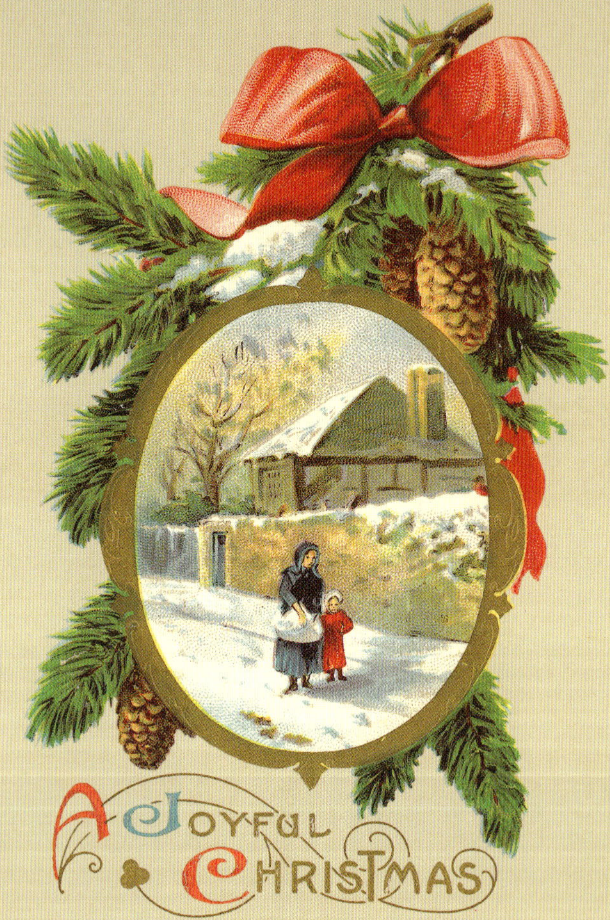
A Joyful
Christmas

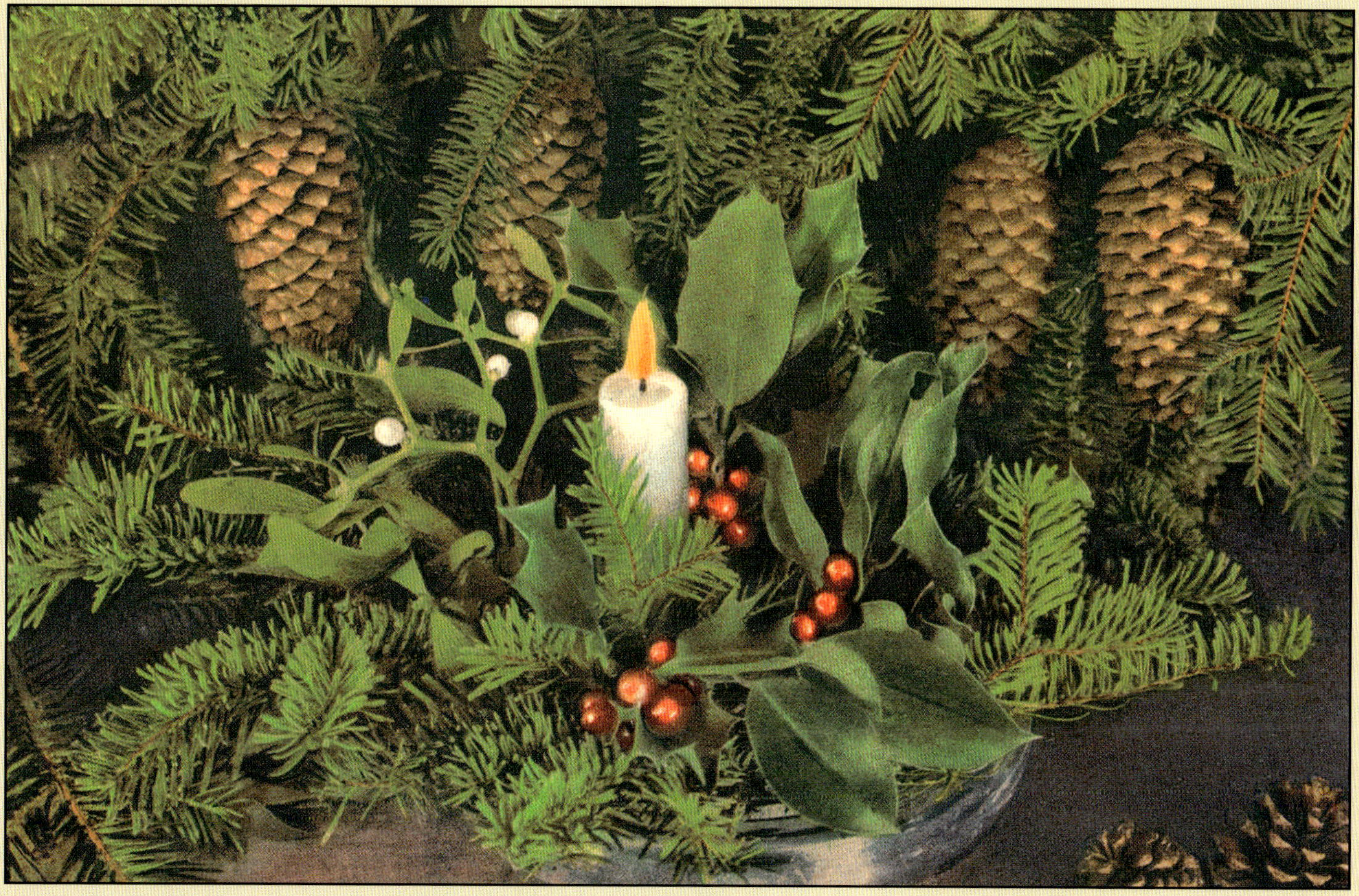

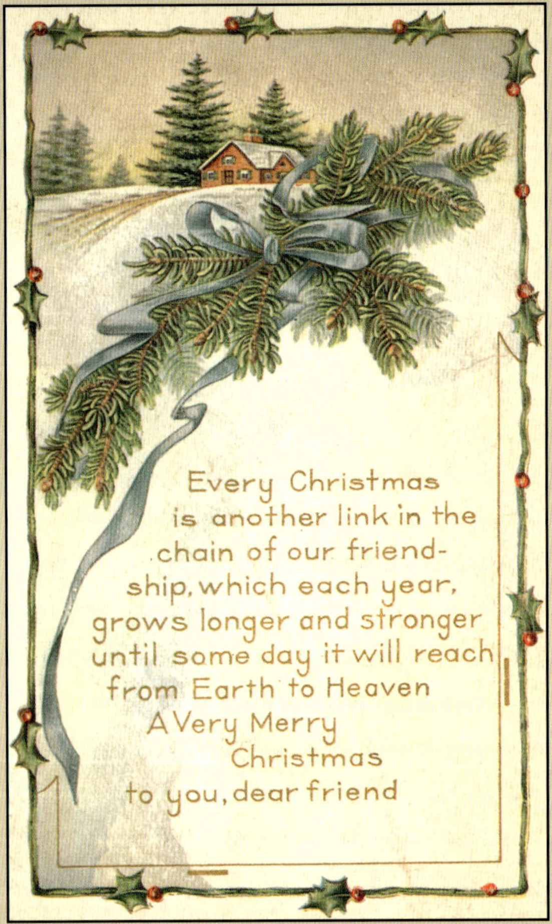
Every Christmas
is another link in the
chain of our friend-
ship, which each year,
grows longer and stronger
until some day it will reach
from Earth to Heaven
A Very Merry
Christmas
to you, dear friend

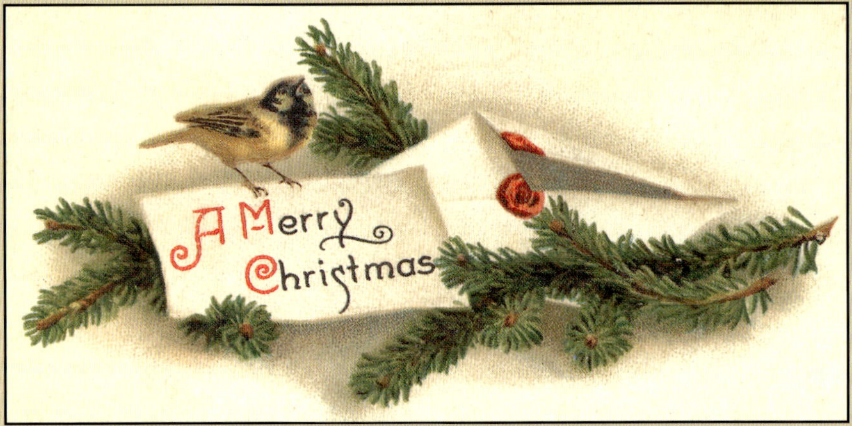
A Merry
Christmas

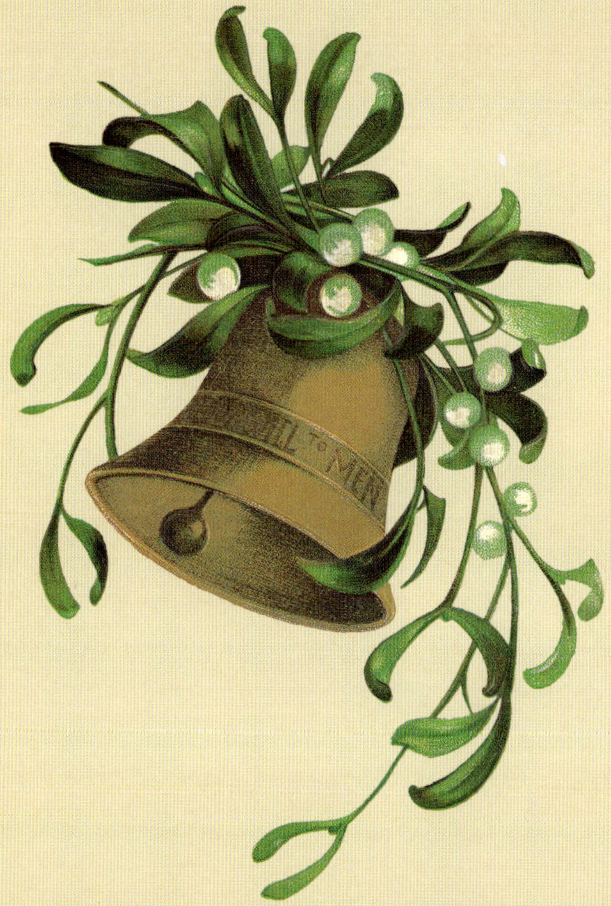

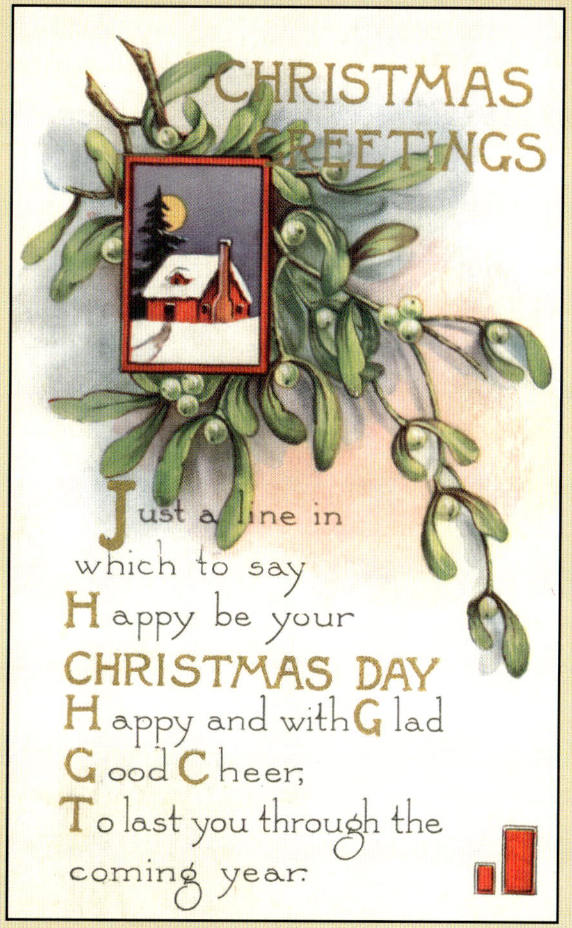
CHRISTMAS GREETINGS
Just a line in
which to say
Happy be your
CHRISTMAS DAY
Happy and with Glad
Good Cheer,
To last you through the
coming year.

I have always thought of Christmas as a good time; a kind, forgiving, charitable time; the only time I know of in the calendar of the year when men and women seem, by one consent to open their shut-up hearts freely. I believe it has done me good, and I say, "God bless it!"

—Chas. Dickens.

No. 573

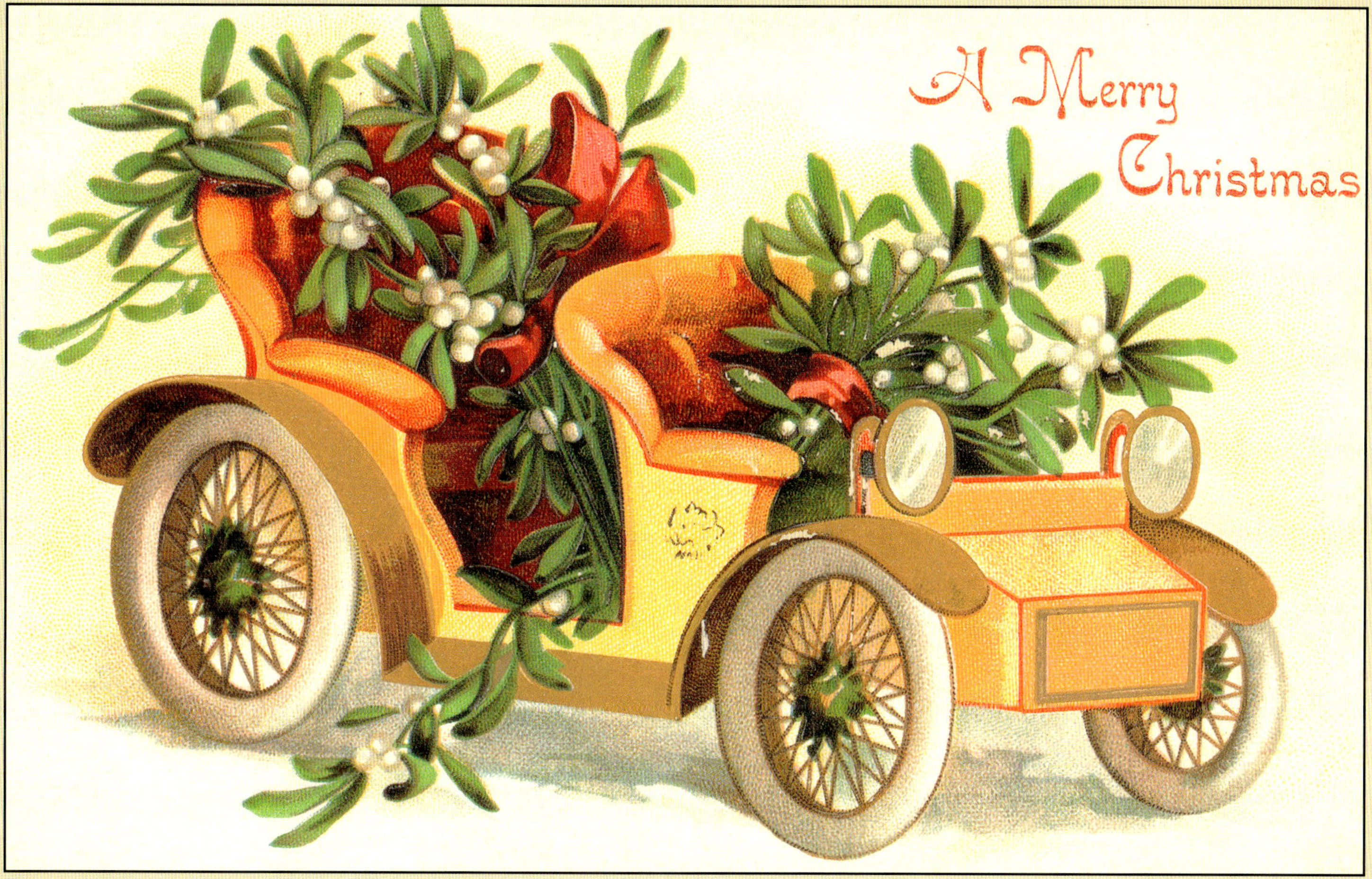
A Merry
Christmas

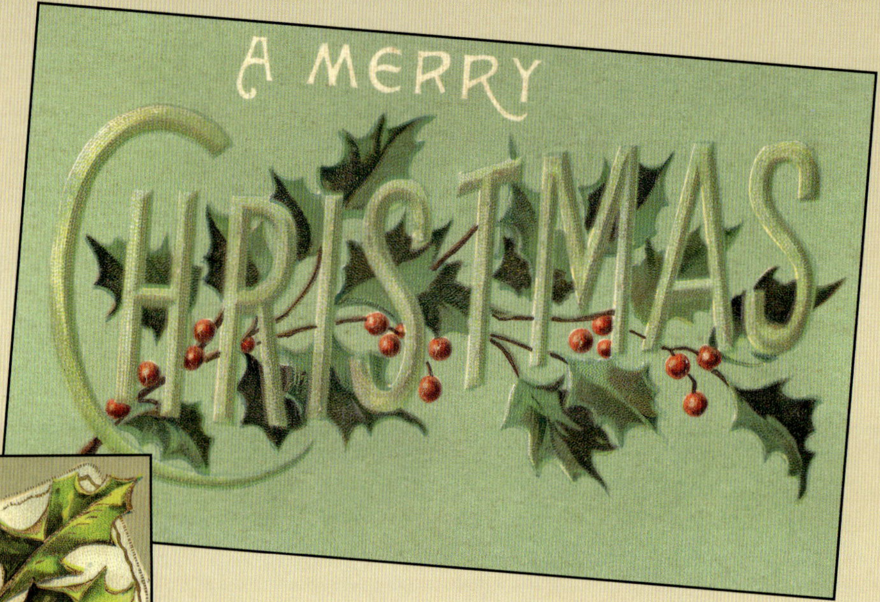
A MERRY
CHRISTMAS

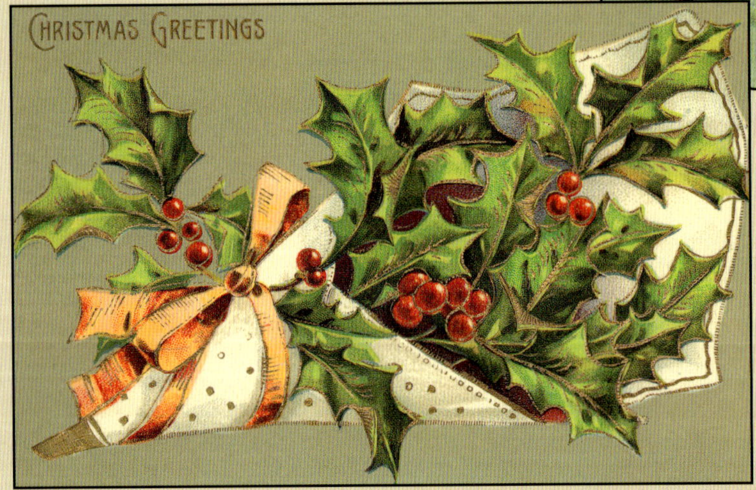
CHRISTMAS GREETINGS

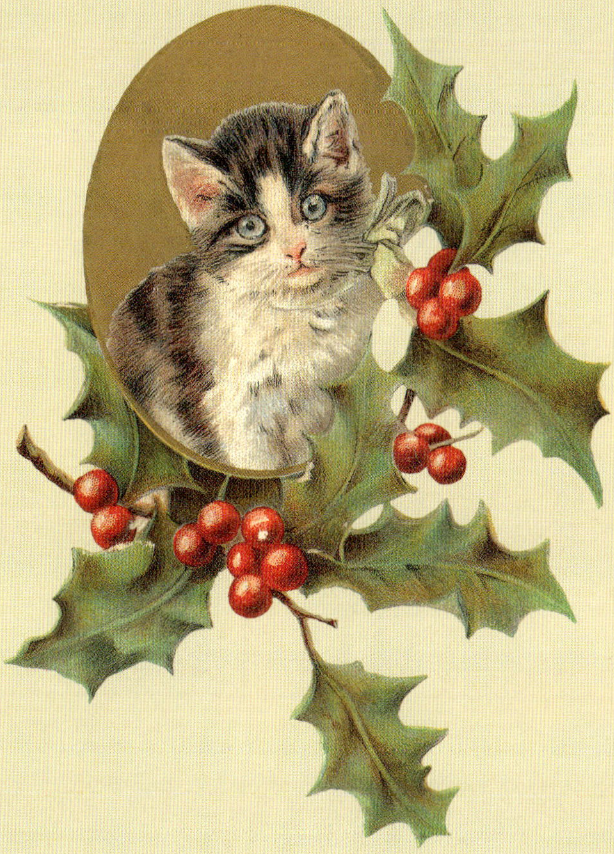

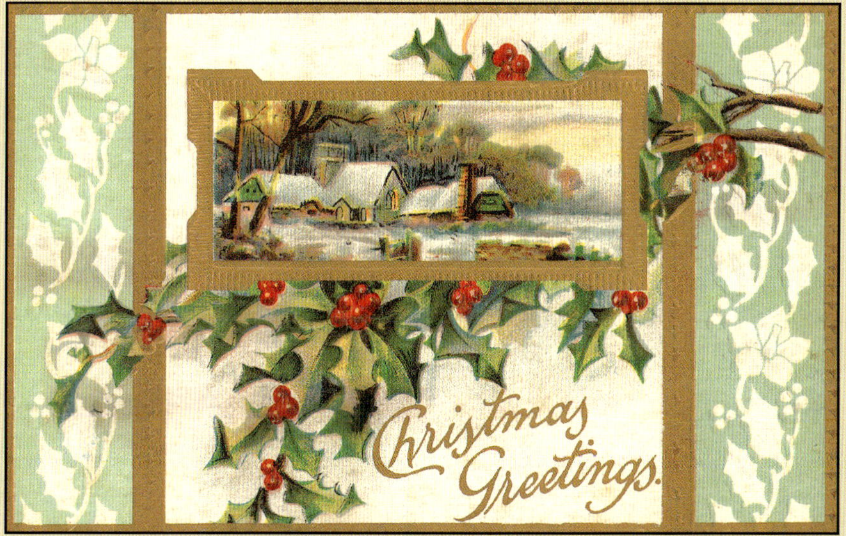
Christmas Greetings.

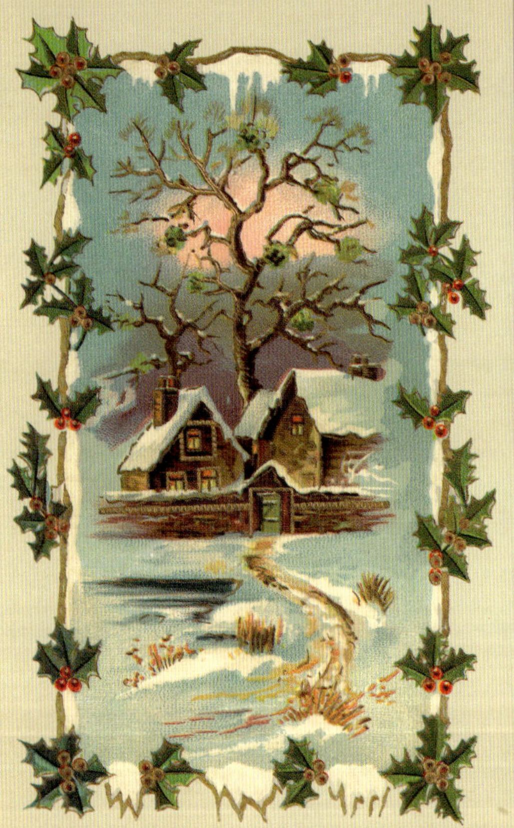

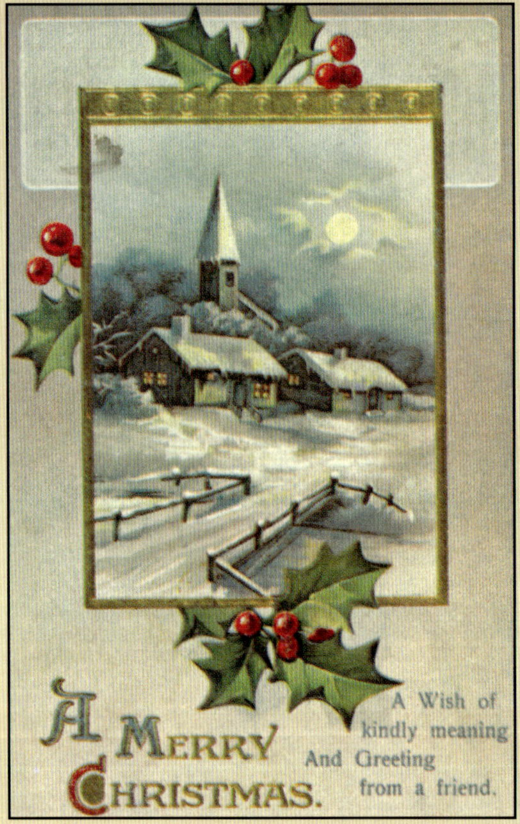
A Merry Christmas.
A Wish of kindly meaning And Greeting from a friend.

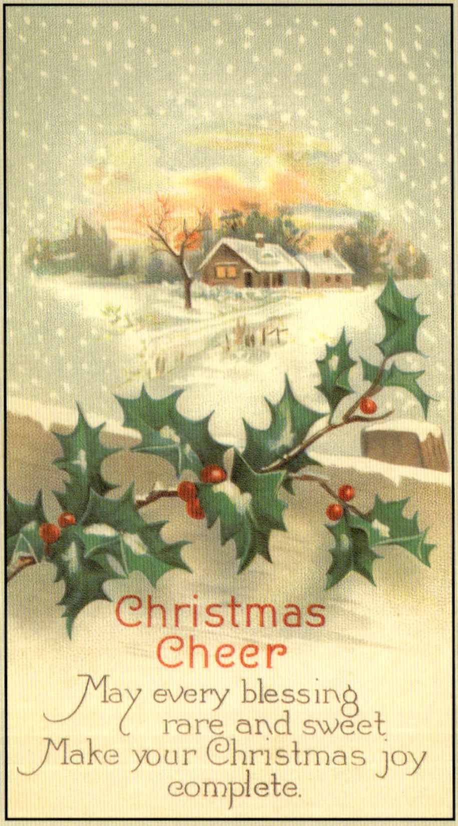
Christmas Cheer
May every blessing rare and sweet Make your Christmas joy complete.

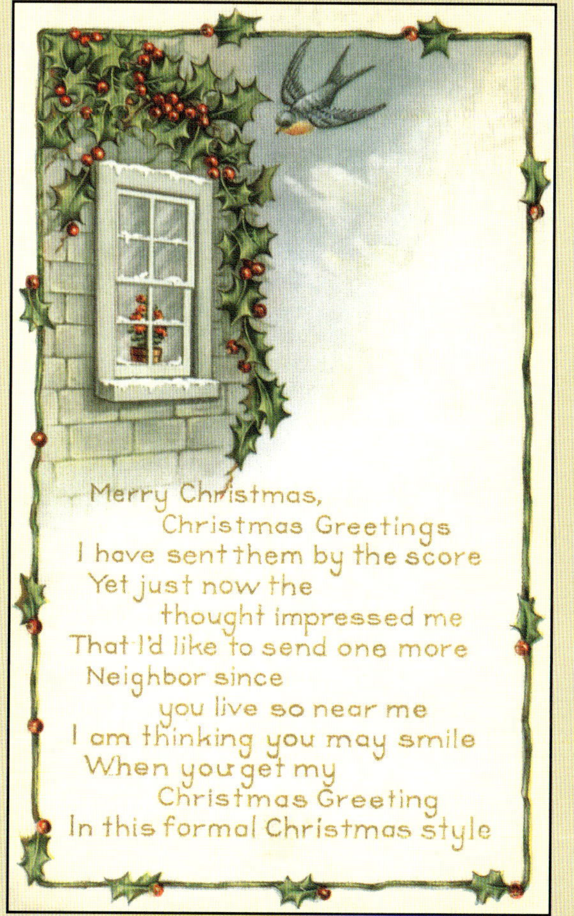
Merry Christmas,
Christmas Greetings
I have sent them by the score
Yet just now the
thought impressed me
That I'd like to send one more
Neighbor since
you live so near me
I am thinking you may smile
When you get my
Christmas Greeting
In this formal Christmas style

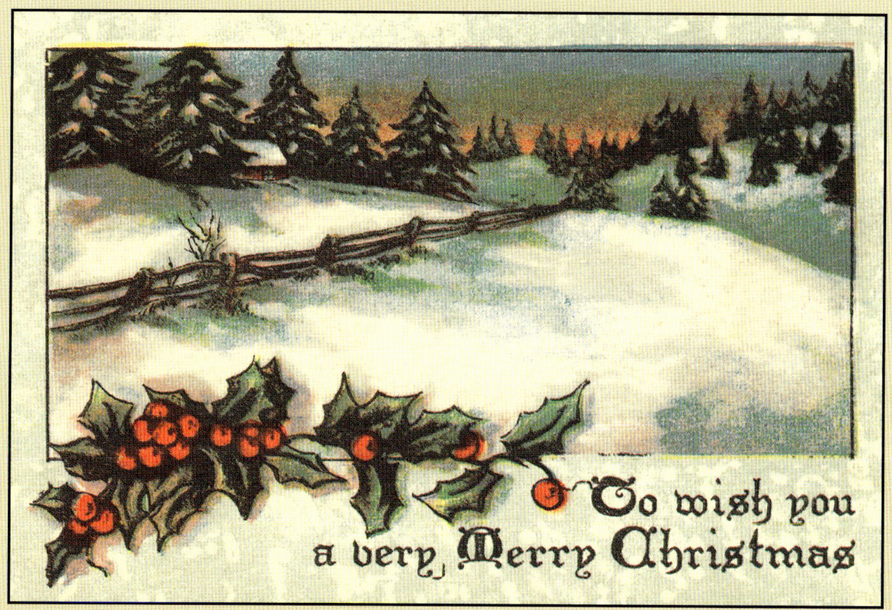
To wish you
a very Merry Christmas

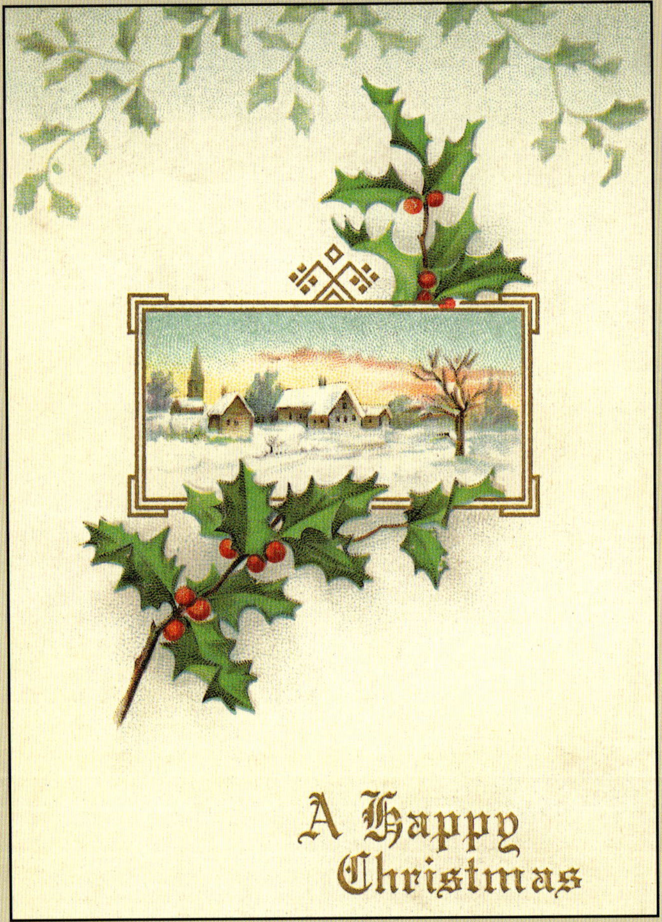
A Happy
Christmas

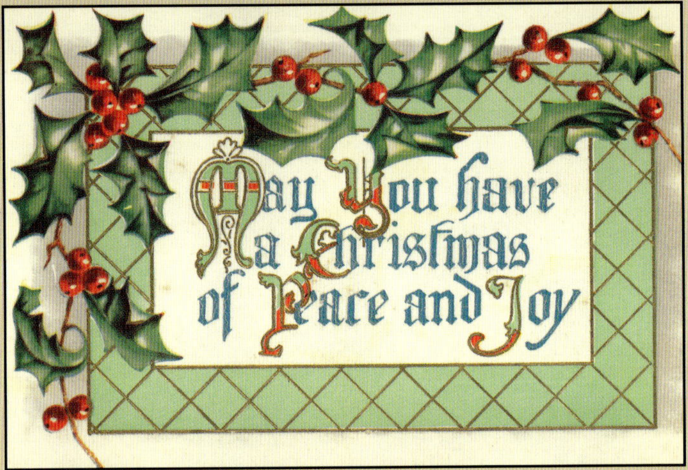
May You have
a Christmas
of Peace and Joy

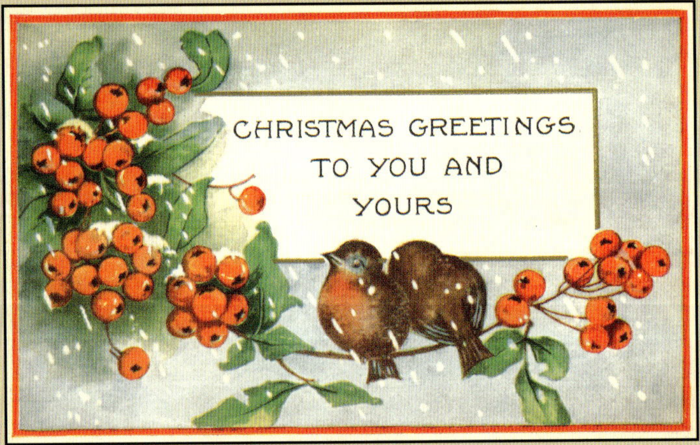
CHRISTMAS GREETINGS
TO YOU AND
YOURS

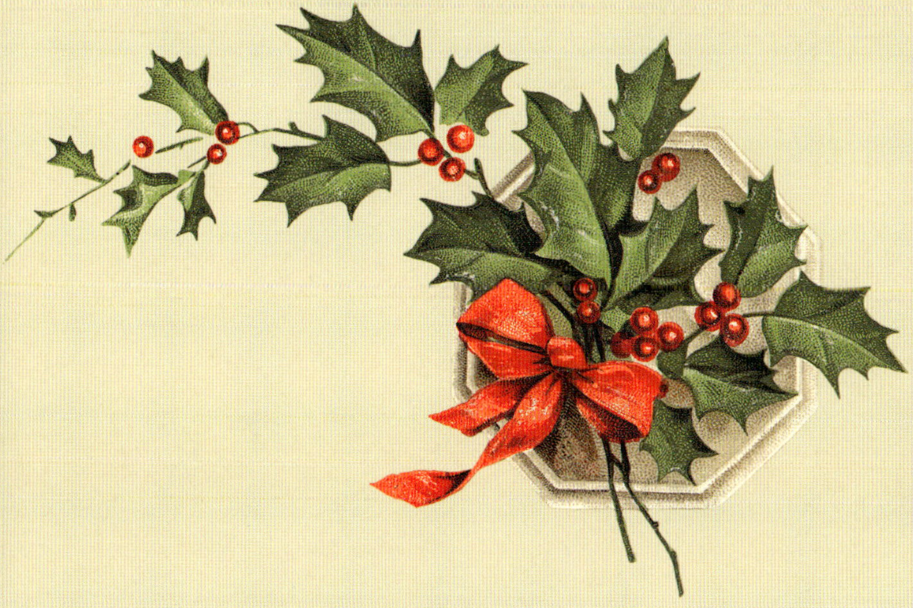

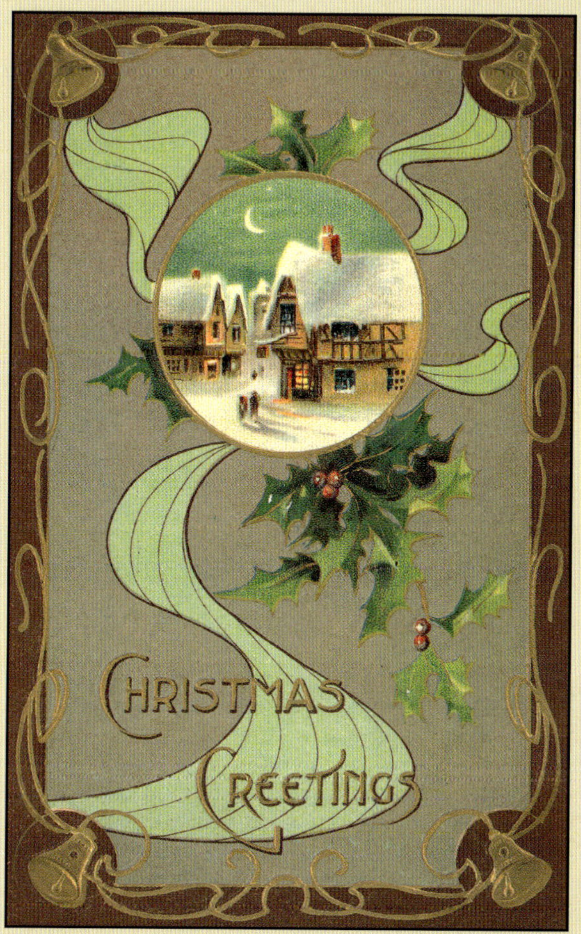
CHRISTMAS
GREETINGS

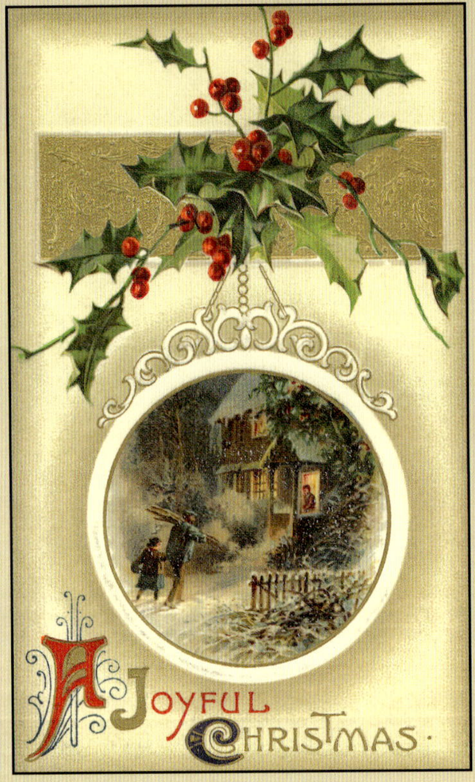
A Joyful Christmas.

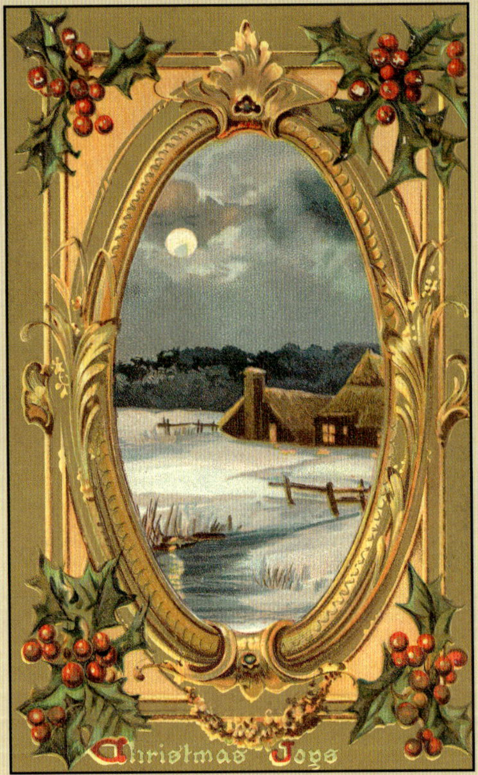
Christmas Joys

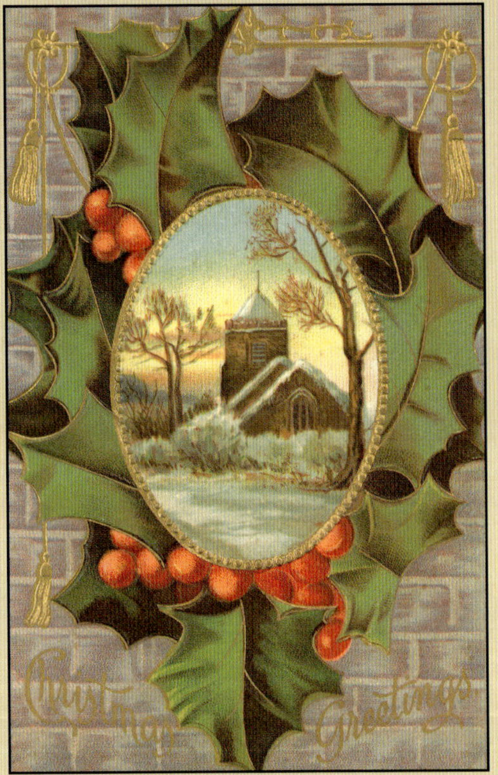
Christmas Greetings

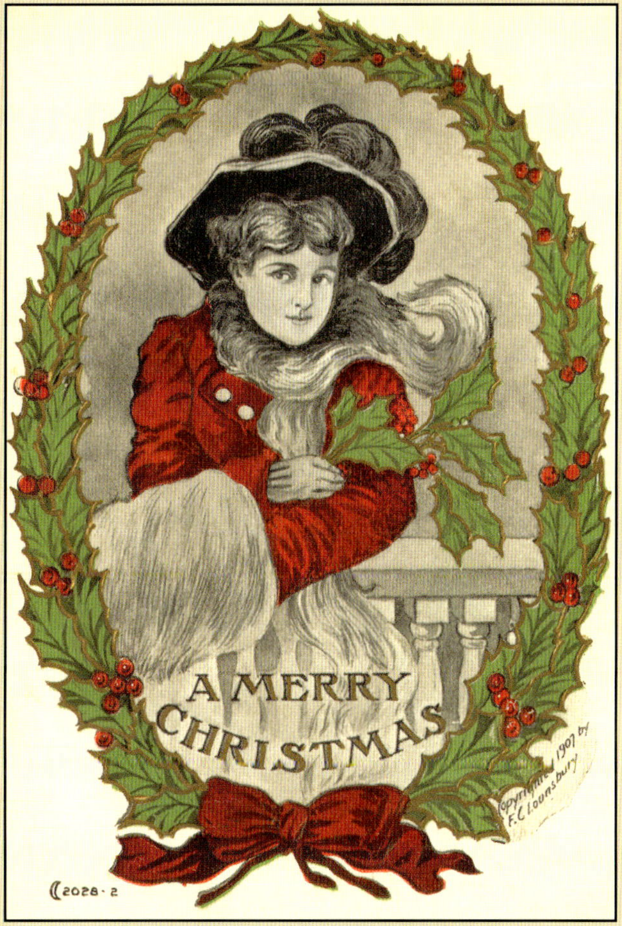
A MERRY CHRISTMAS
Copyrighted 1907 by F.C. Lounsbury
2028-2

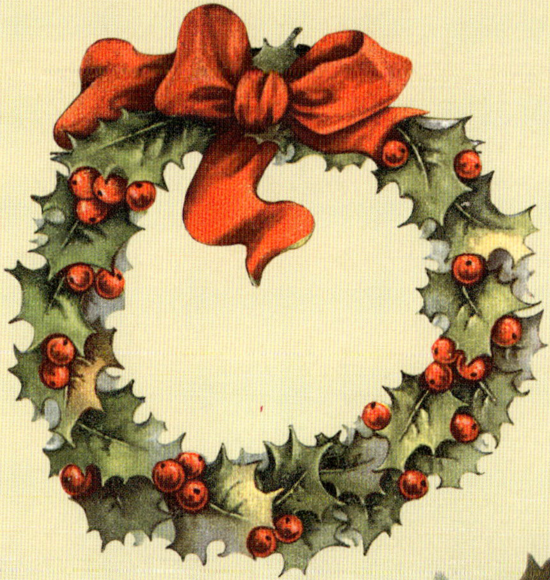

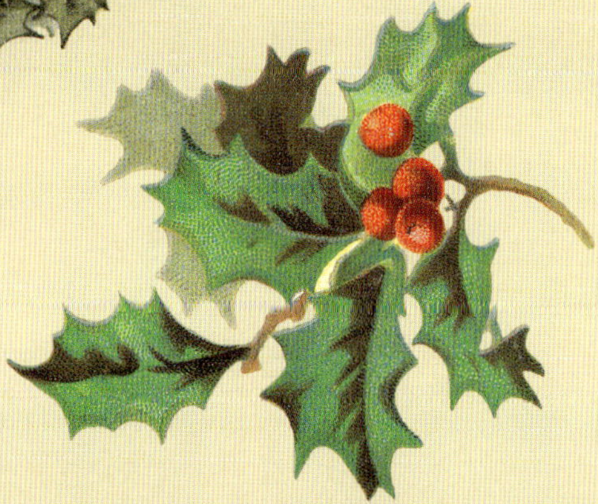

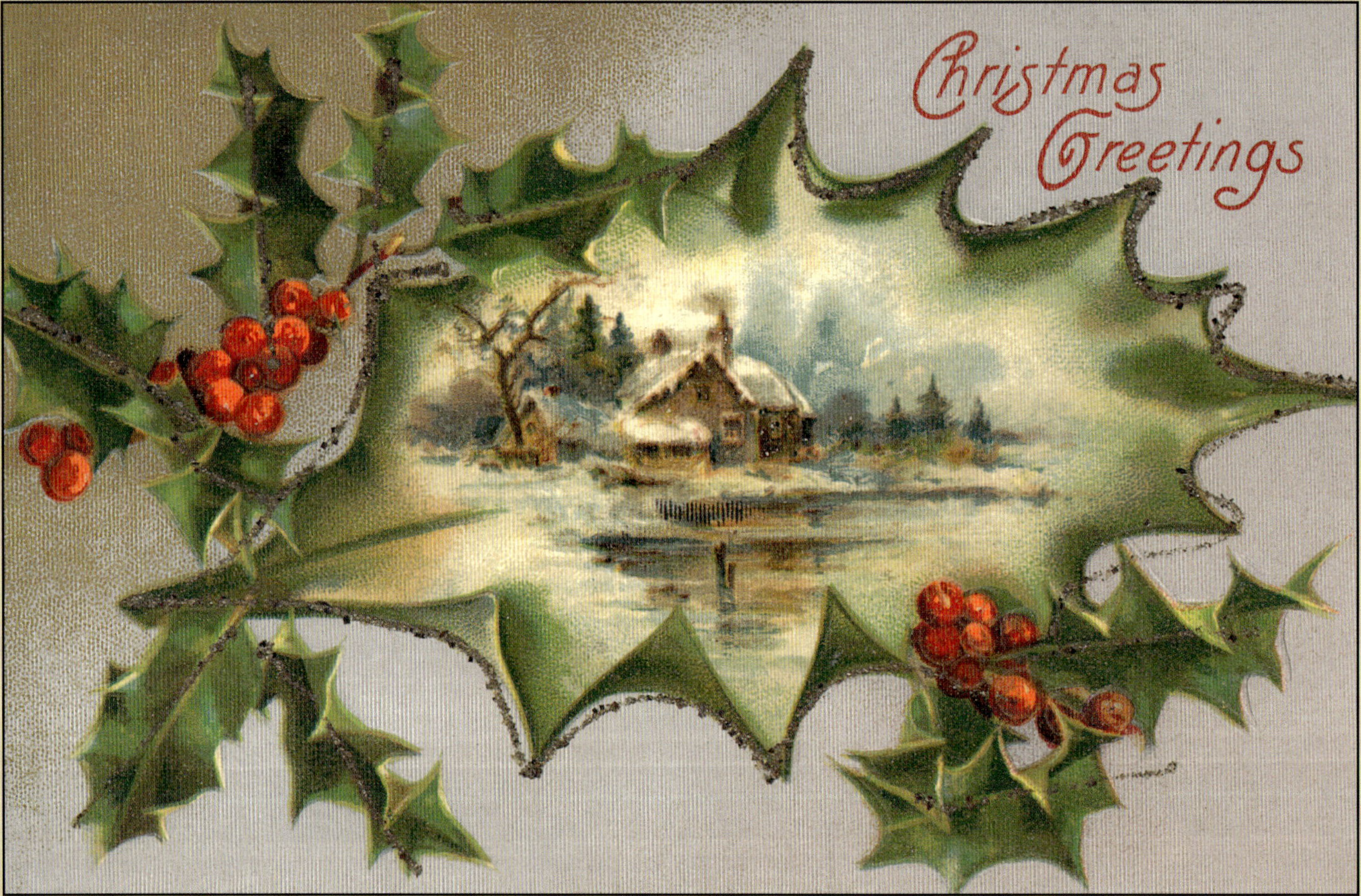
Christmas Greetings

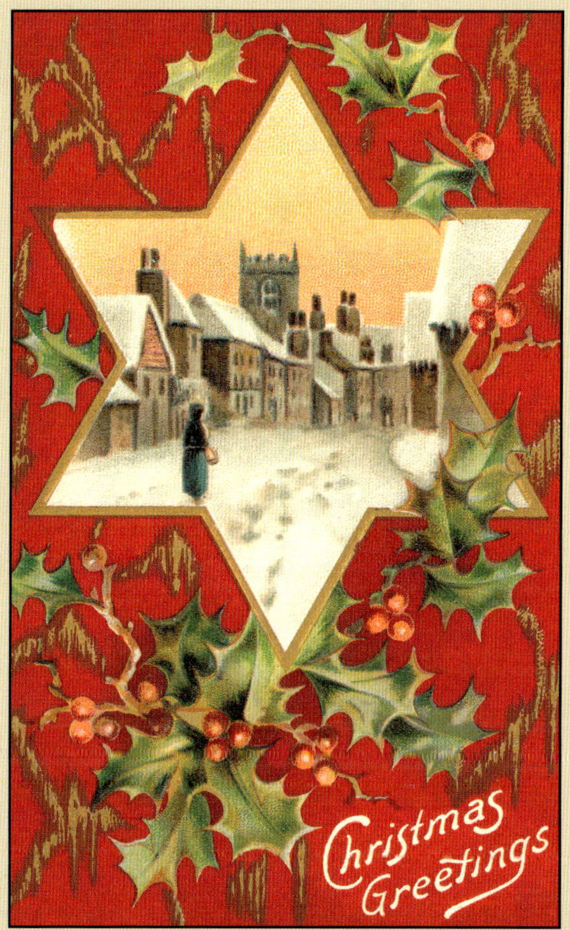
Christmas
Greetings

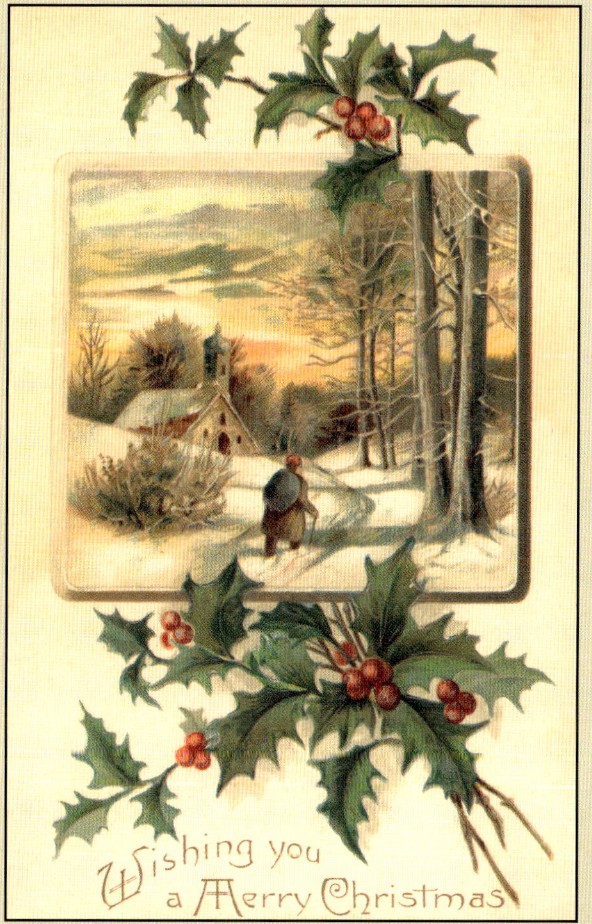
Wishing you
a Merry Christmas

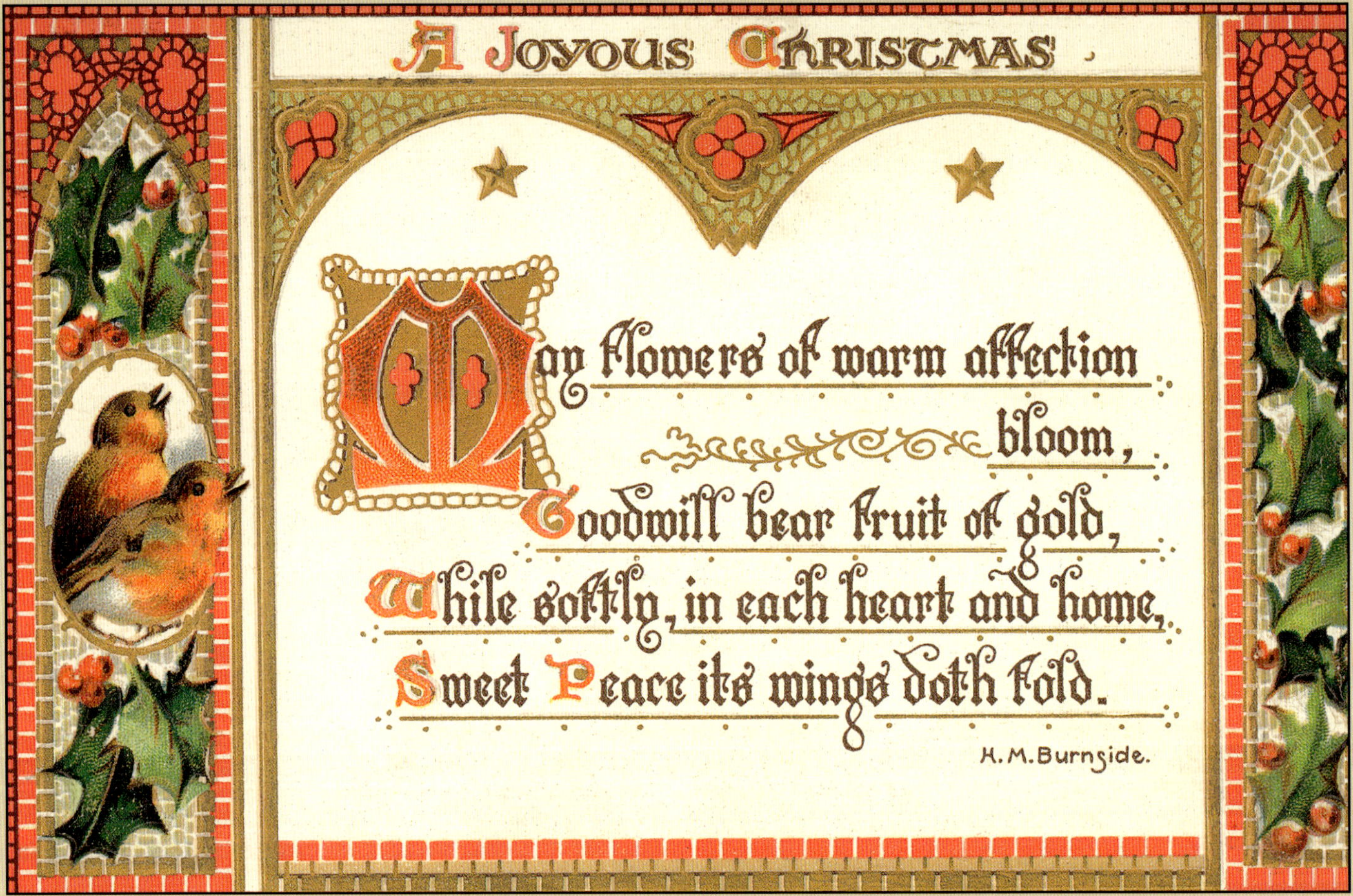
A Joyous Christmas
May flowers of warm affection
bloom,
Goodwill bear fruit of gold,
While softly, in each heart and home,
Sweet Peace its wings doth fold.
H.M.Burnside.

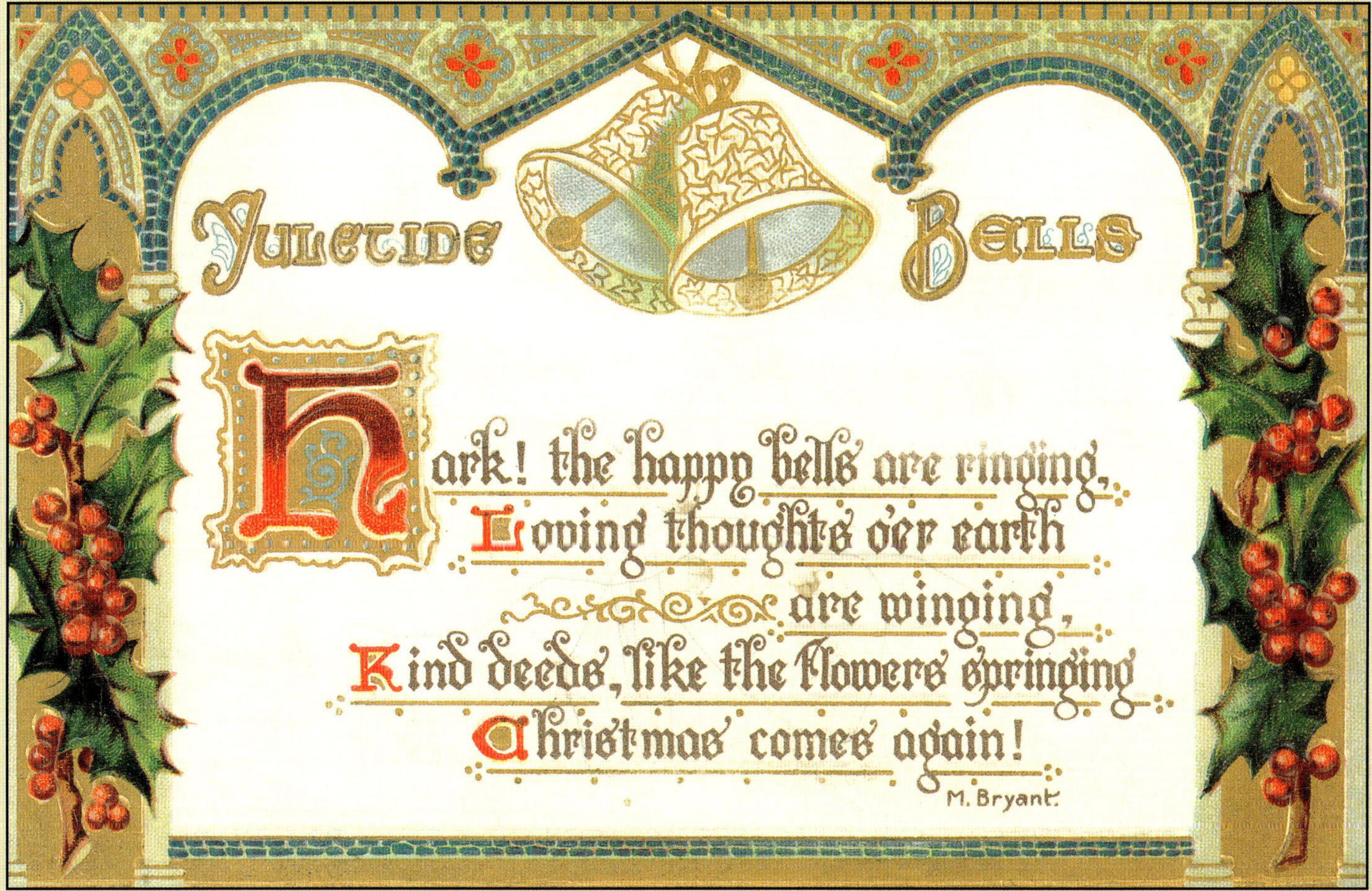
Yuletide Bells
Hark! the happy bells are ringing,
Loving thoughts o'er earth
are winging,
Kind deeds, like the flowers springing
Christmas comes again!
M. Bryant.

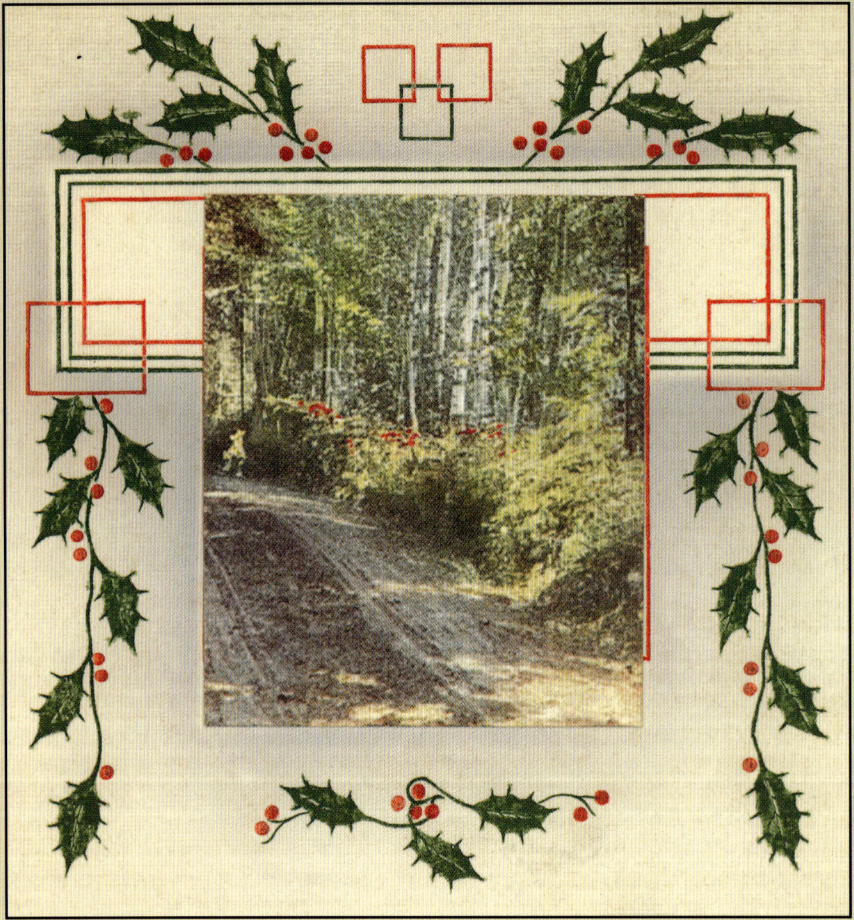

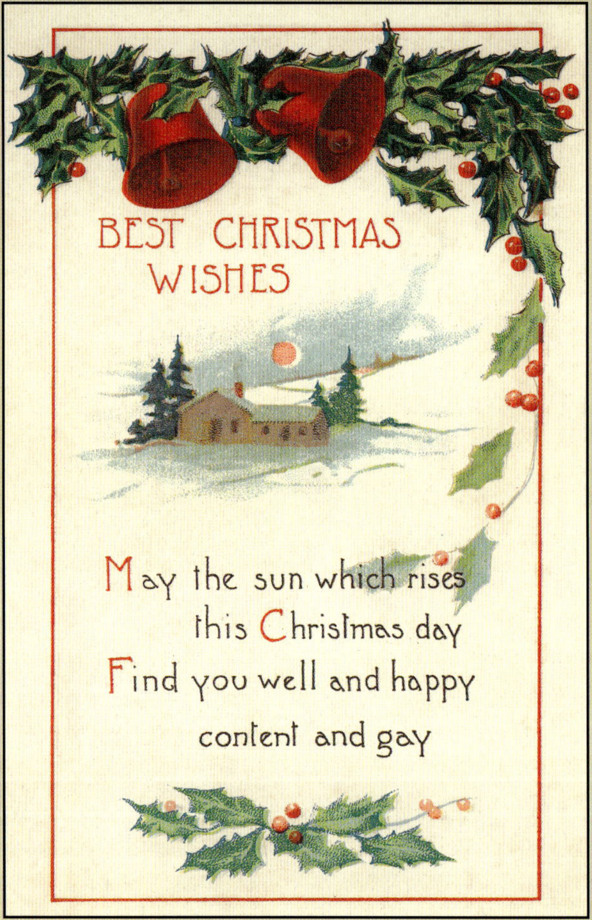
BEST CHRISTMAS WISHES
May the sun which rises
this Christmas day
Find you well and happy
content and gay

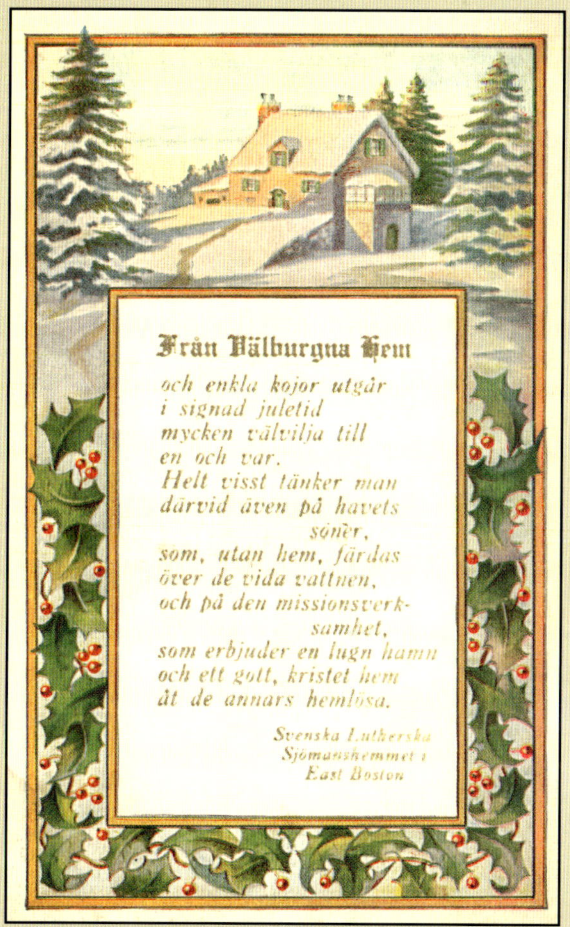
Från Välburgna Hem
och enkla kojor utgår
i signad juletid
mycken välvilja till
en och var.
Helt visst tänker man
därvid även på havets
söner,
som, utan hem, färdas
över de vida vattnen,
och på den missionsverk-
samhet,
som erbjuder en lugn hamn
och ett gott, kristet hem
åt de annars hemlösa.
Svenska Lutherska
Sjömanshemmet i
East Boston

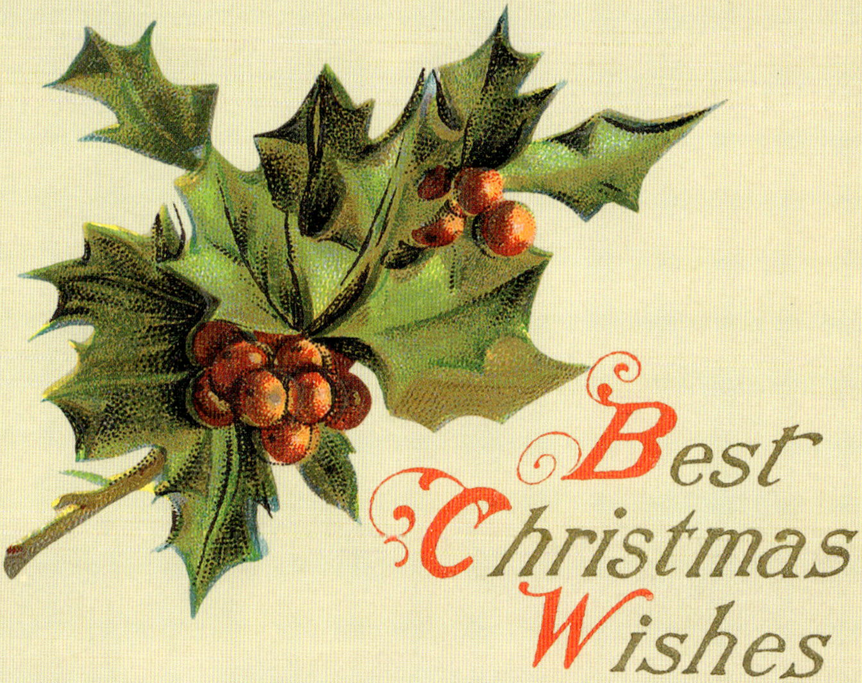
Best
Christmas
Wishes

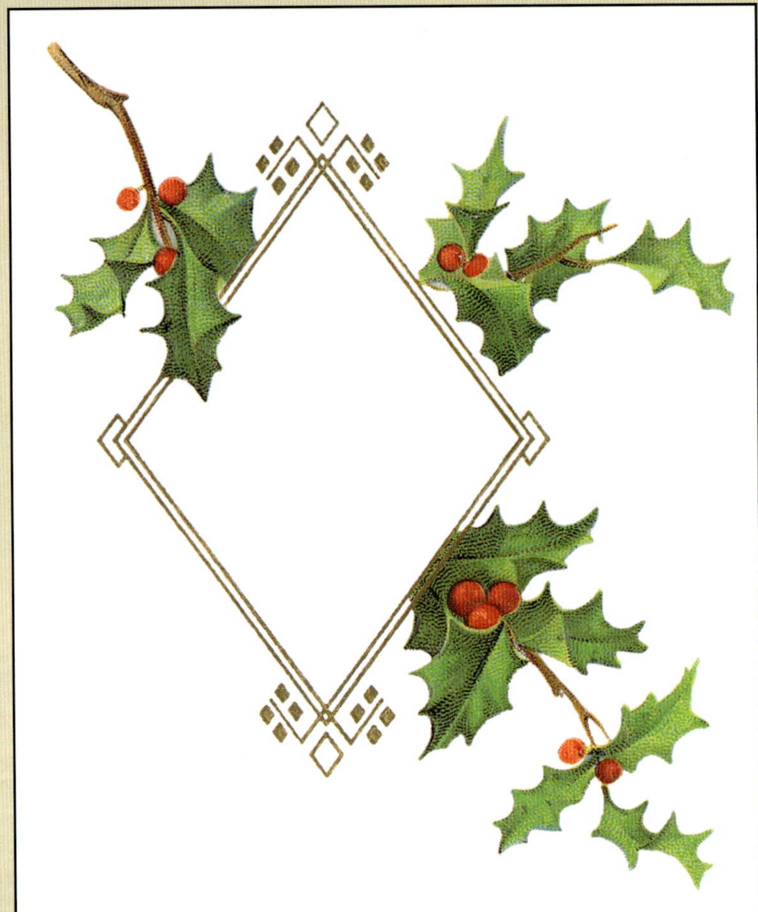

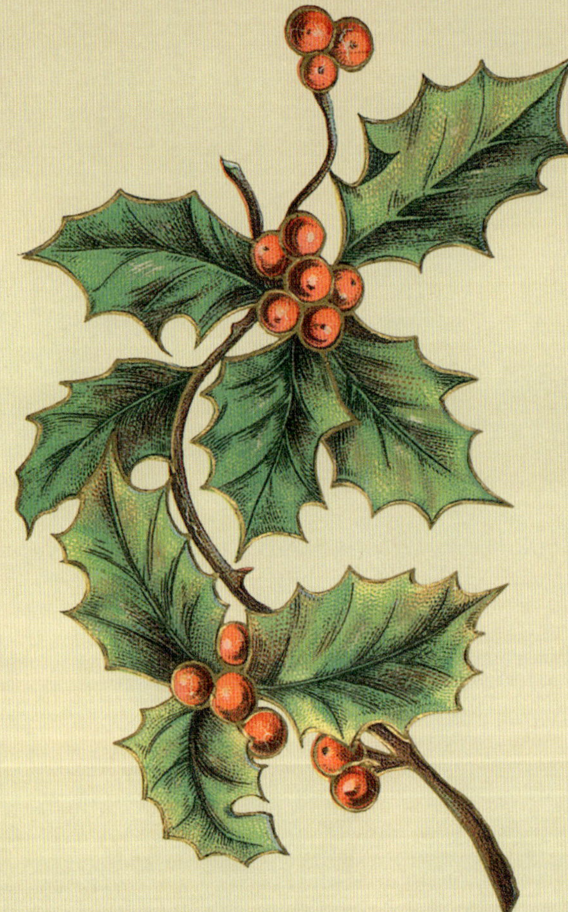

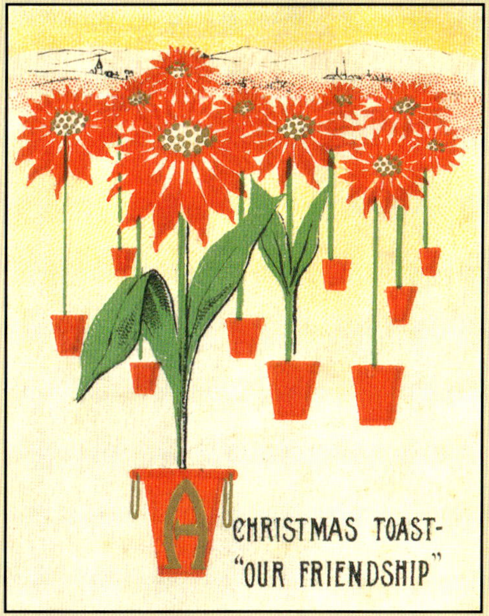
A CHRISTMAS TOAST-
"OUR FRIENDSHIP"

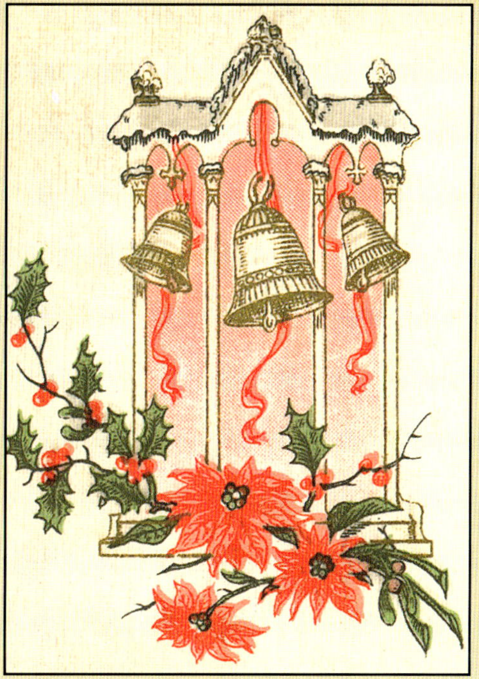

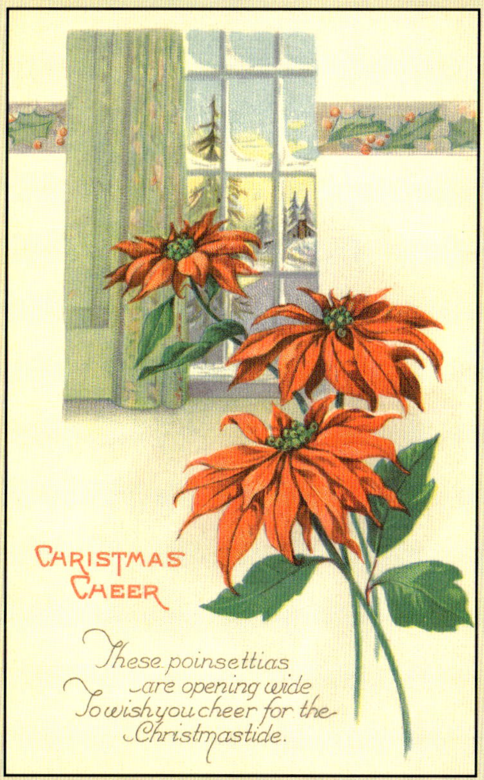
CHRISTMAS
CHEER
These poinsettias
are opening wide
To wish you cheer for the
Christmastide.

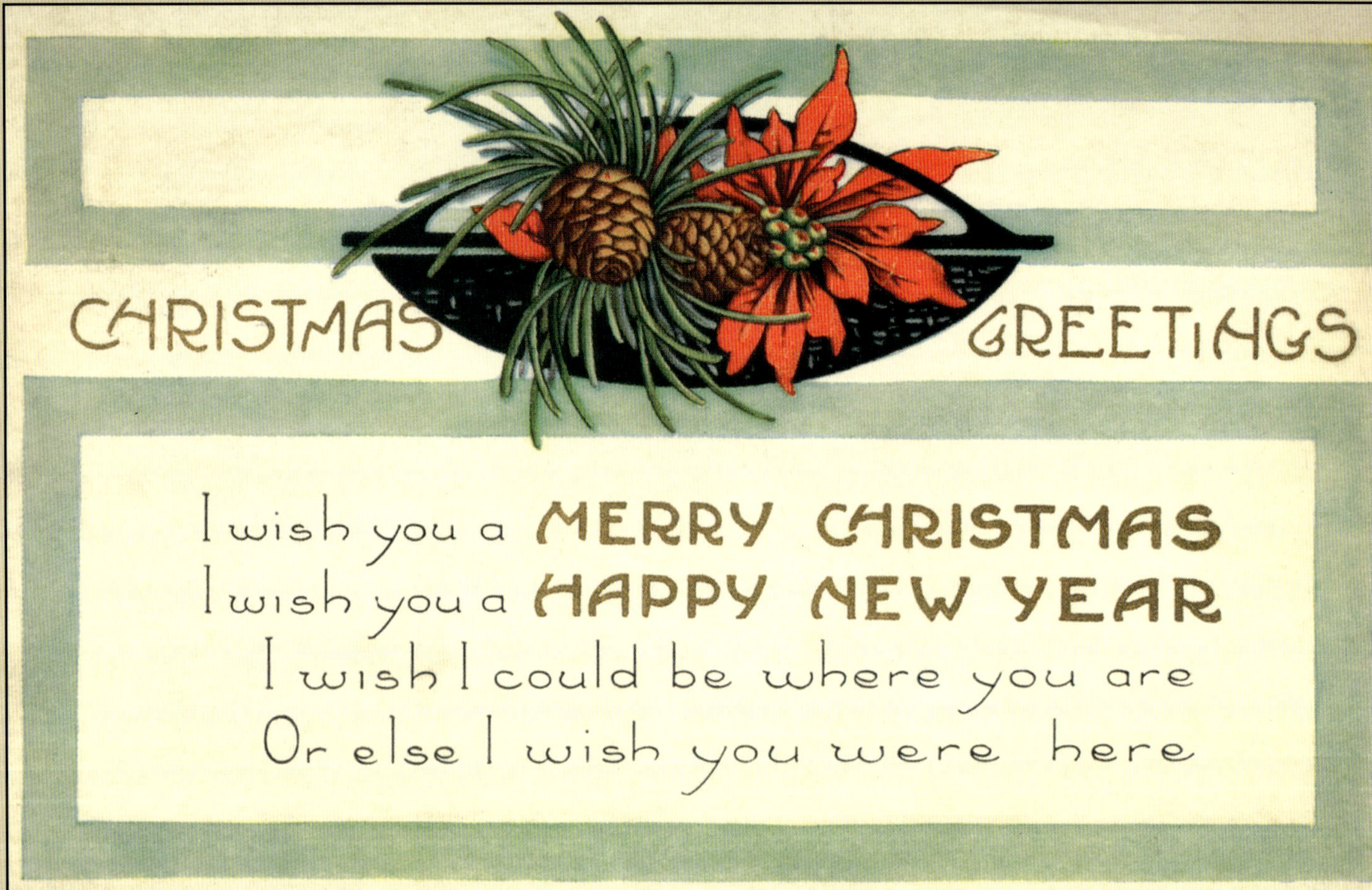
CHRISTMAS GREETINGS
I wish you a MERRY CHRISTMAS
I wish you a HAPPY NEW YEAR
I wish I could be where you are
Or else I wish you were here

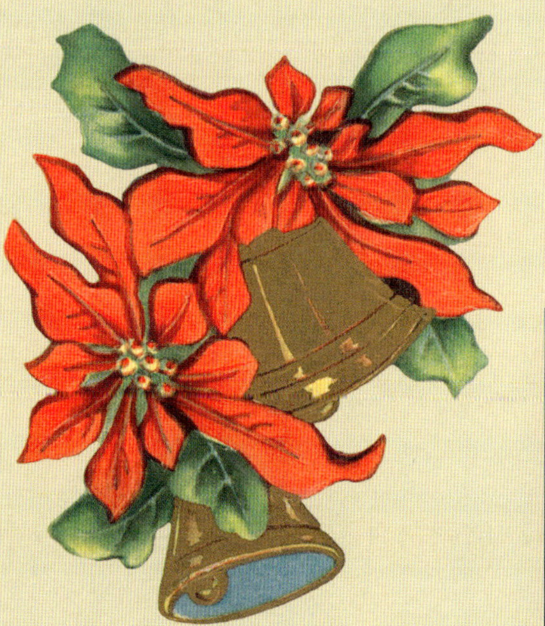

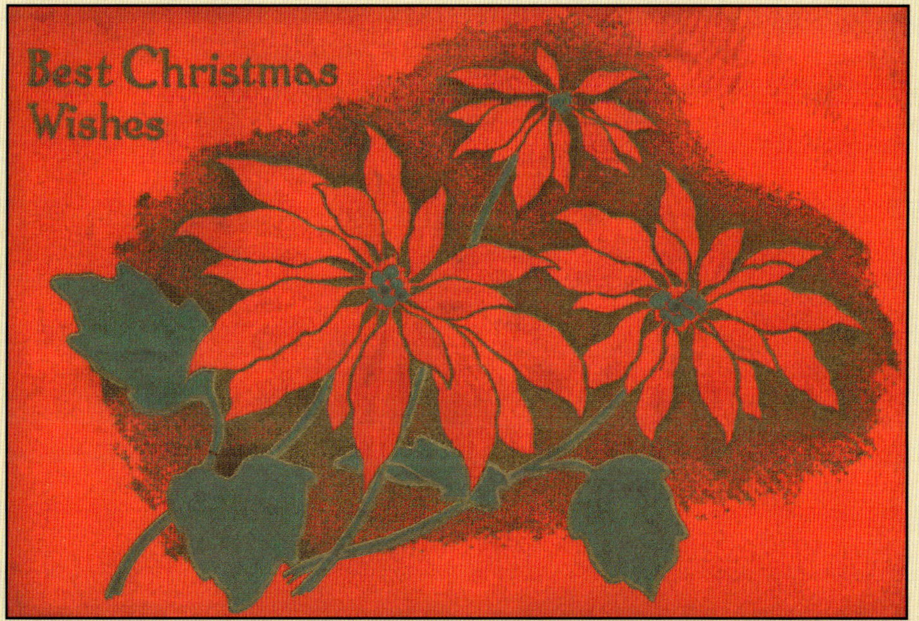
Best Christmas
Wishes

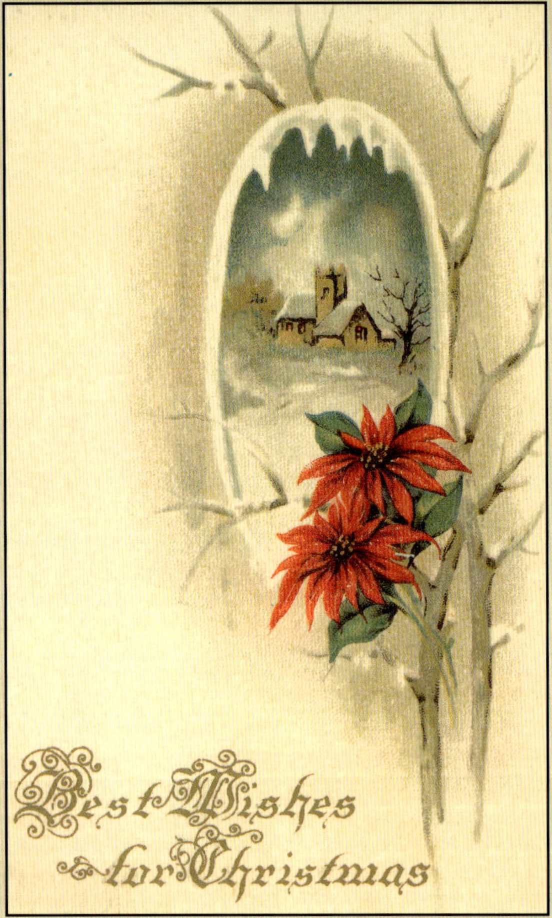
Best Wishes
for Christmas

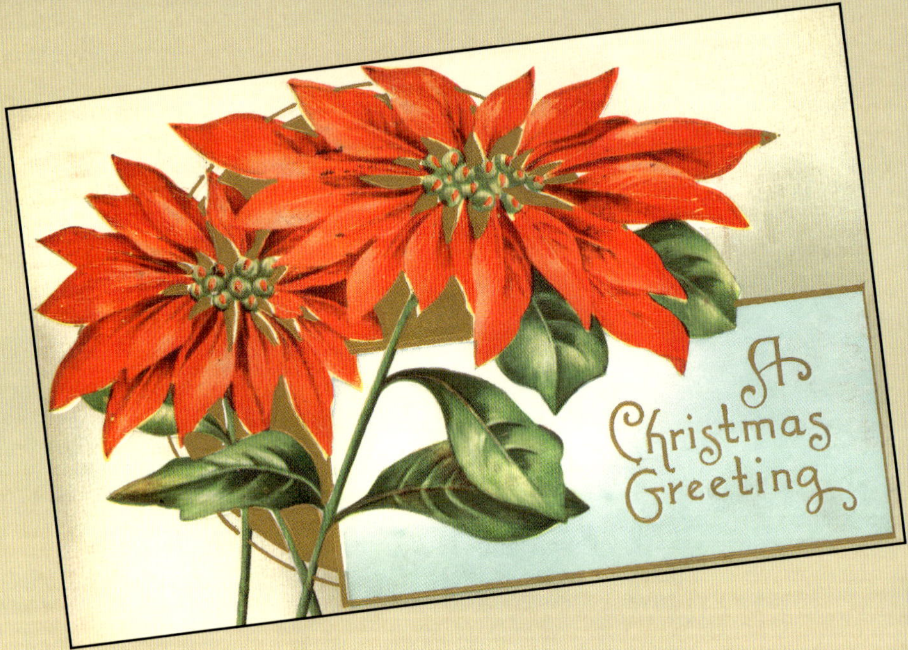
A
Christmas
Greeting

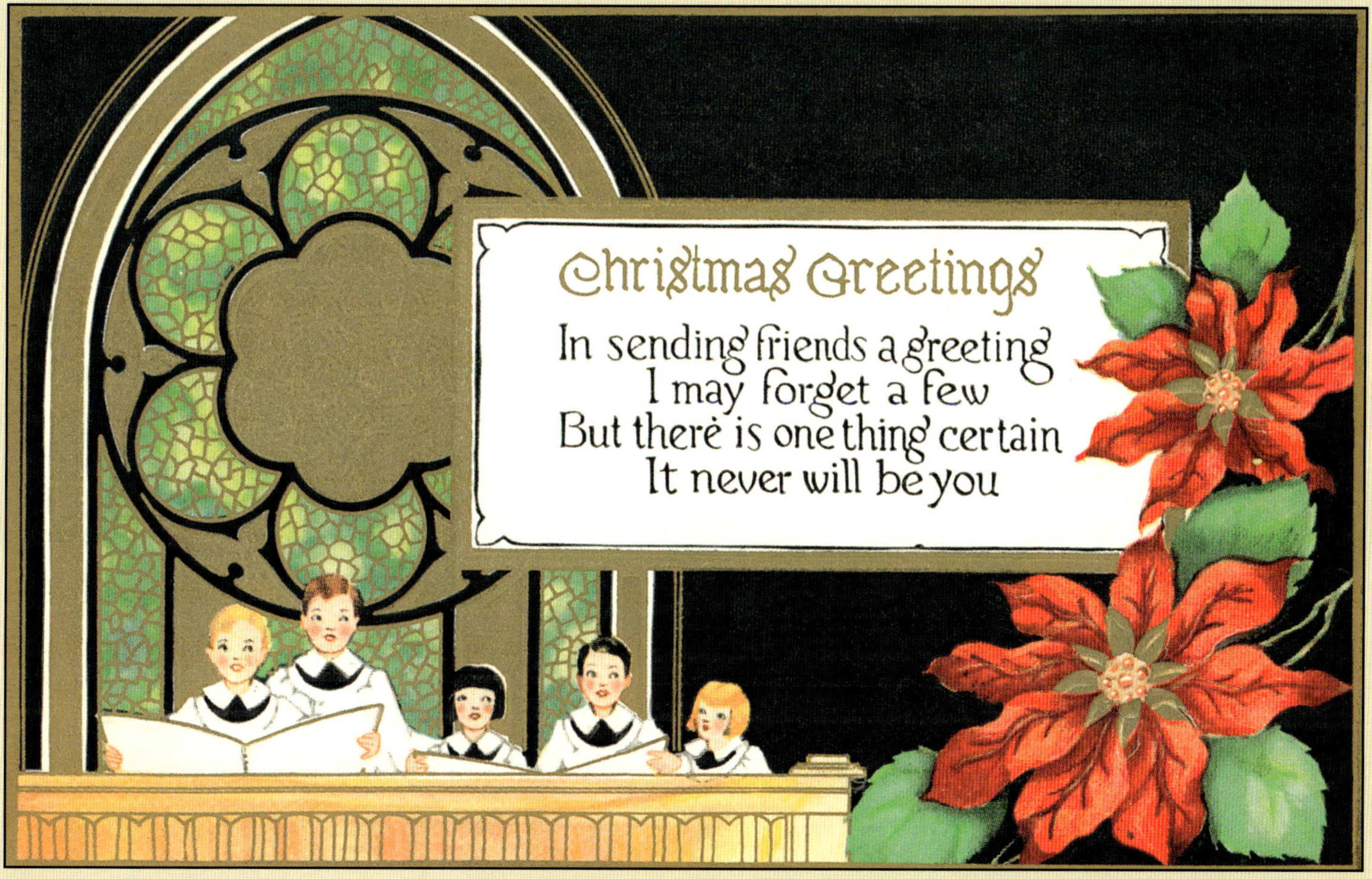
Christmas Greetings
In sending friends a greeting
I may forget a few
But there is one thing certain
It never will be you

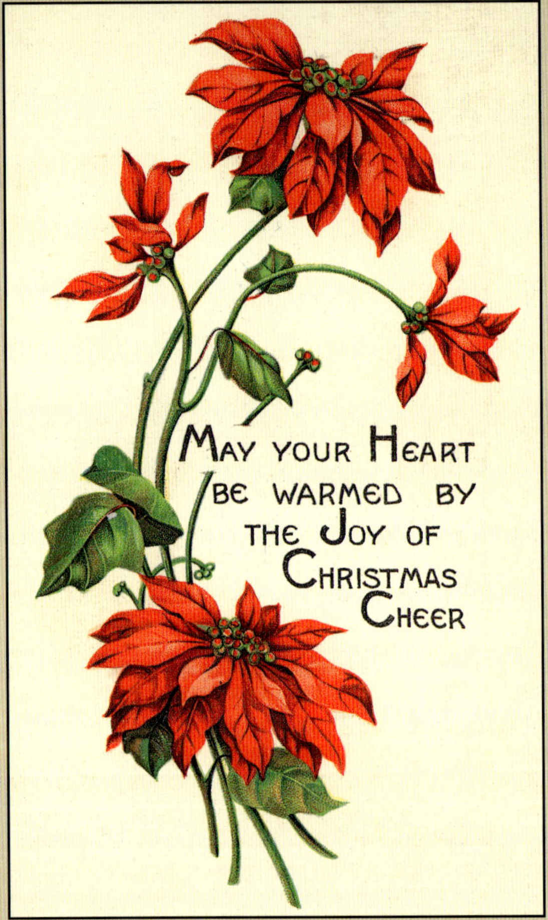
May your Heart
be warmed by
the Joy of
Christmas
Cheer

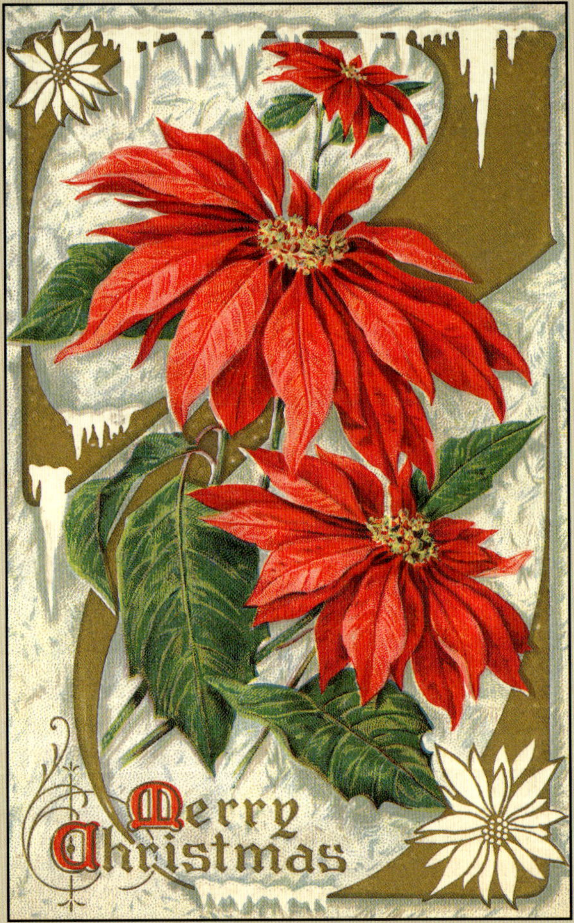
Merry
Christmas

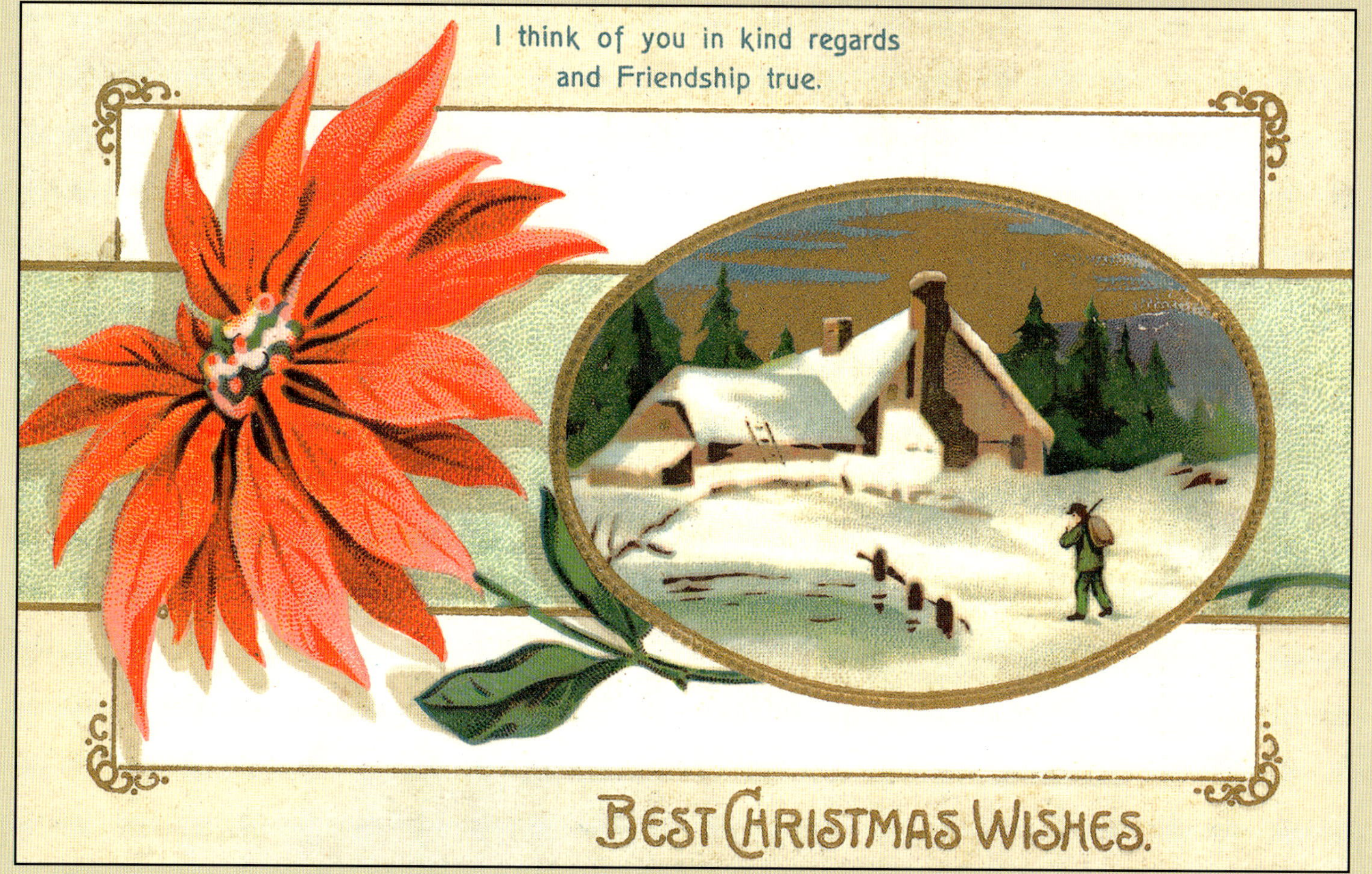
I think of you in kind regards
and Friendship true.
BEST CHRISTMAS WISHES.

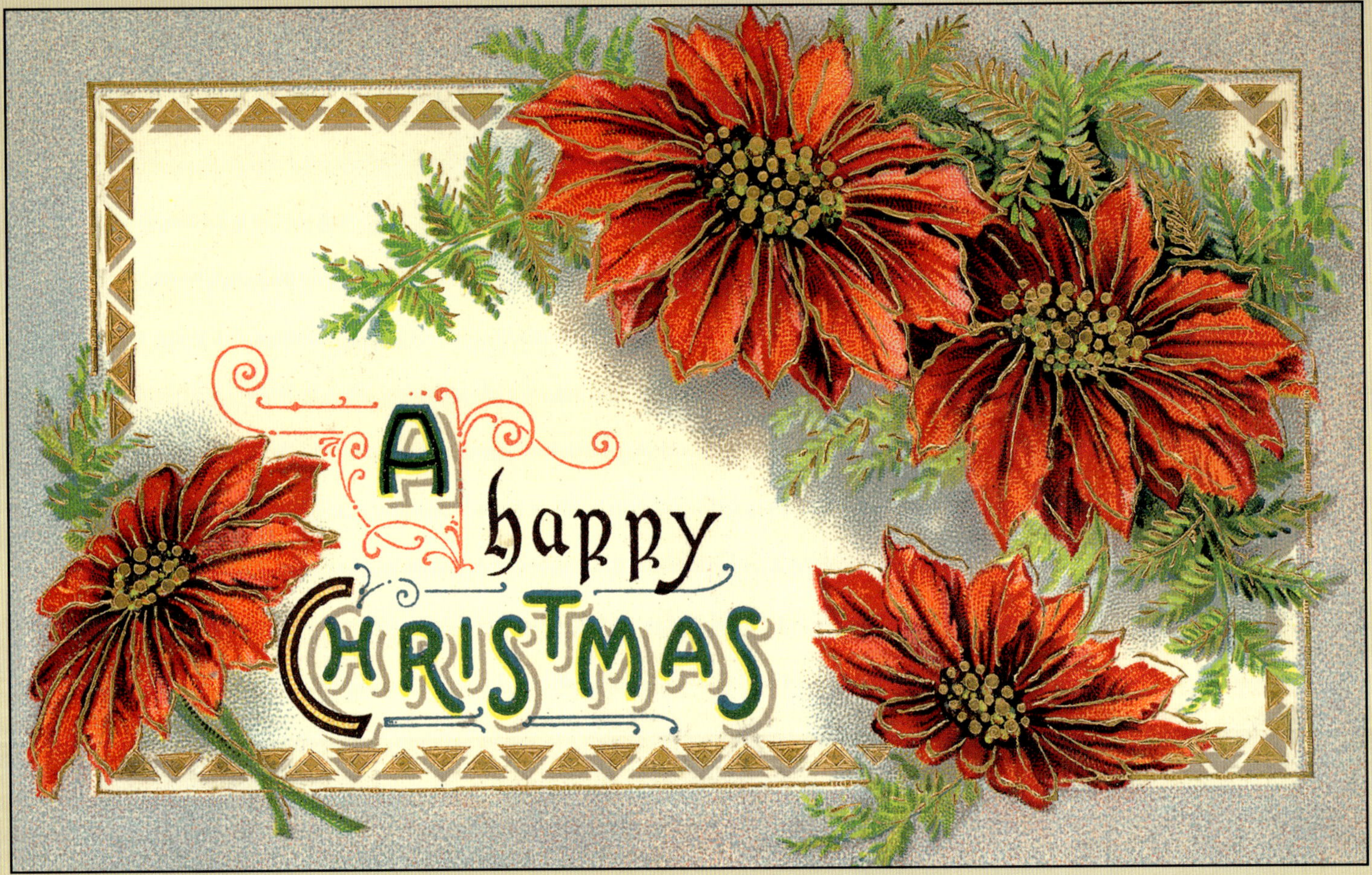
A happy
Christmas

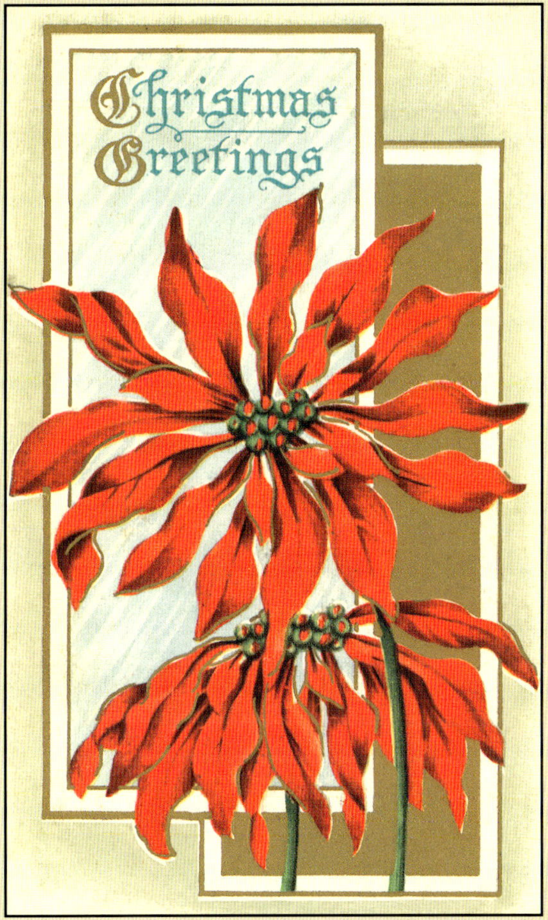
Christmas
Greetings

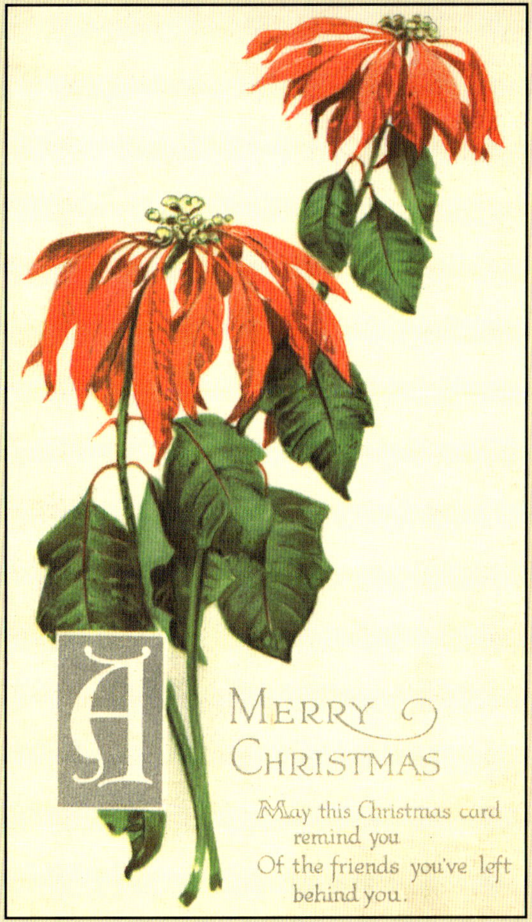
A Merry Christmas
May this Christmas card
remind you
Of the friends you've left
behind you.

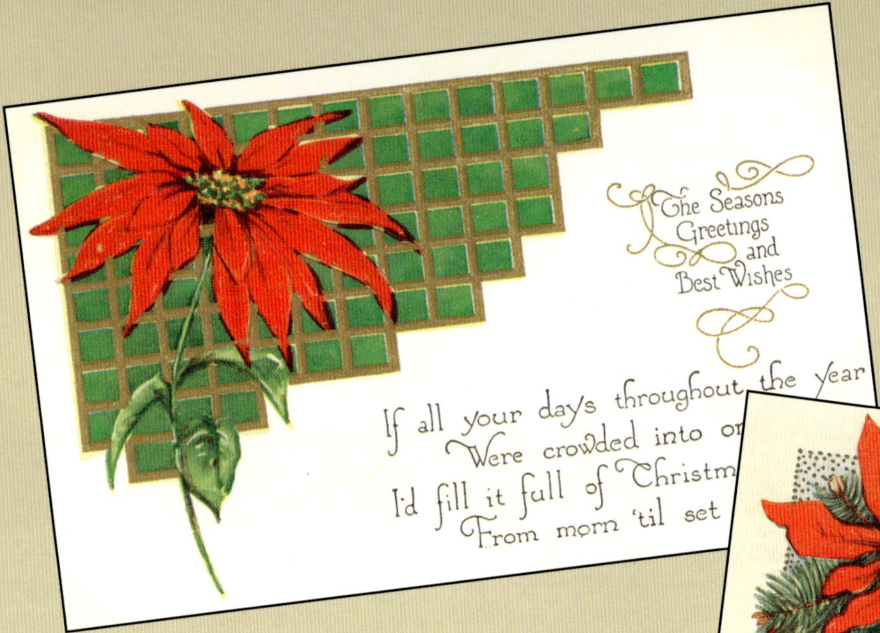
The Seasons Greetings and Best Wishes
If all your days throughout the year
Were crowded into o
I'd fill it full of Christm
From morn 'til set

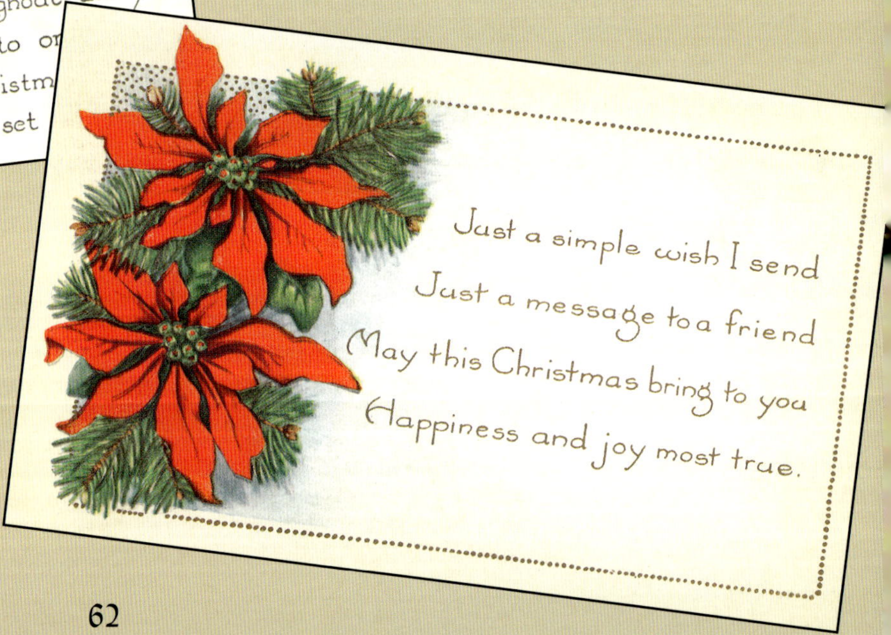
Just a simple wish I send
Just a message to a friend
May this Christmas bring to you
Happiness and joy most true.

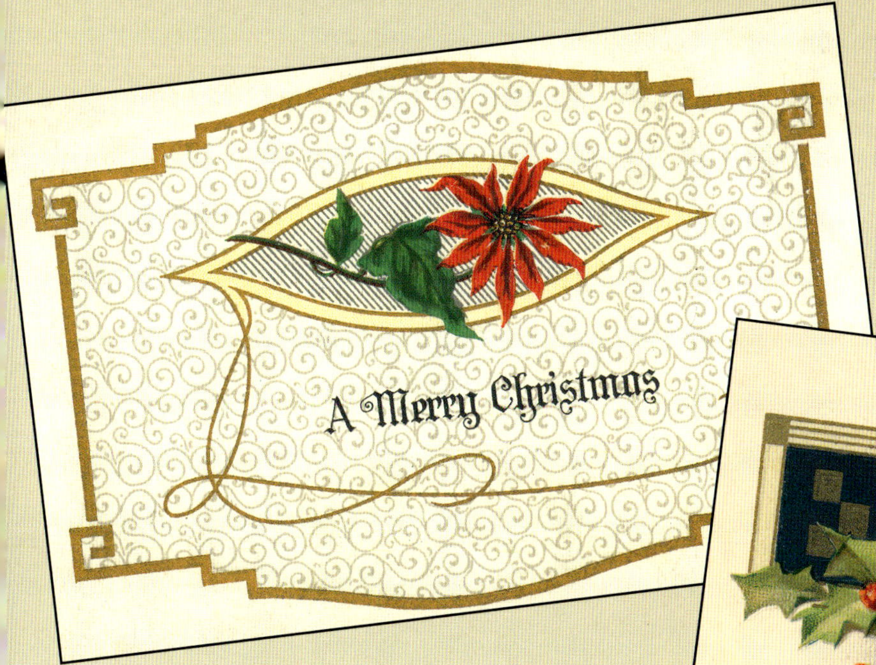
A Merry Christmas

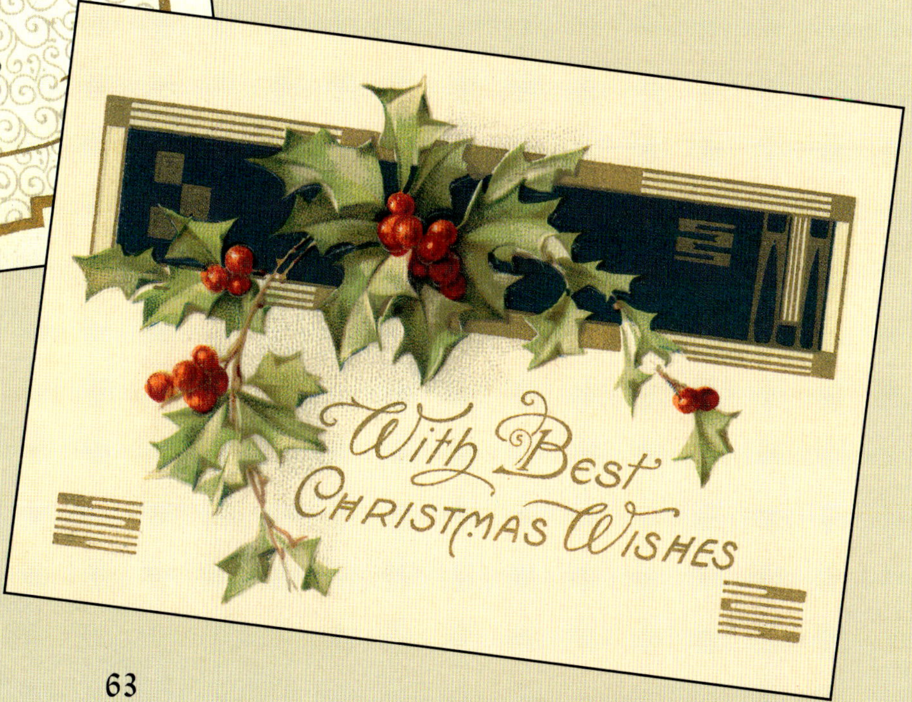
With Best
Christmas Wishes

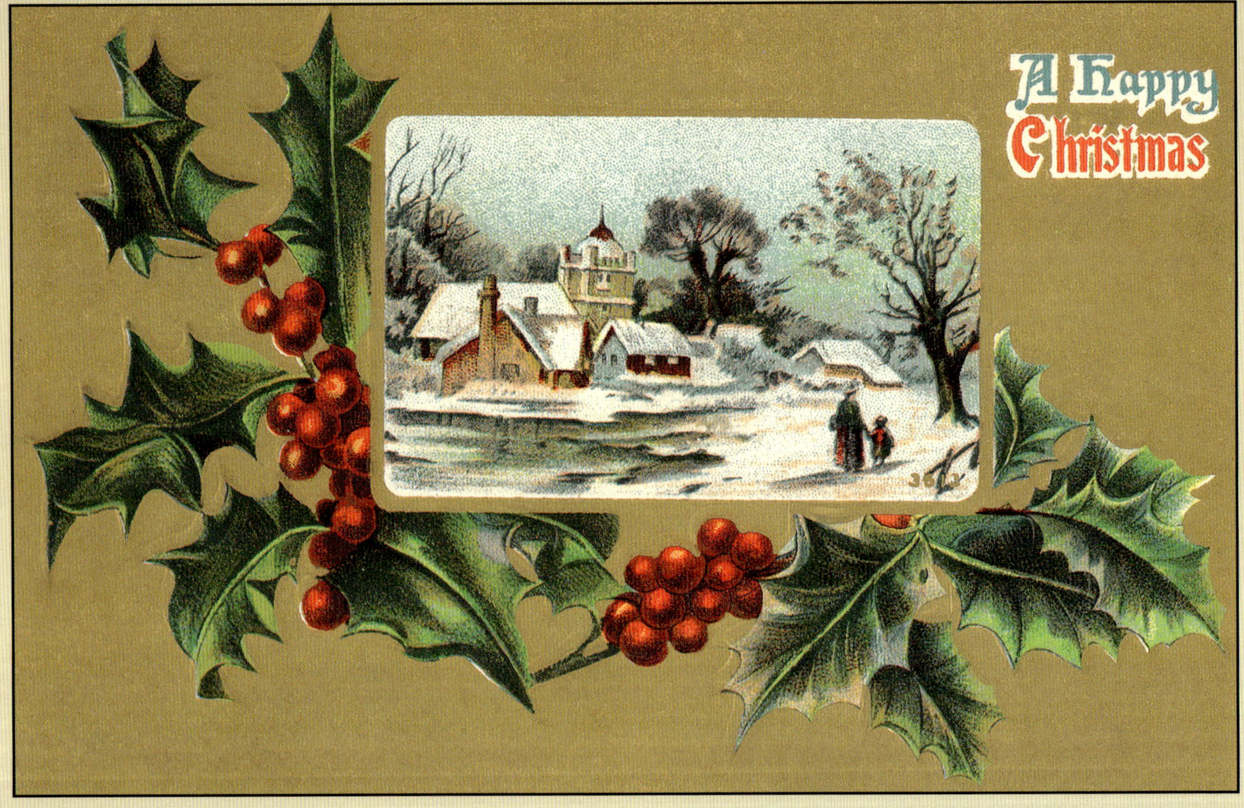
A Happy
Christmas

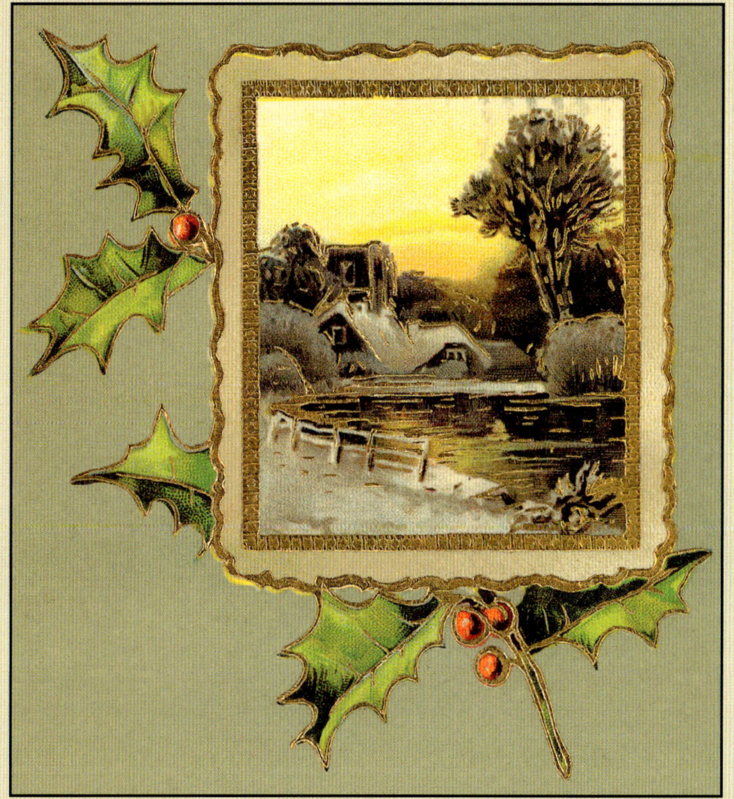

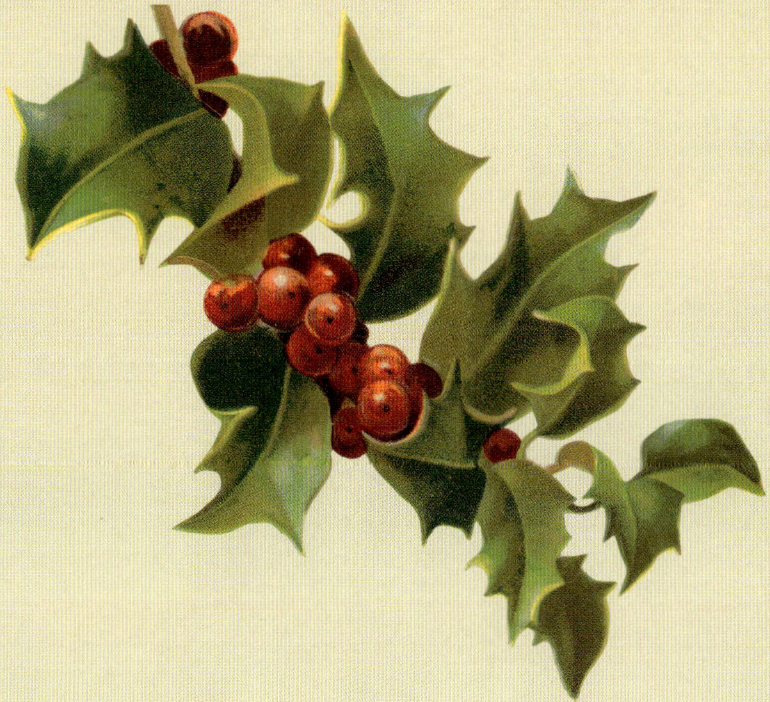

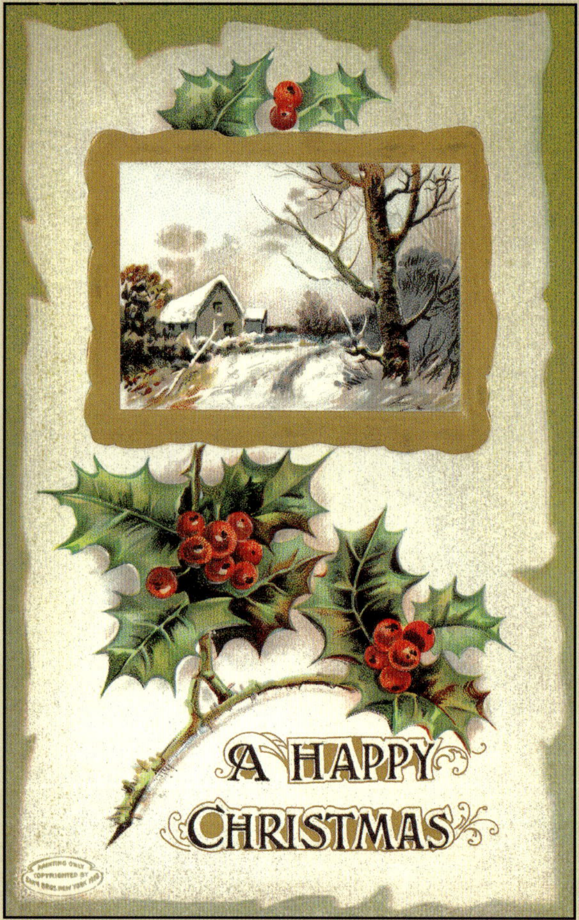
A HAPPY
CHRISTMAS

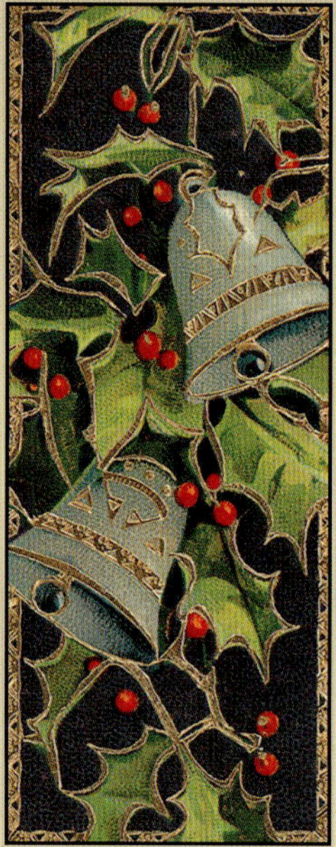

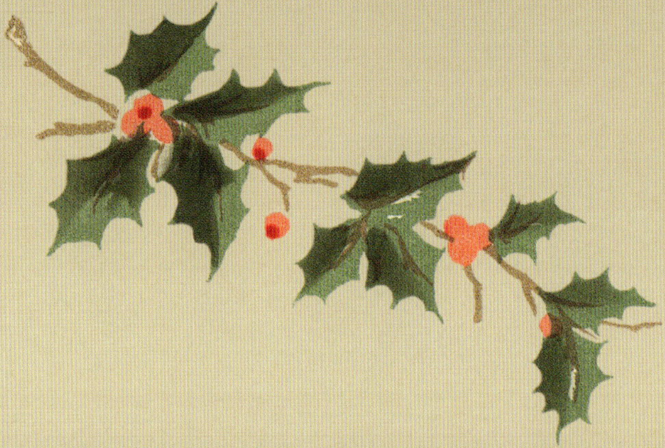

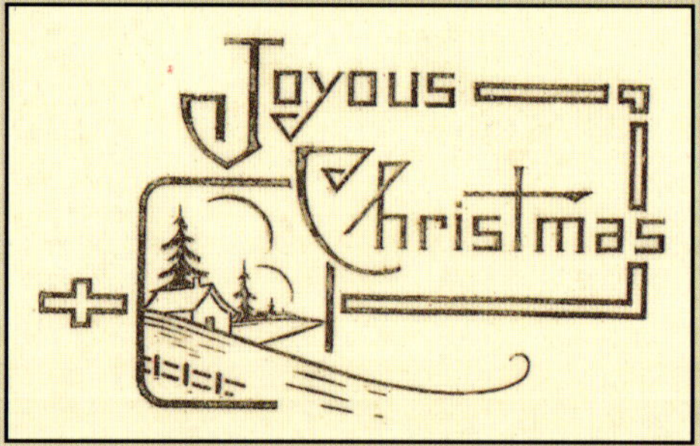
Joyous
Christmas

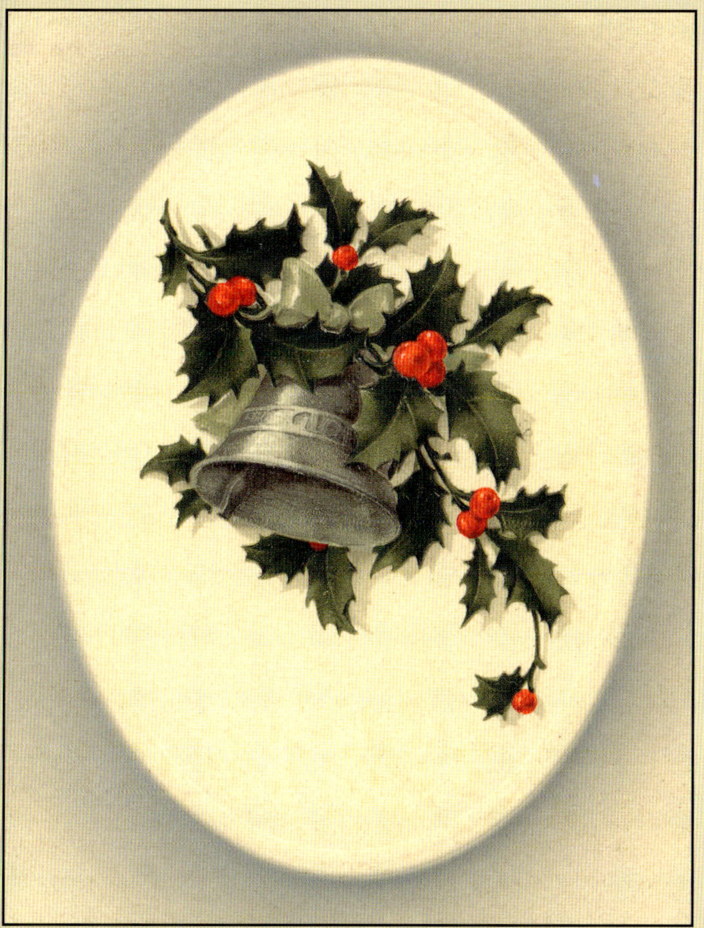

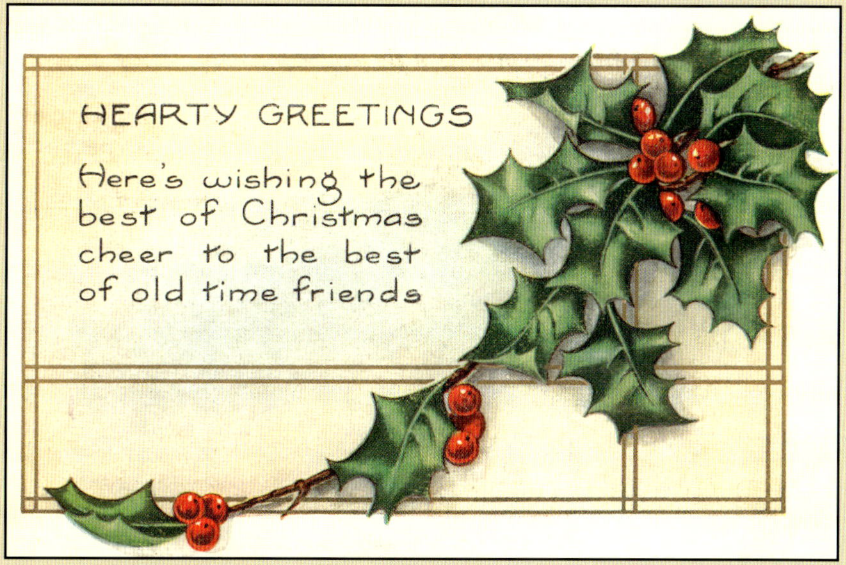
HEARTY GREETINGS
Here's wishing the
best of Christmas
cheer to the best
of old time friends

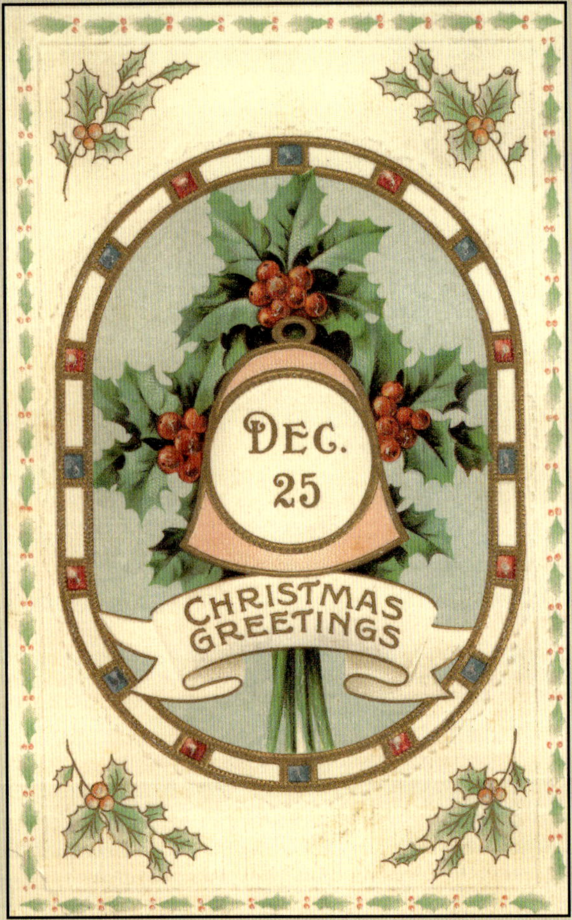
DEC.
25
CHRISTMAS
GREETINGS

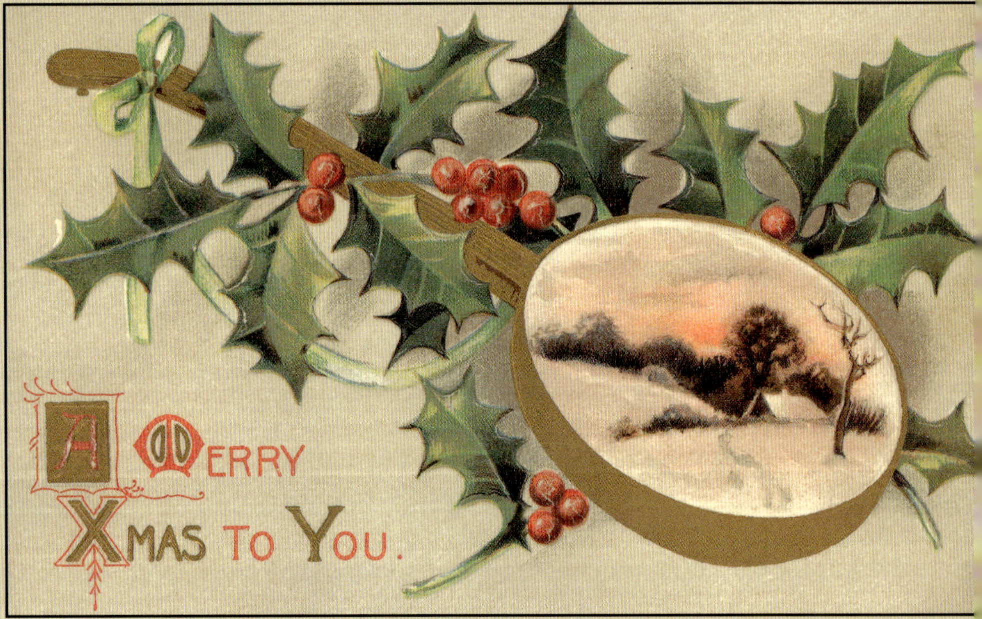
A MERRY
XMAS TO YOU.

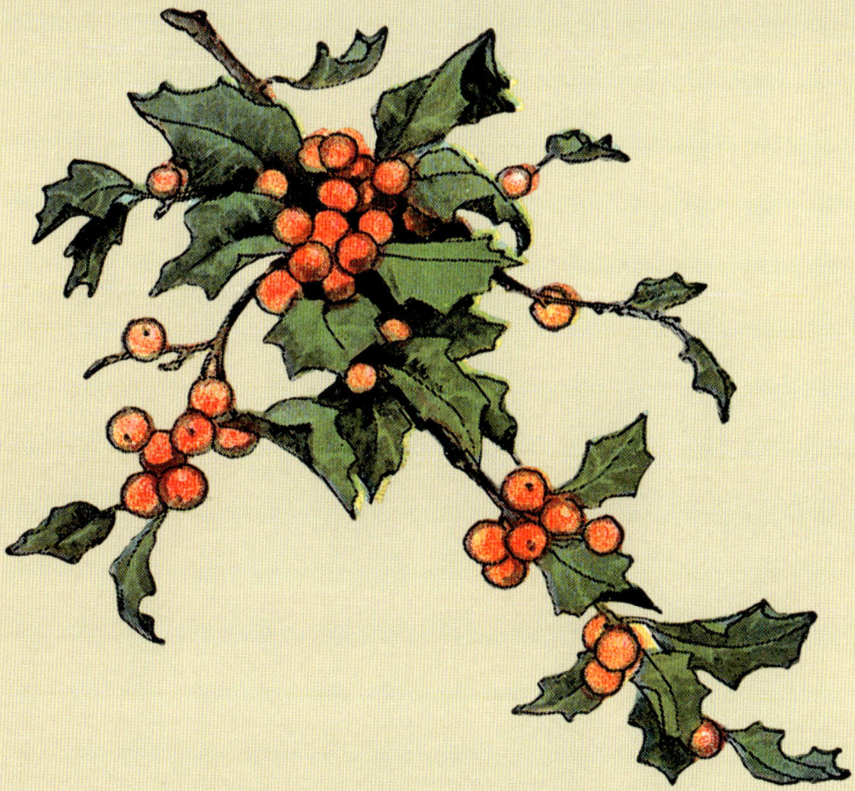

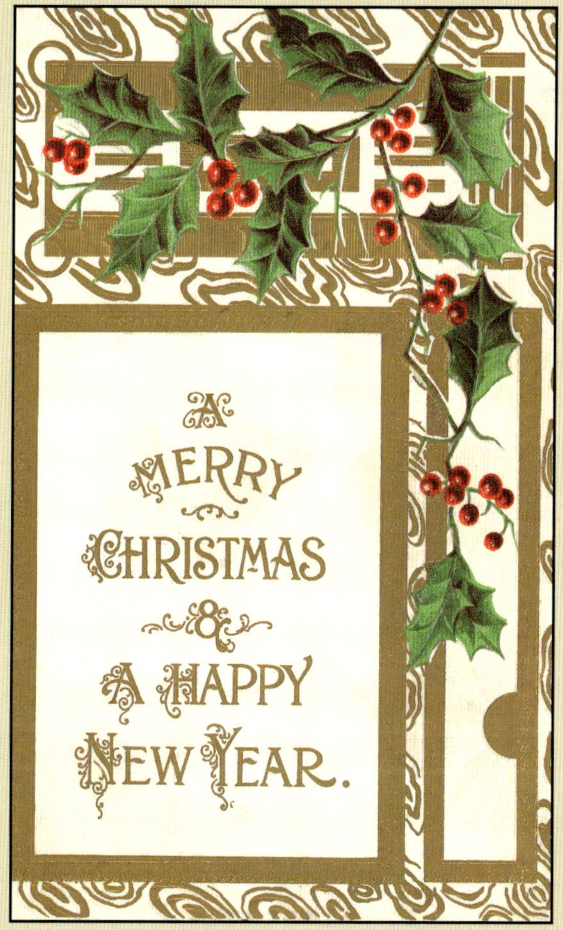
A
MERRY
CHRISTMAS
&
A HAPPY
NEW YEAR.

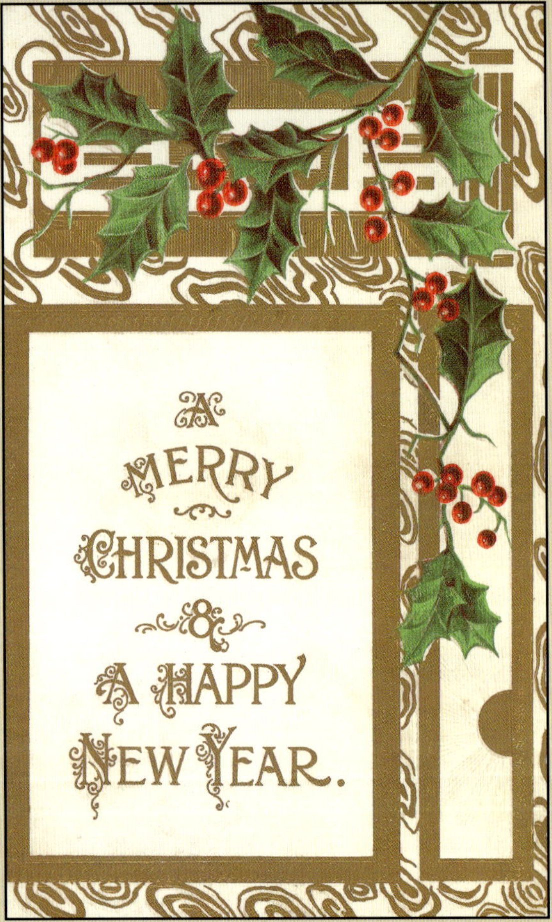
A
MERRY
CHRISTMAS
&
A HAPPY
NEW YEAR.

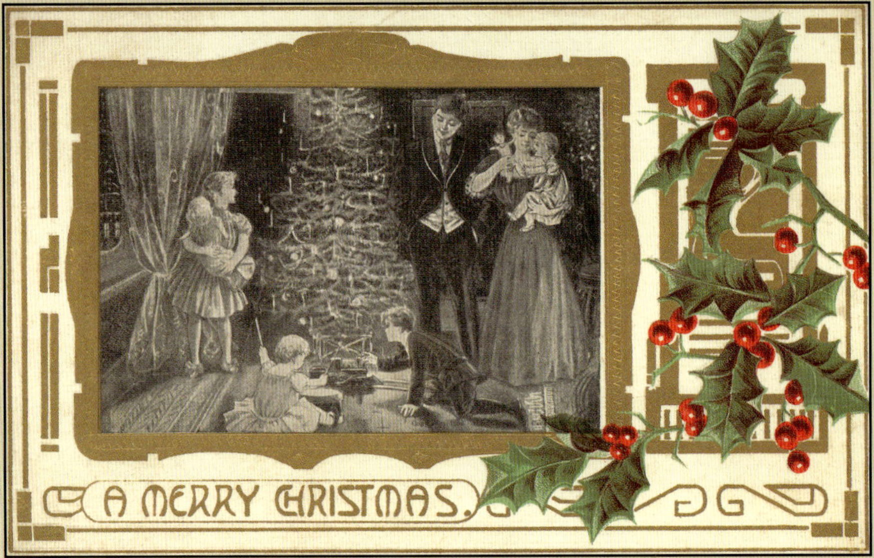
A MERRY CHRISTMAS.

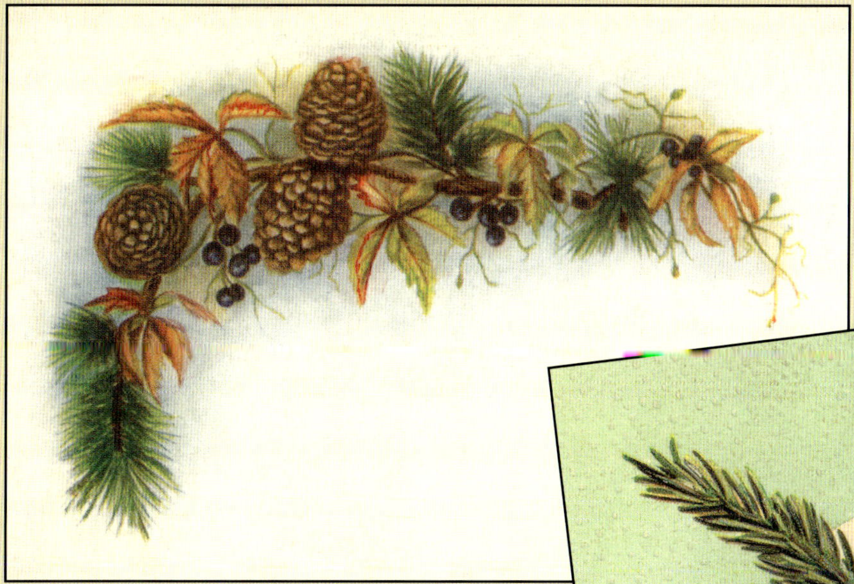

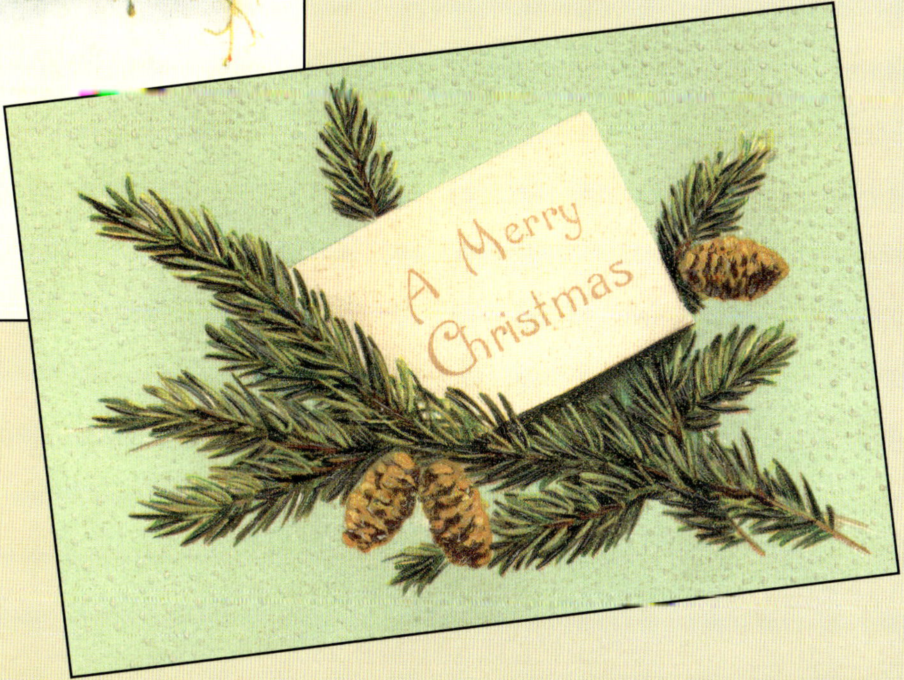
A Merry
Christmas

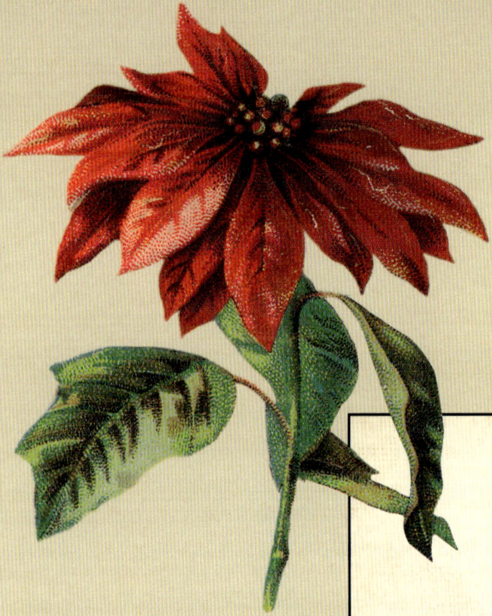

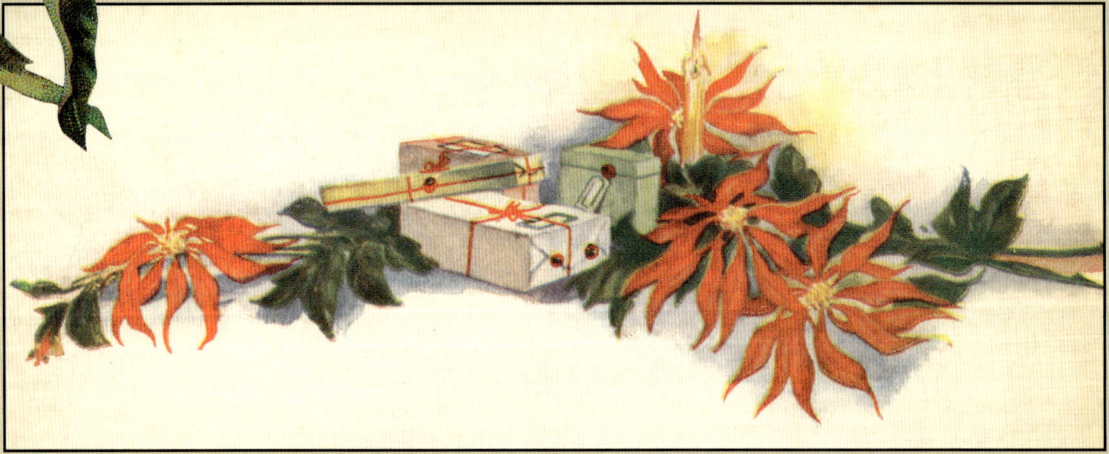

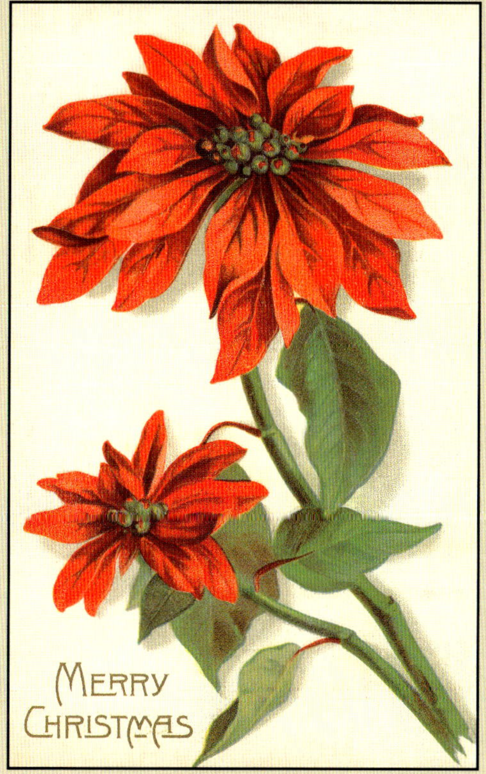
MERRY
CHRISTMAS

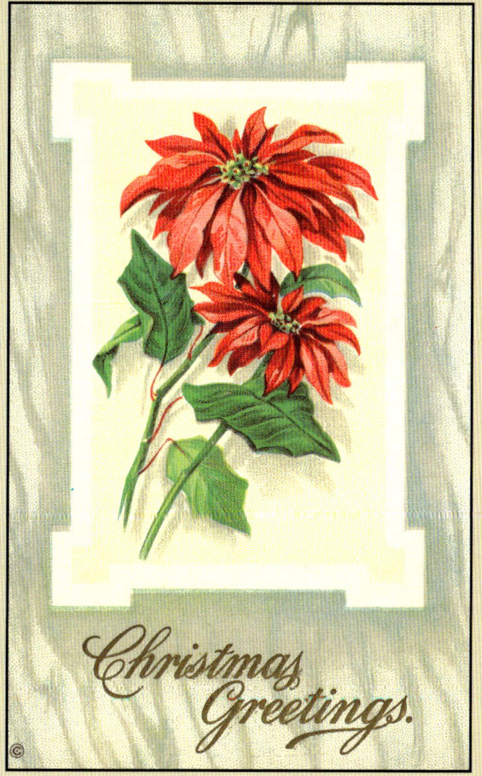
Christmas
Greetings.

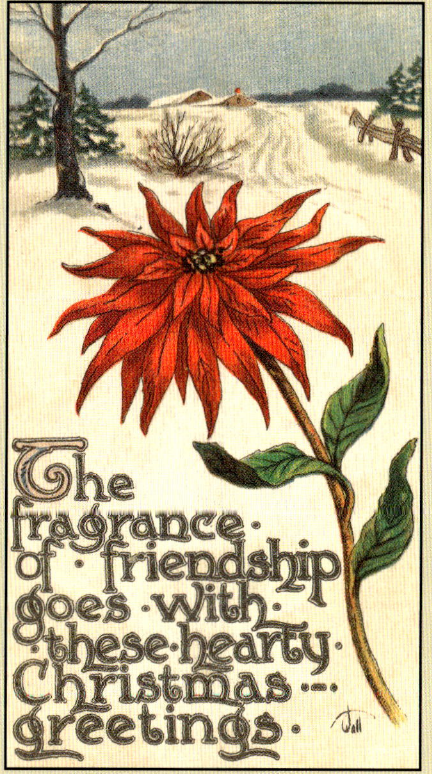
The
fragrance·
of·friendship
goes·with·
·these·hearty·
Christmas
greetings·

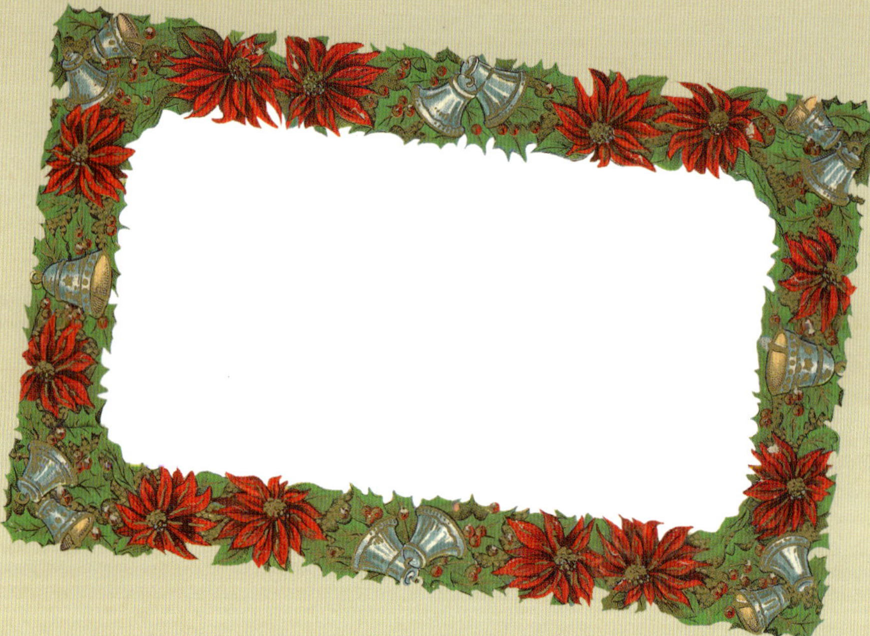

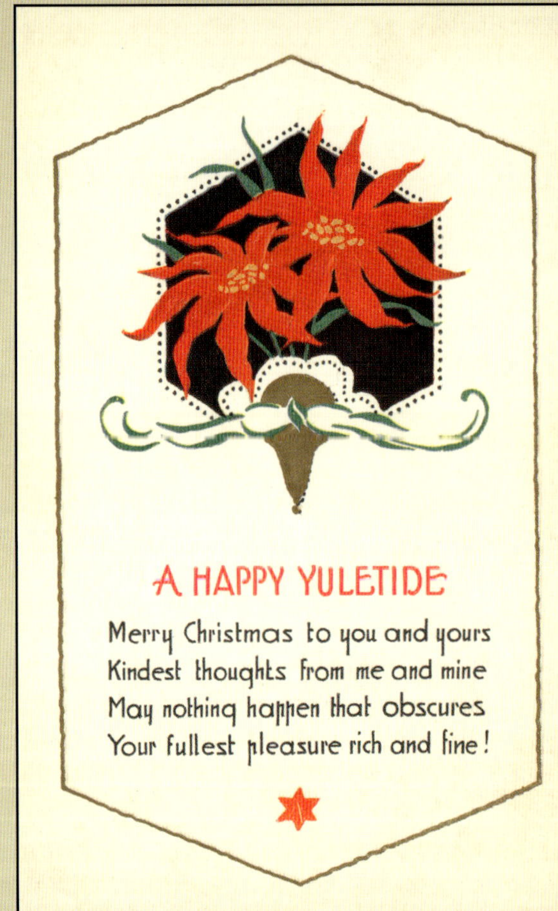
A HAPPY YULETIDE
Merry Christmas to you and yours
Kindest thoughts from me and mine
May nothing happen that obscures
Your fullest pleasure rich and fine!

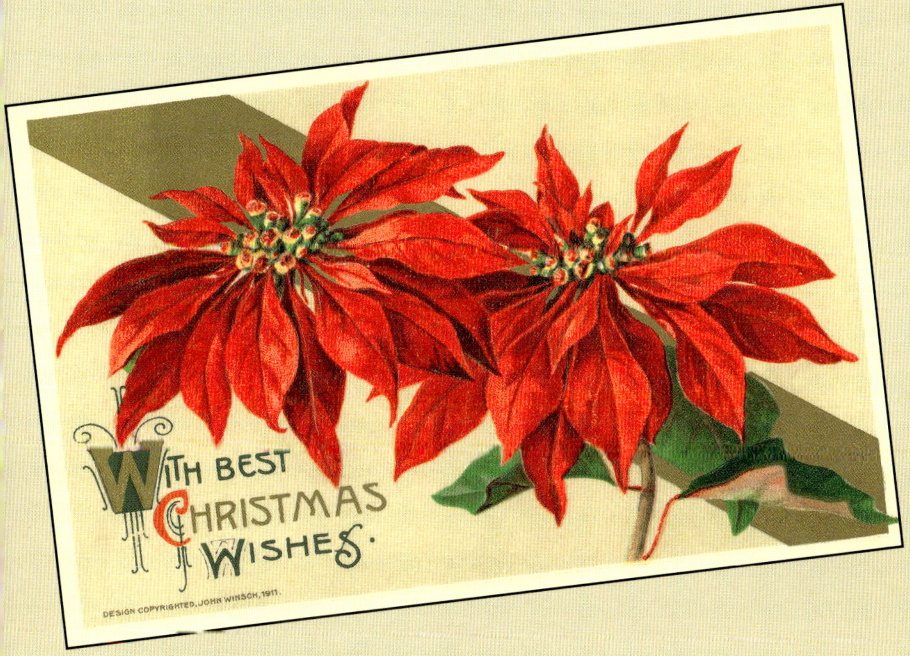
WITH BEST
CHRISTMAS
WISHES.
DESIGN COPYRIGHTED, JOHN WINSCH, 1911.

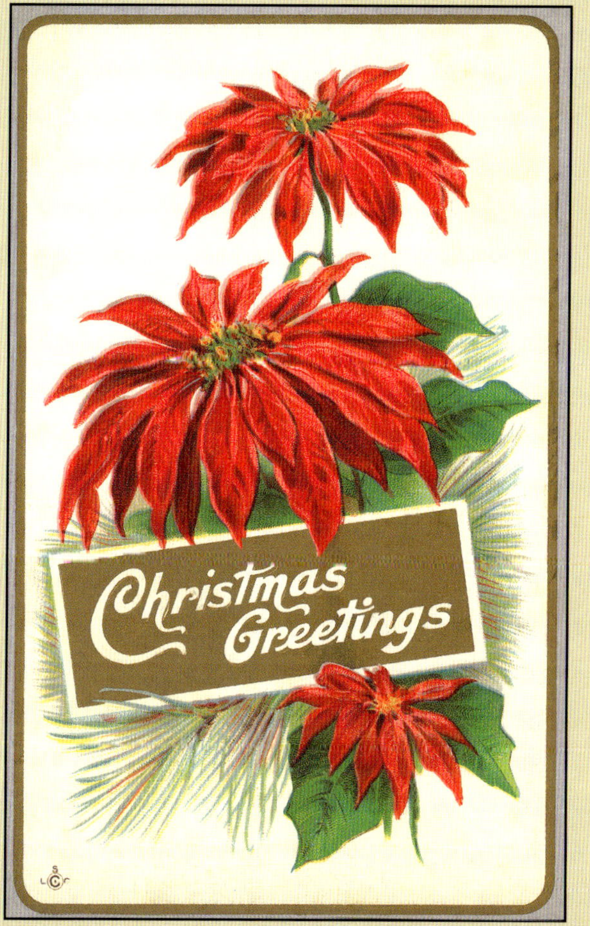
Christmas
Greetings

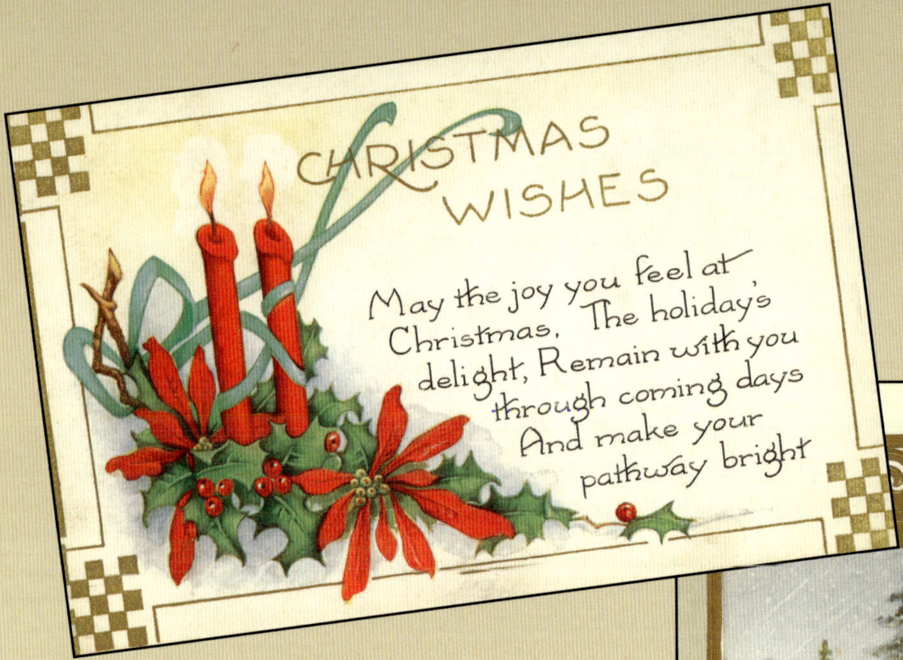
CHRISTMAS WISHES
May the joy you feel at Christmas, The holiday's delight, Remain with you through coming days And make your pathway bright

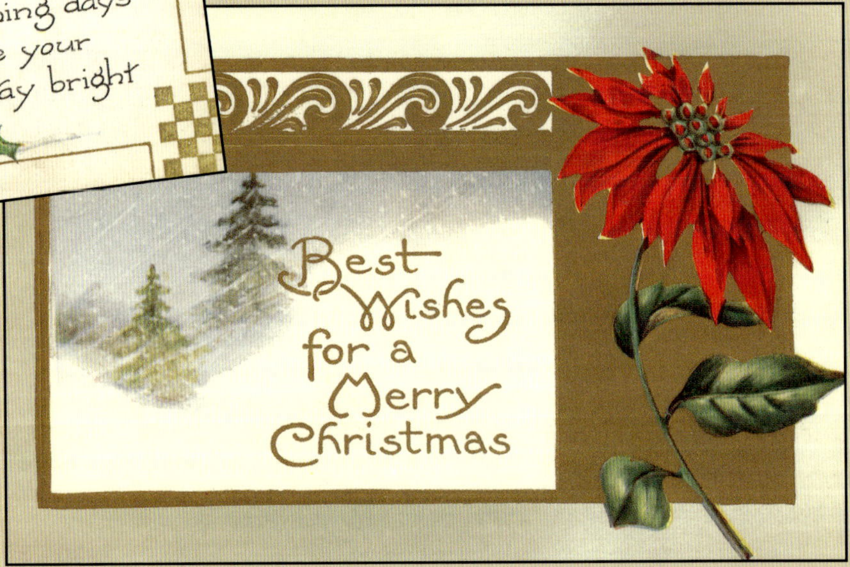
Best Wishes for a Merry Christmas

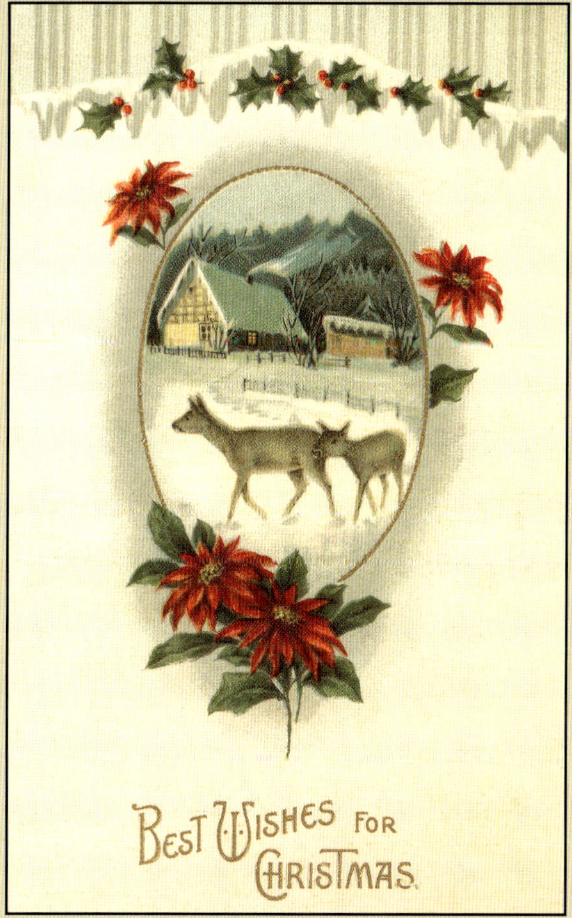
Best Wishes for
Christmas

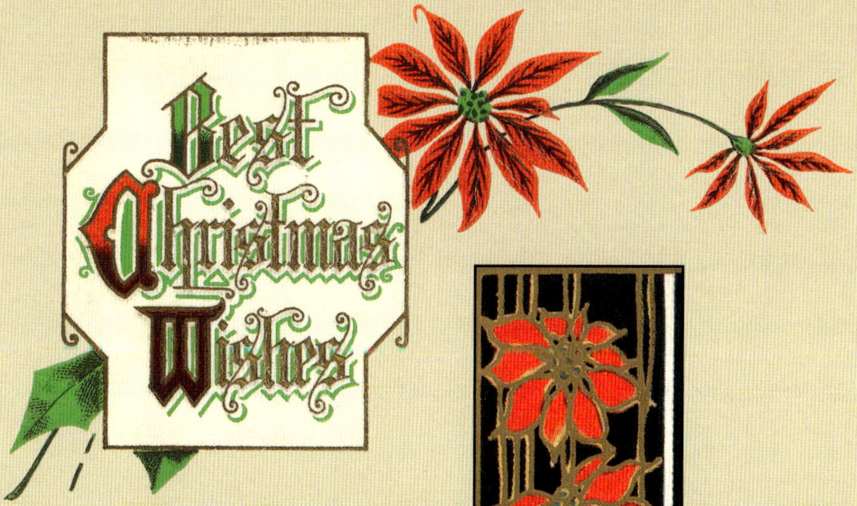
Best
Christmas
Wishes

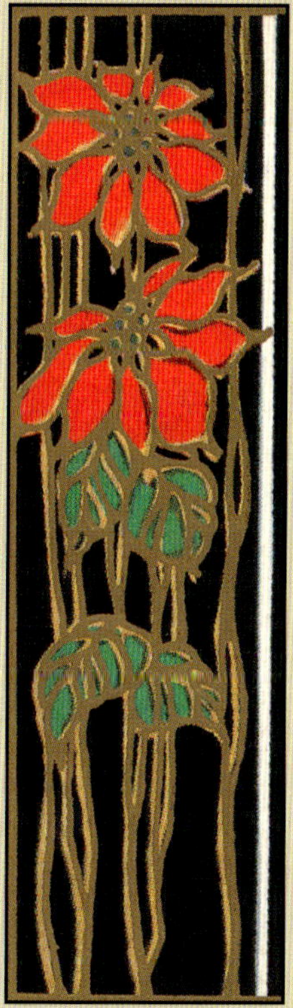

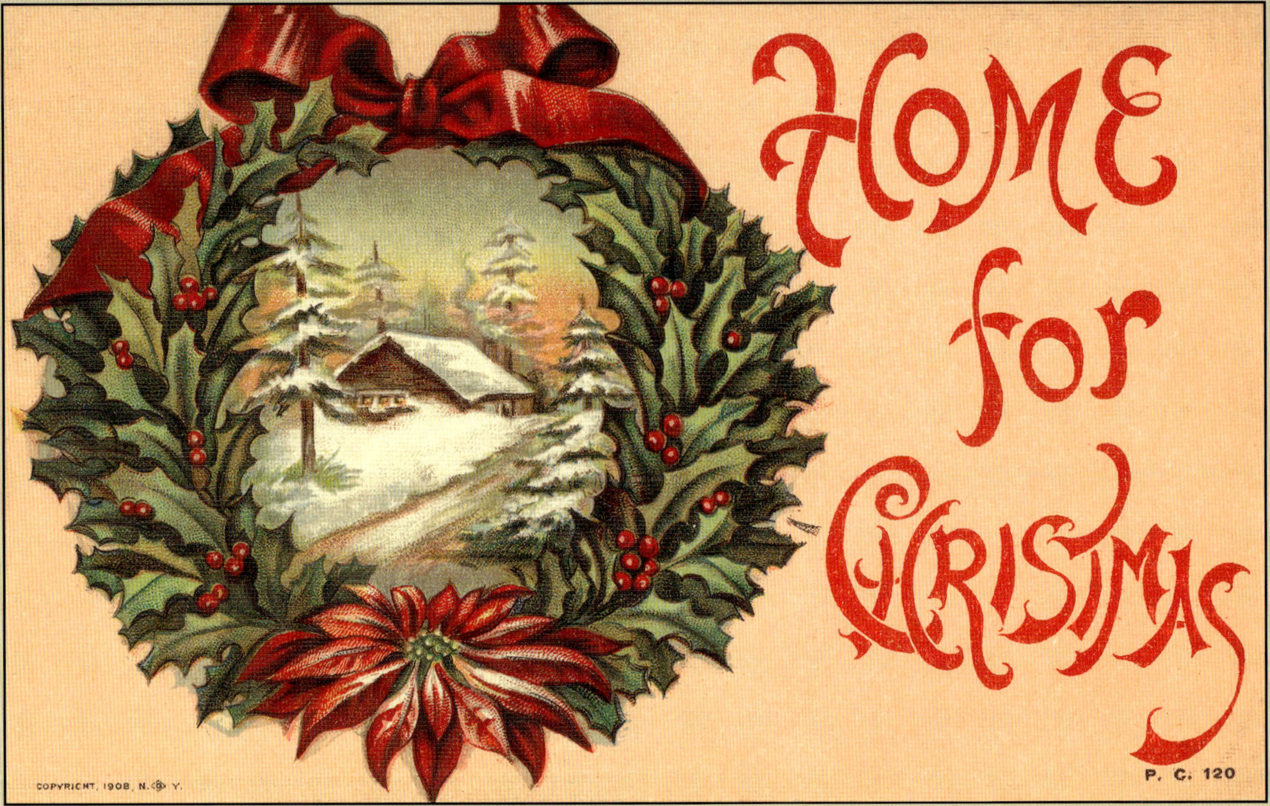
Home for Christmas
COPYRIGHT, 1908, N. Y.
P. C. 120

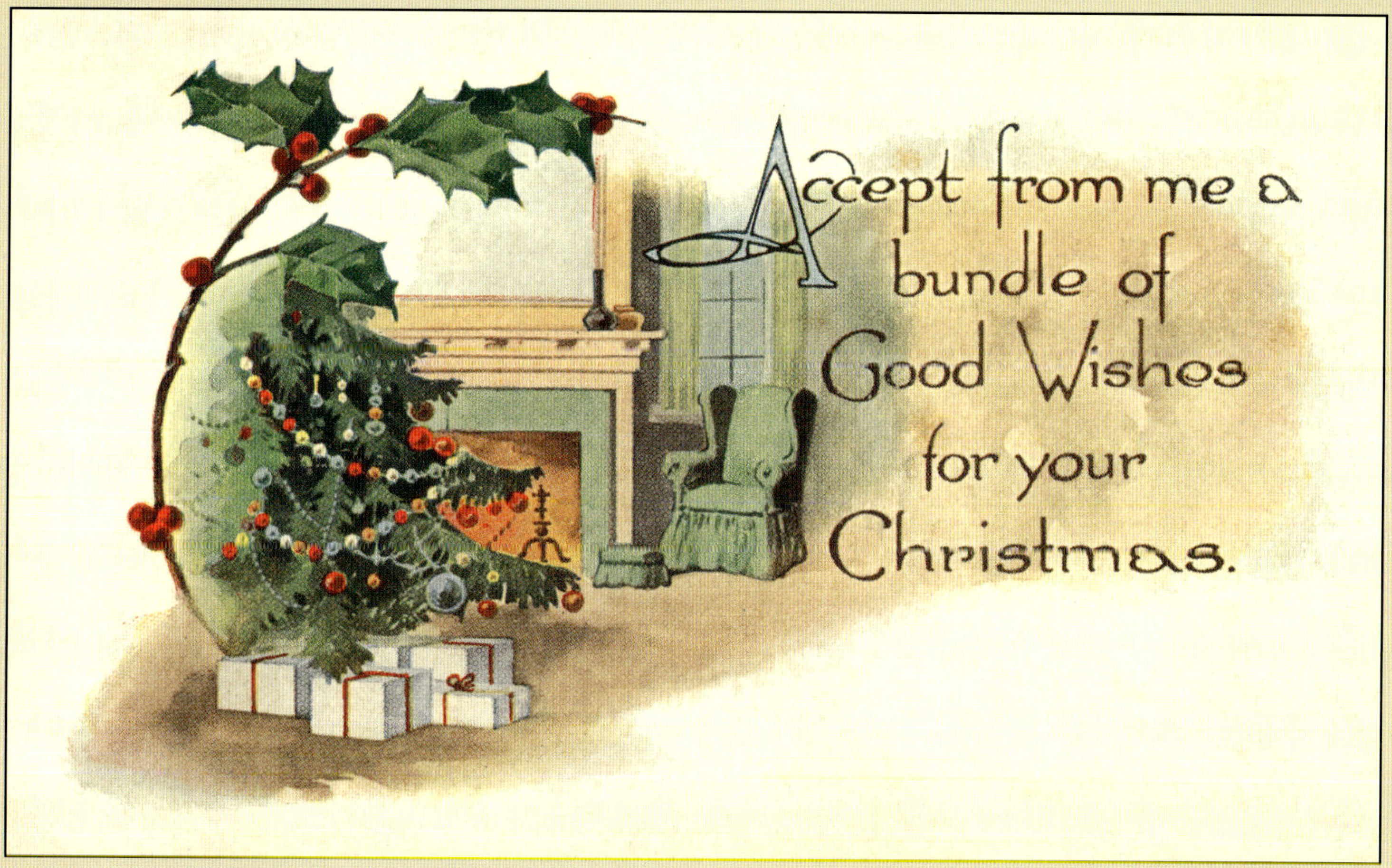
Accept from me a
bundle of
Good Wishes
for your
Christmas.

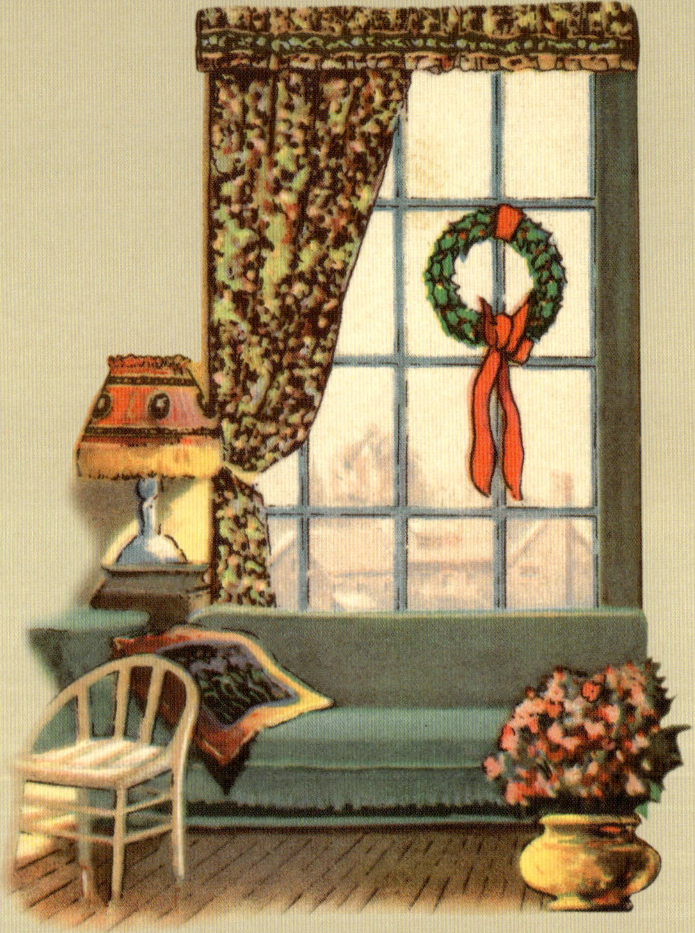

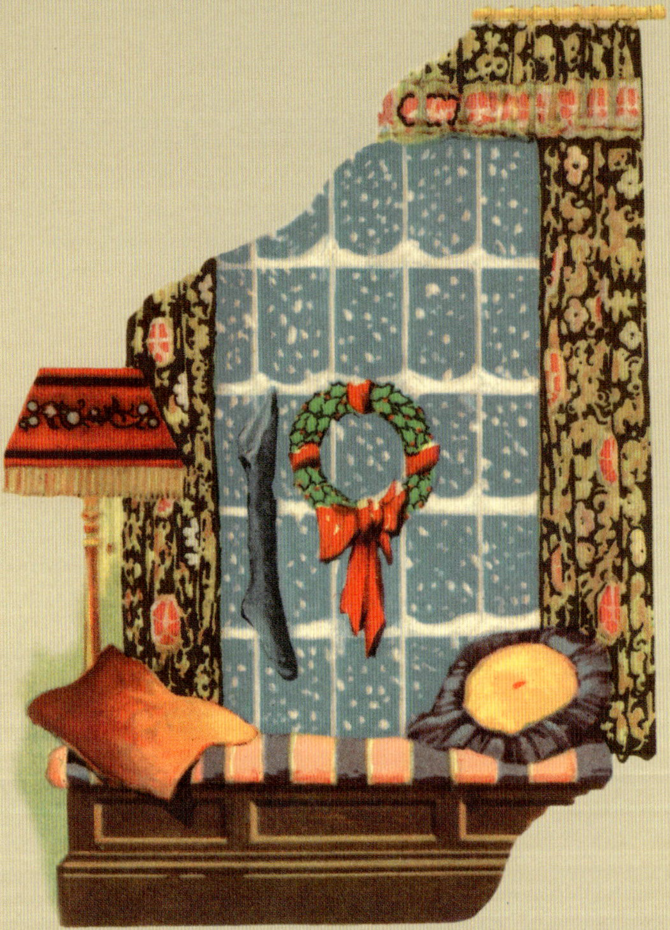

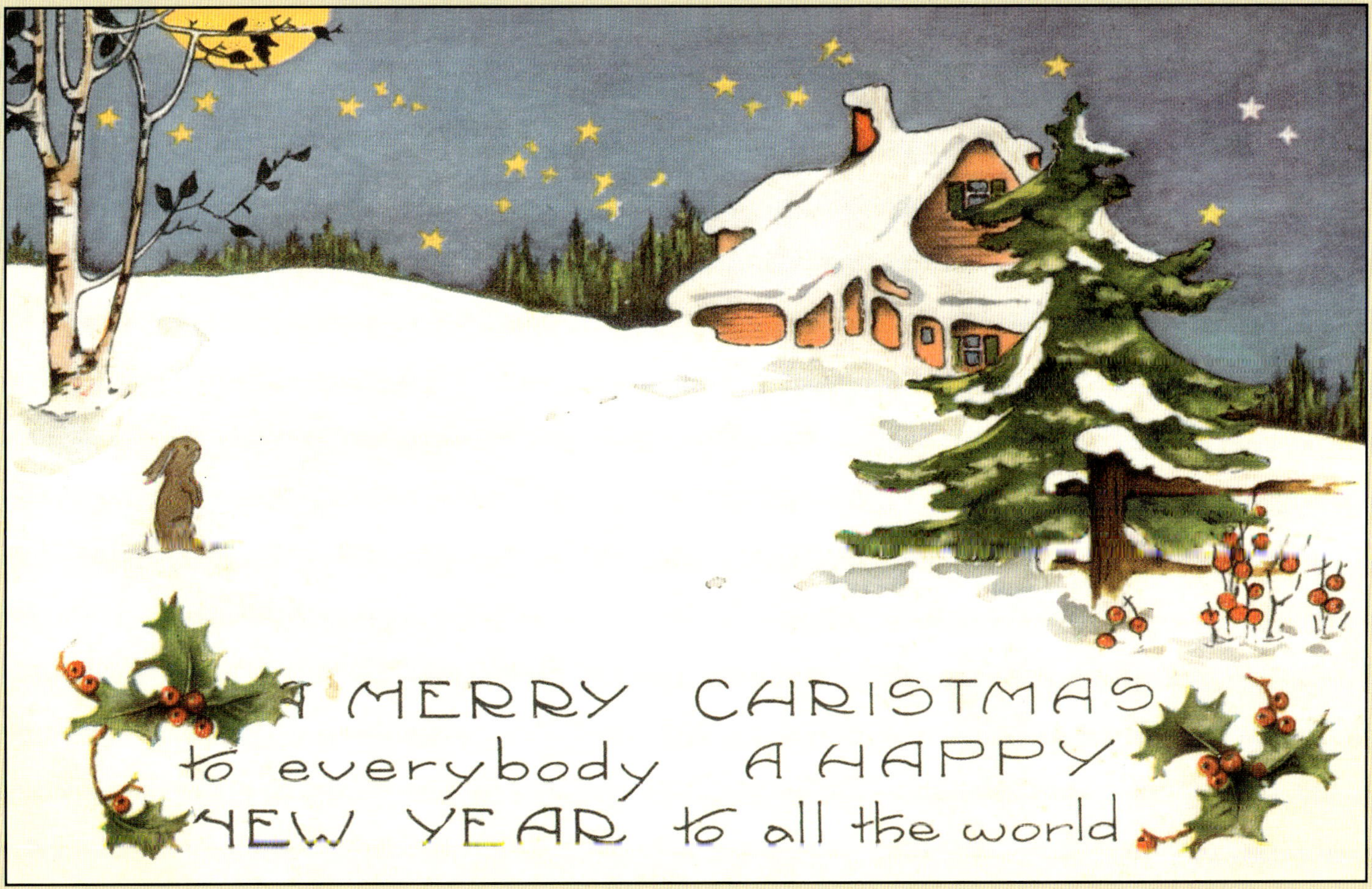
A MERRY CHRISTMAS
to everybody A HAPPY
NEW YEAR to all the world

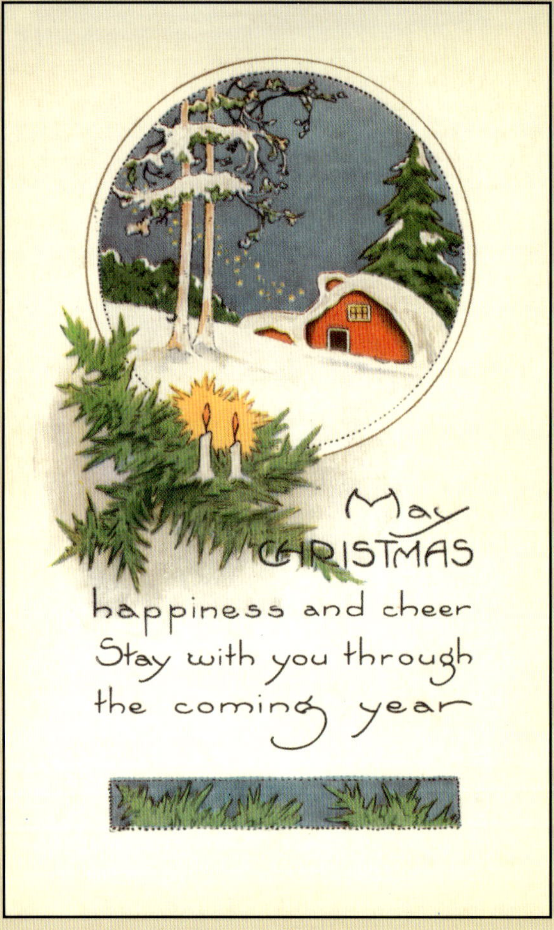
May
CHRISTMAS
happiness and cheer
Stay with you through
the coming year

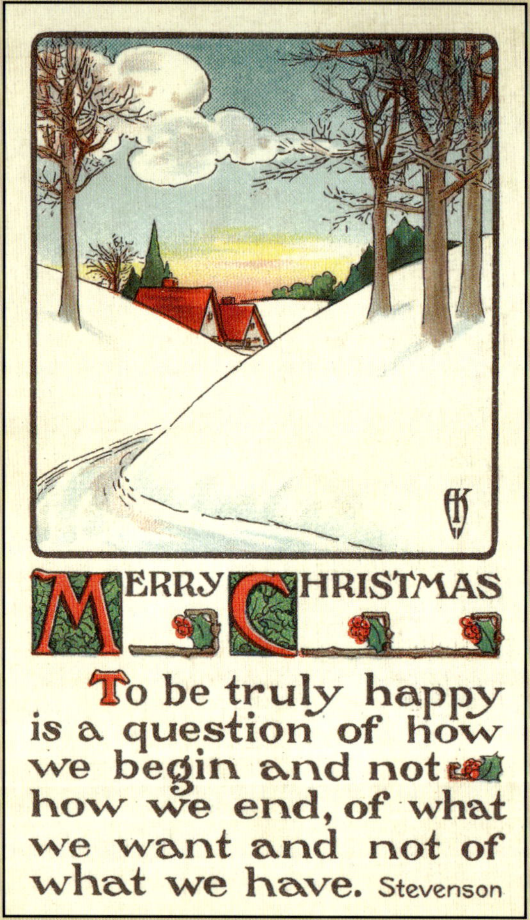
MERRY CHRISTMAS
To be truly happy
is a question of how
we begin and not
how we end, of what
we want and not of
what we have. Stevenson

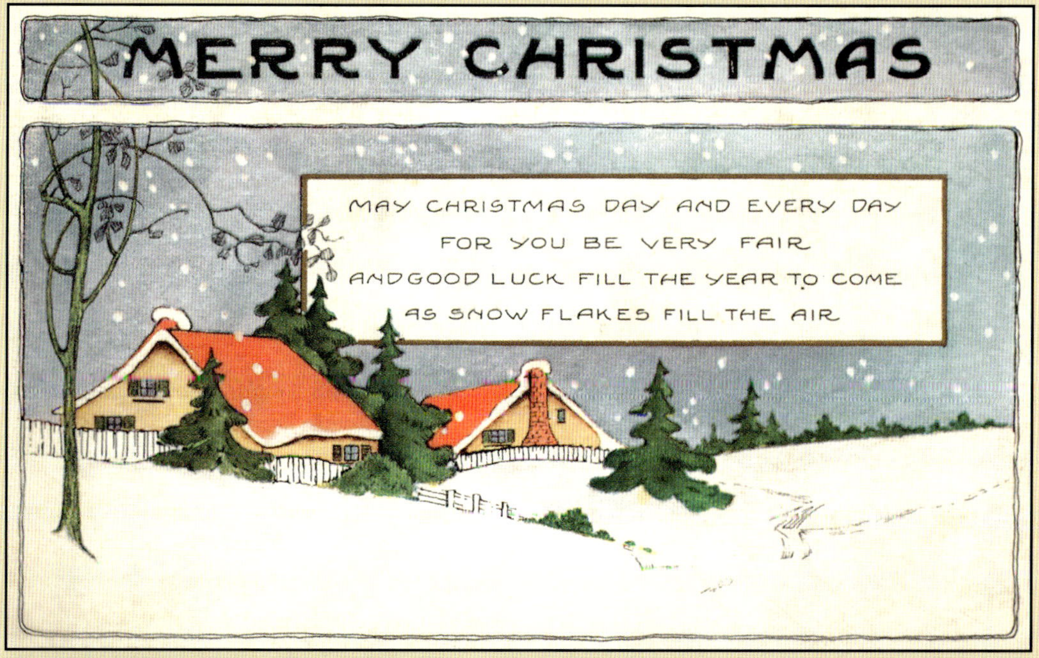
MERRY CHRISTMAS
MAY CHRISTMAS DAY AND EVERY DAY
FOR YOU BE VERY FAIR
AND GOOD LUCK FILL THE YEAR TO COME
AS SNOW FLAKES FILL THE AIR

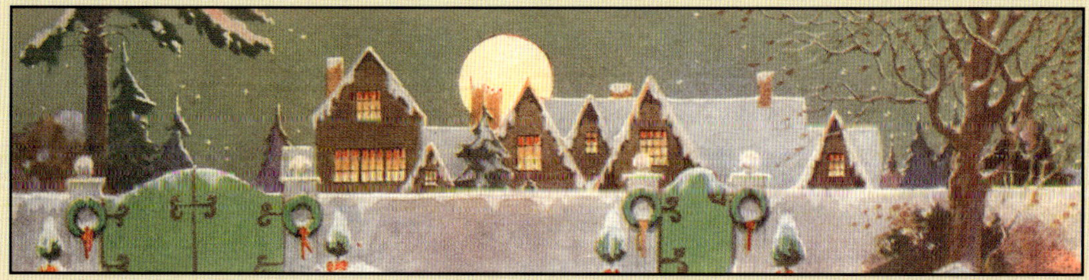

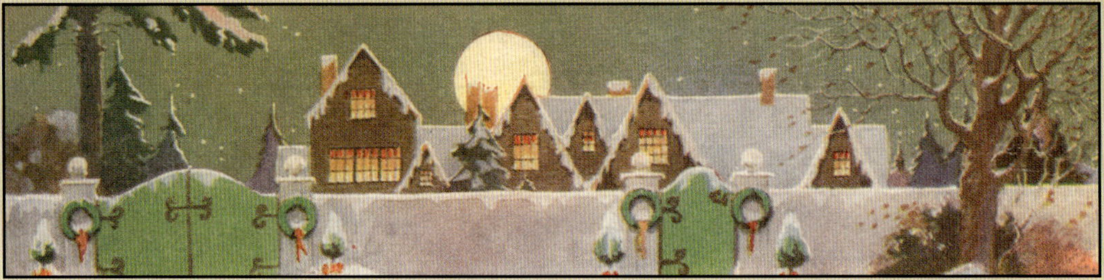

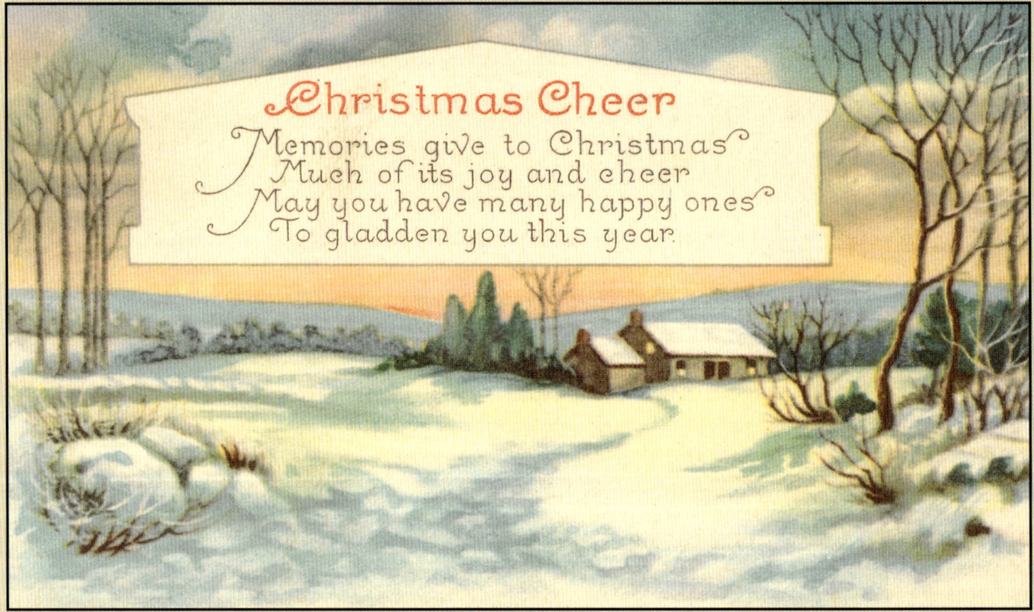
Christmas Cheer
Memories give to Christmas
Much of its joy and cheer
May you have many happy ones
To gladden you this year.

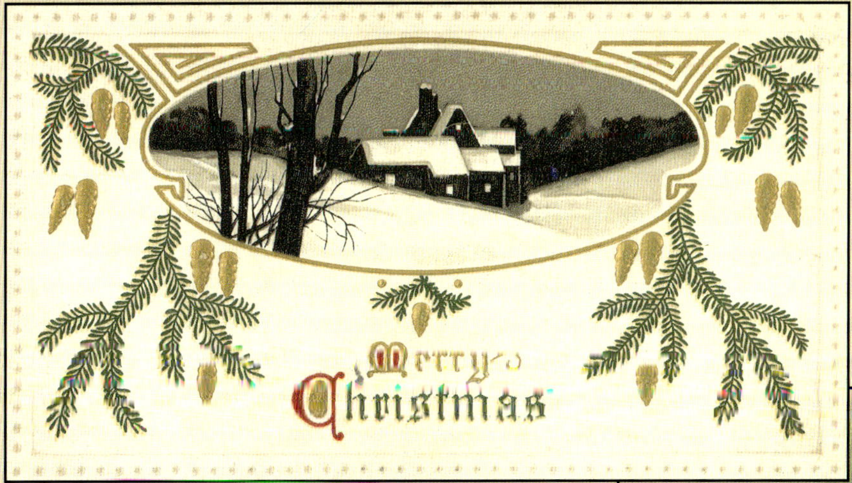
Merry
Christmas

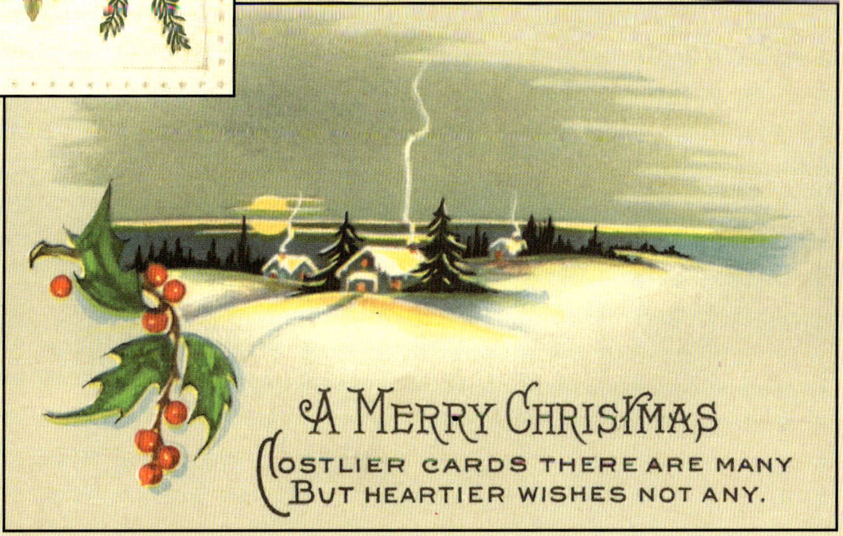
A MERRY CHRISTMAS
COSTLIER CARDS THERE ARE MANY
BUT HEARTIER WISHES NOT ANY.

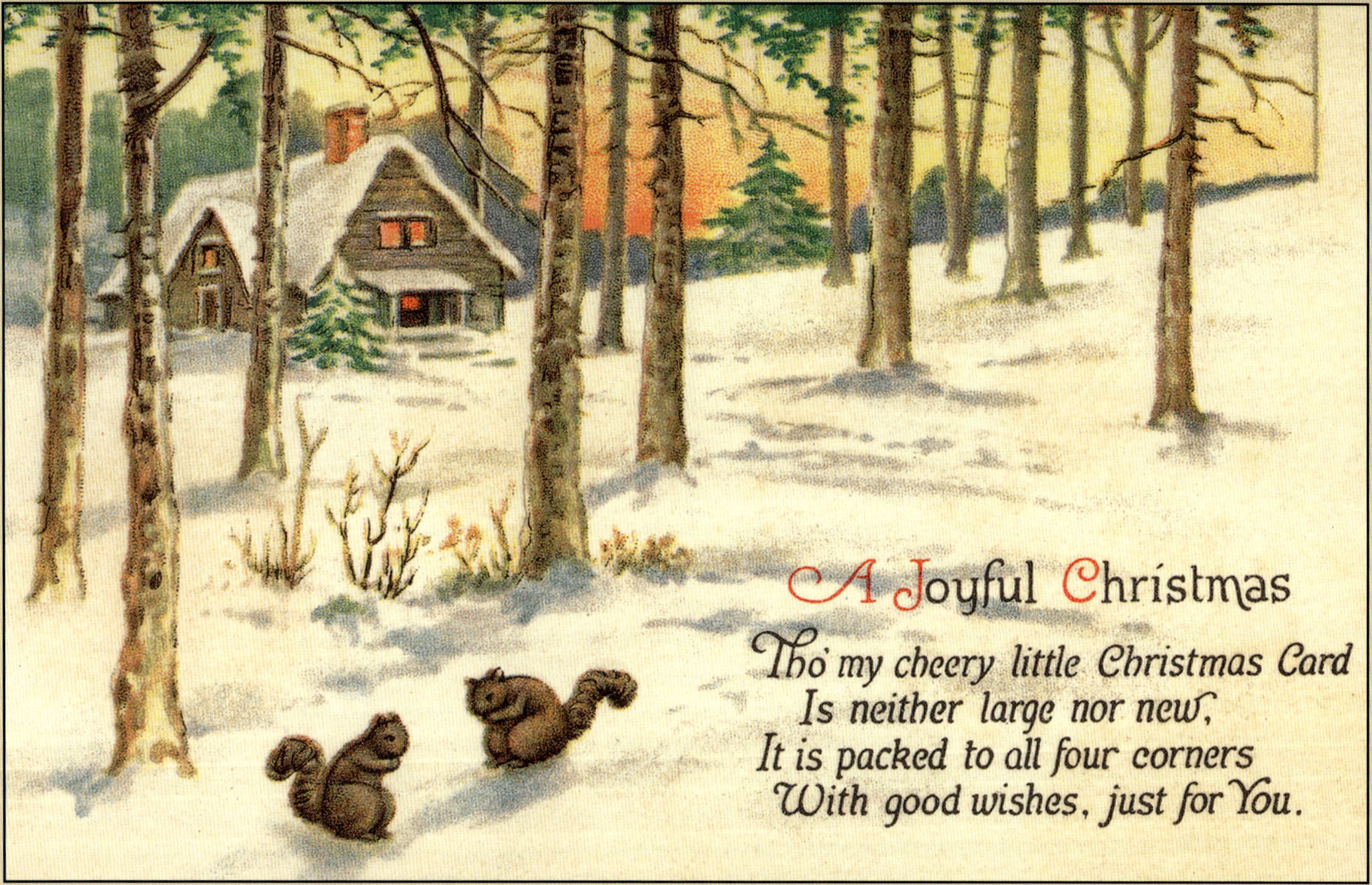
A Joyful Christmas
Tho' my cheery little Christmas Card
Is neither large nor new,
It is packed to all four corners
With good wishes, just for You.

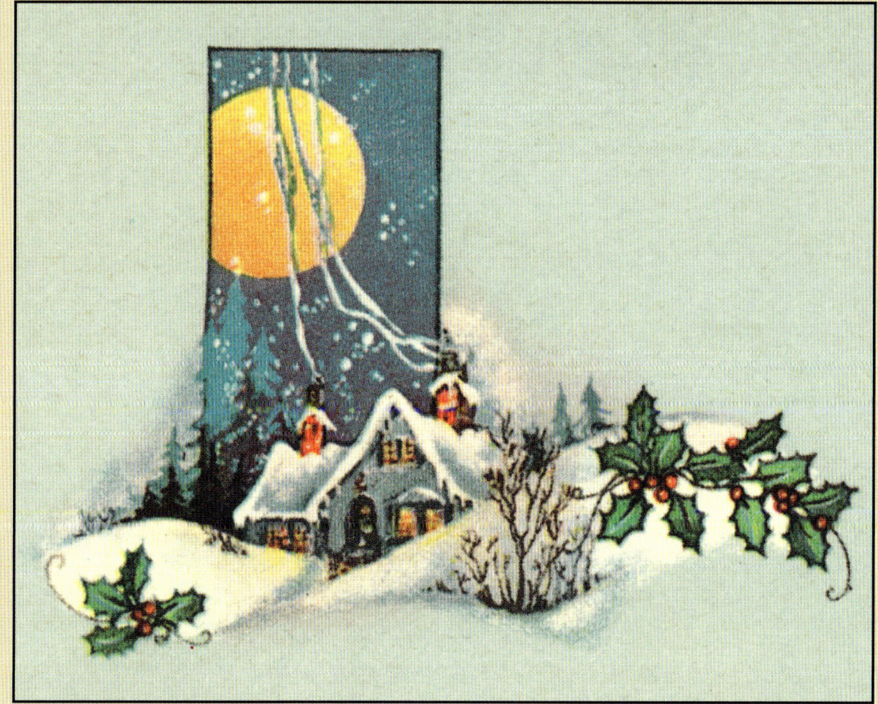

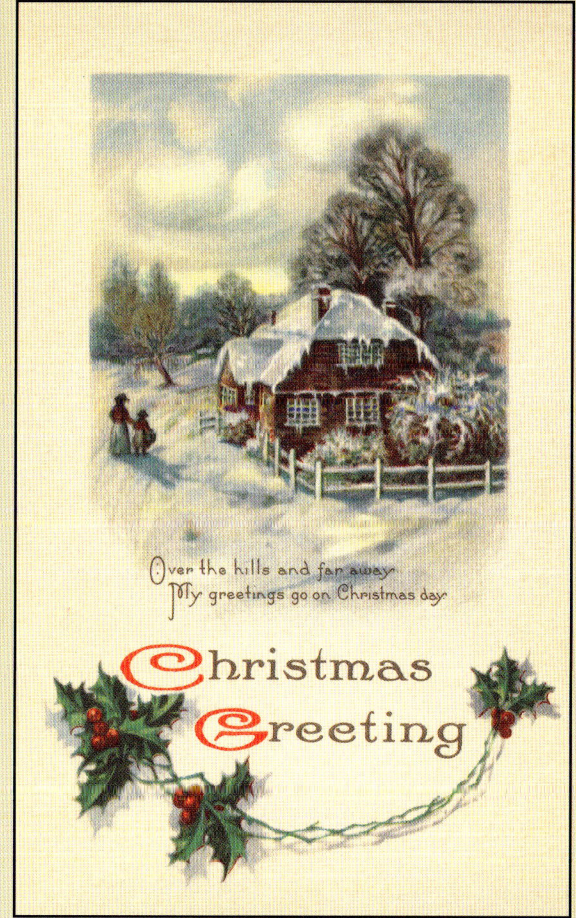
Over the hills and far away
My greetings go on Christmas day.
Christmas
Greeting

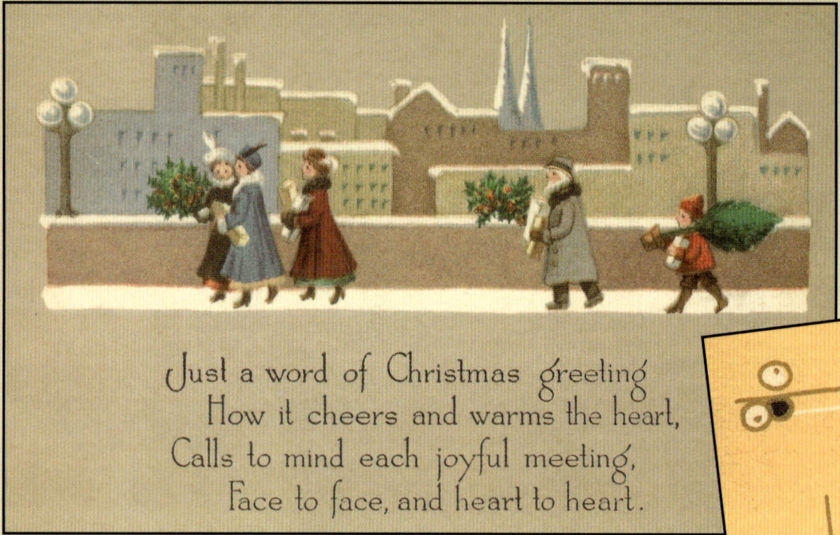
Just a word of Christmas greeting
How it cheers and warms the heart,
Calls to mind each joyful meeting,
Face to face, and heart to heart.

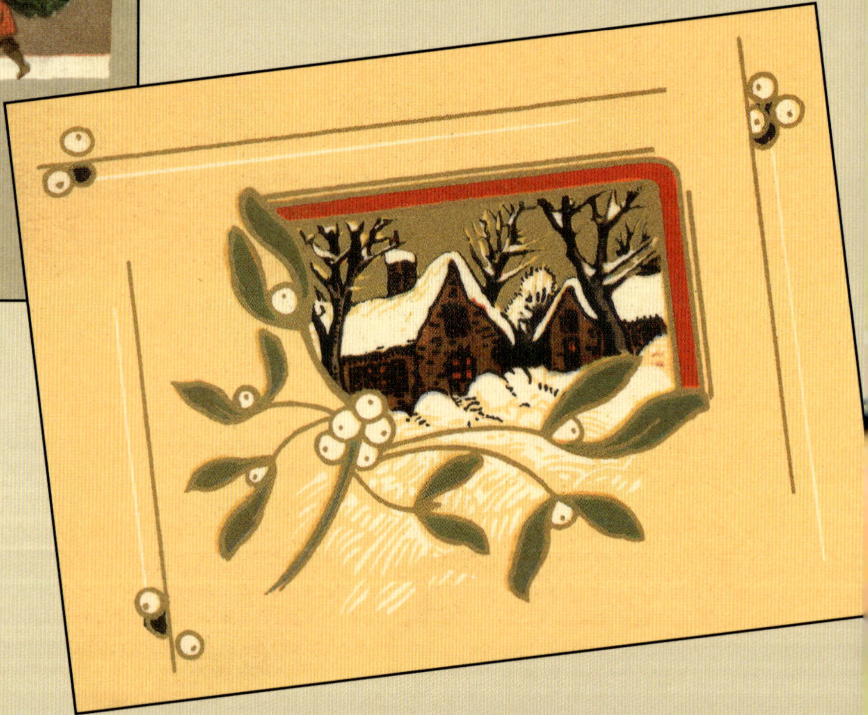

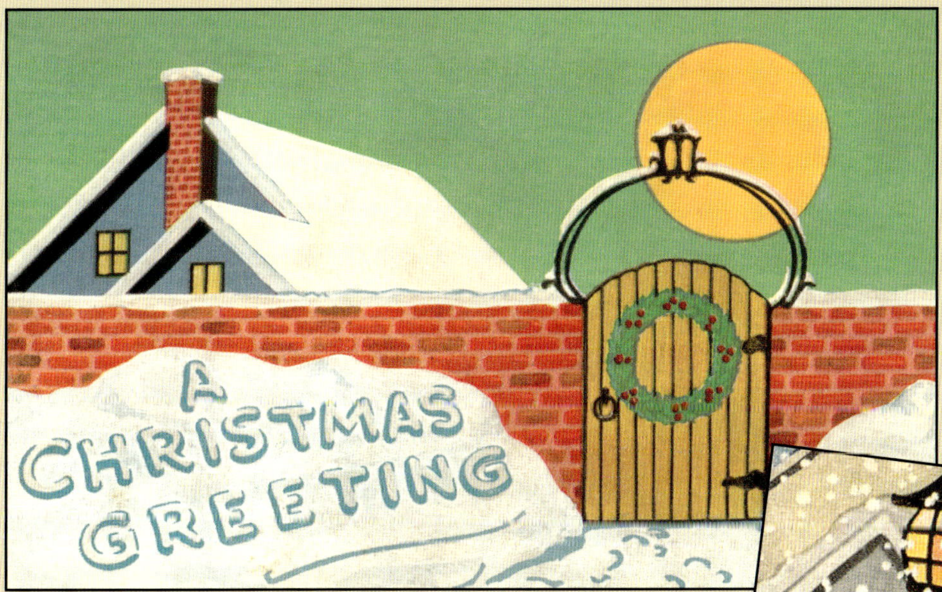
A
CHRISTMAS
GREETING

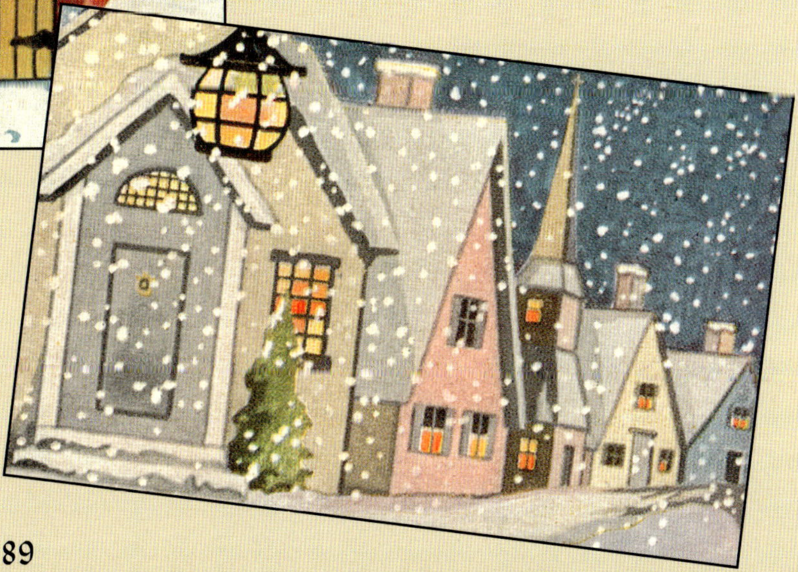

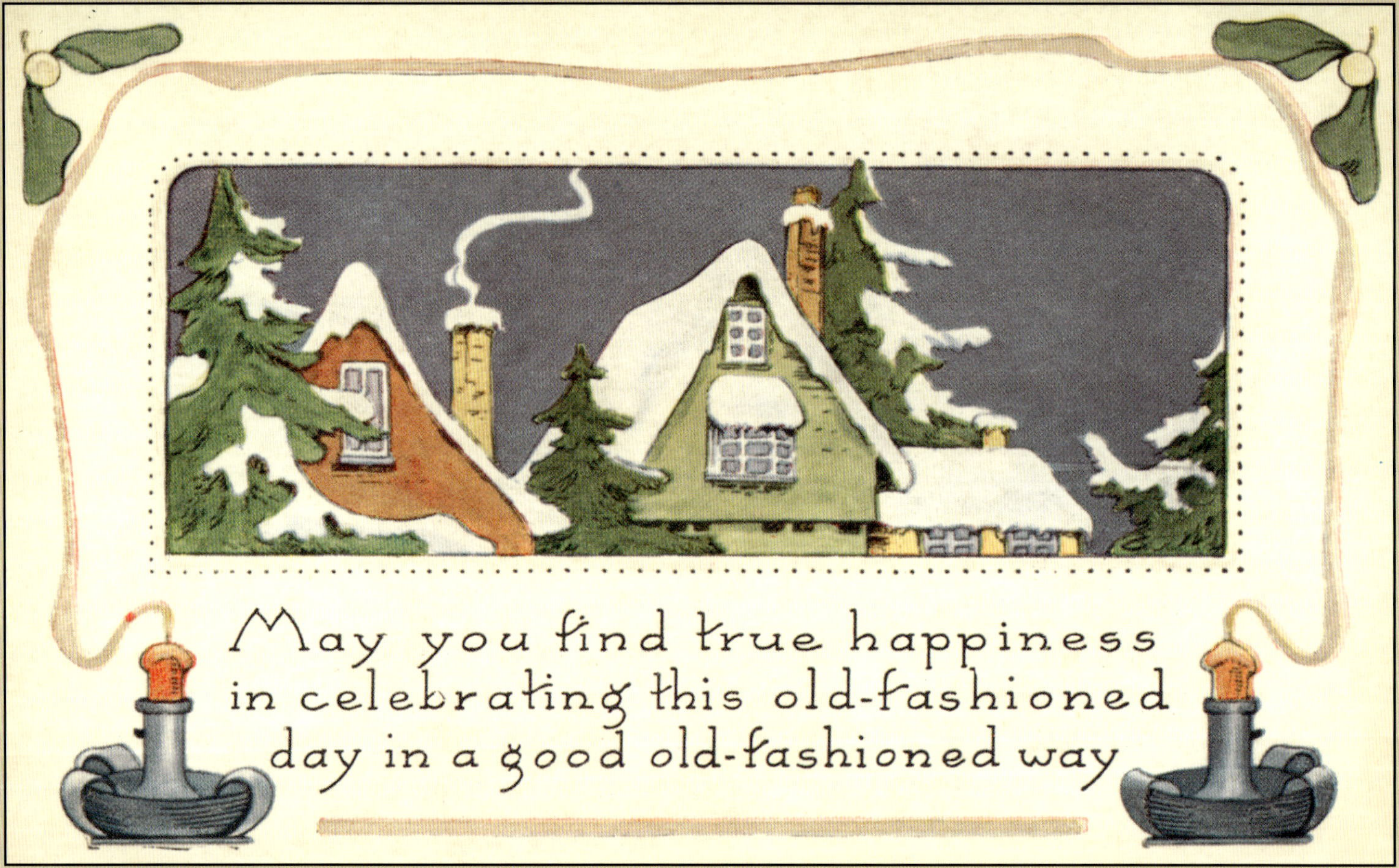
May you find true happiness
in celebrating this old-fashioned
day in a good old-fashioned way

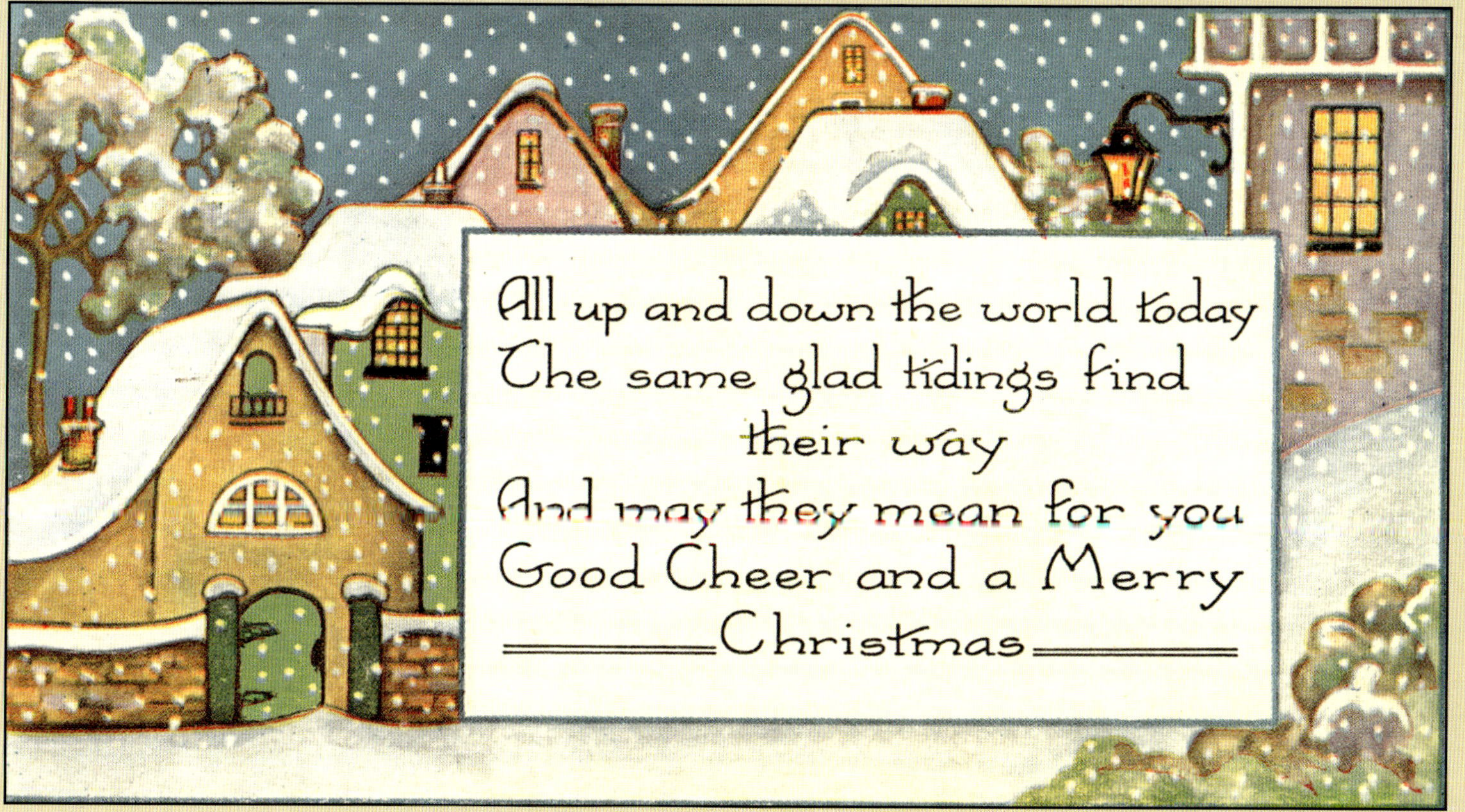
All up and down the world today
The same glad tidings find
their way
And may they mean for you
Good Cheer and a Merry
Christmas

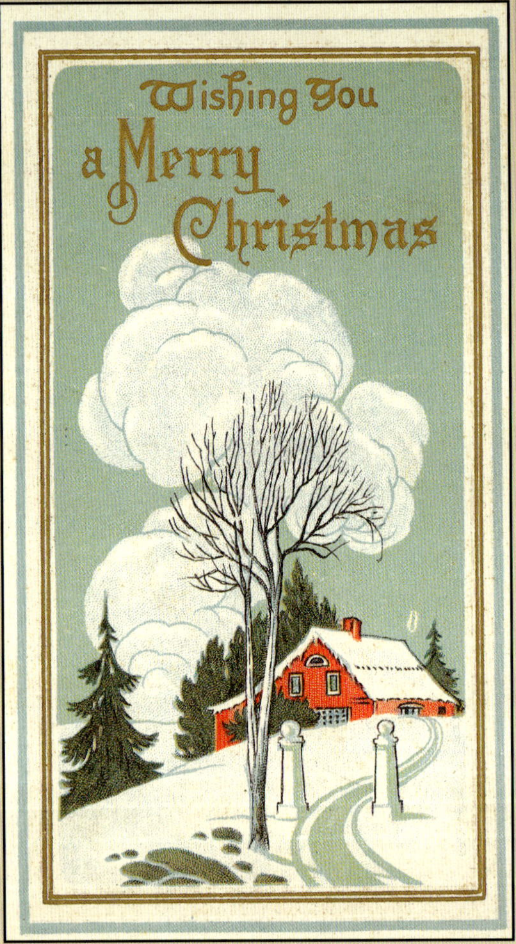
Wishing You
a Merry
Christmas

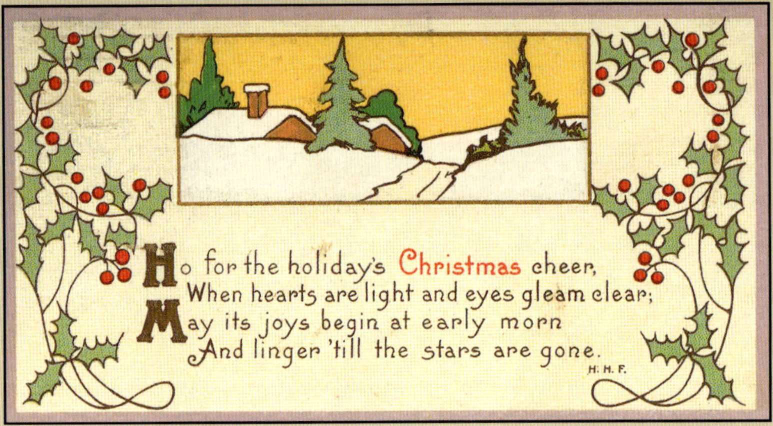
Ho for the holiday's Christmas cheer,
When hearts are light and eyes gleam clear;
May its joys begin at early morn
And linger 'till the stars are gone.
H. H. F.

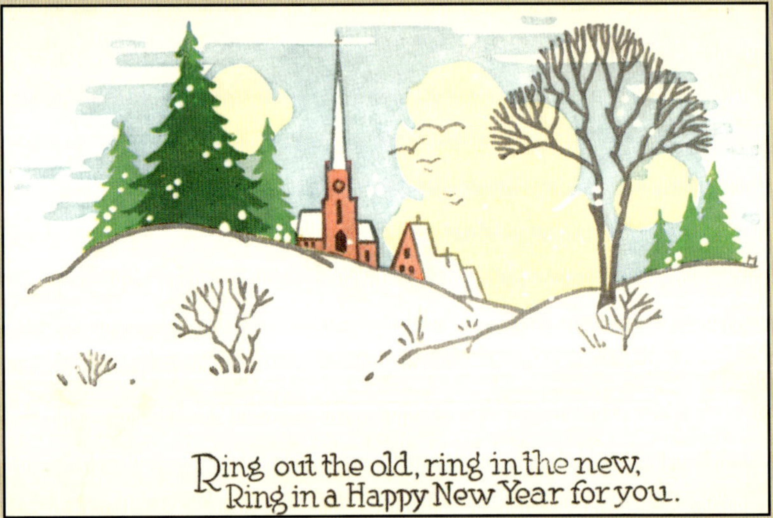
Ring out the old, ring in the new,
Ring in a Happy New Year for you.

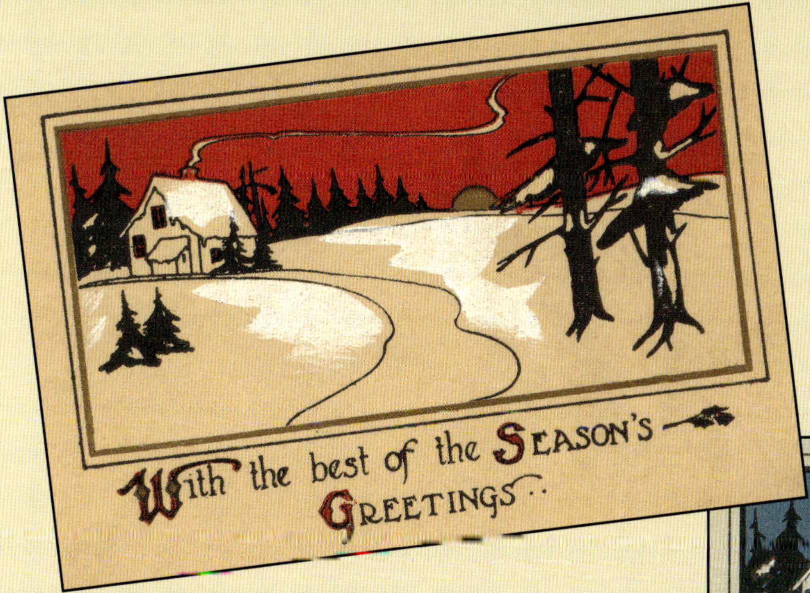
With the best of the Season's
Greetings..

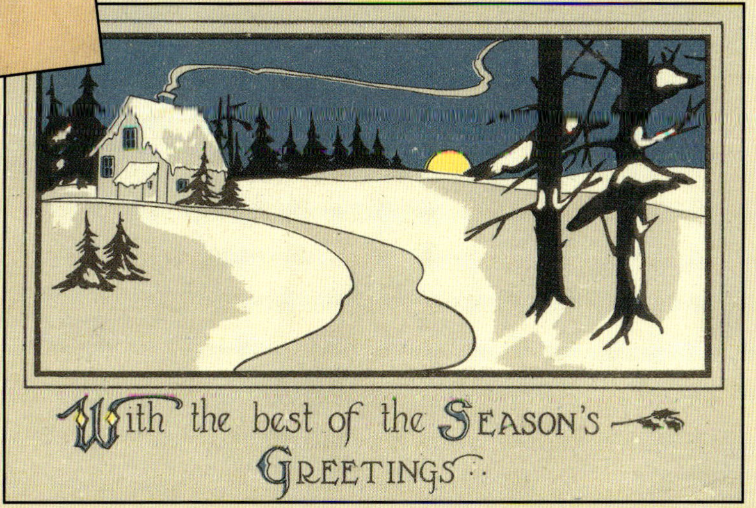
With the best of the Season's
Greetings..

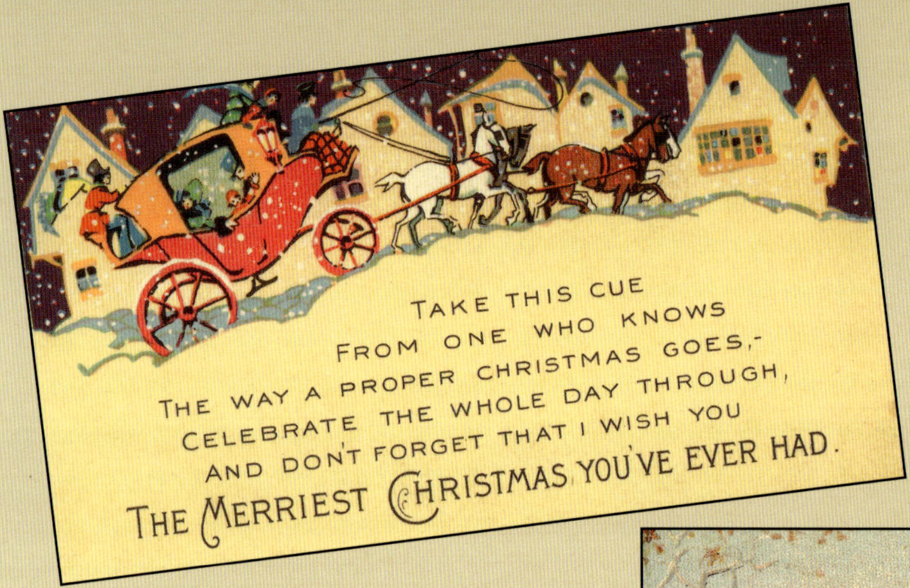
Take this cue
From one who knows
The way a proper Christmas goes,-
Celebrate the whole day through,
And don't forget that I wish you
The Merriest Christmas you've ever had.

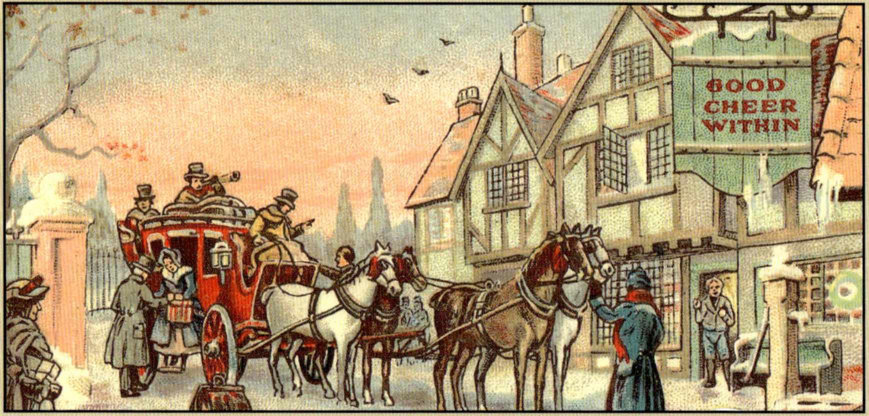
Good
Cheer
Within

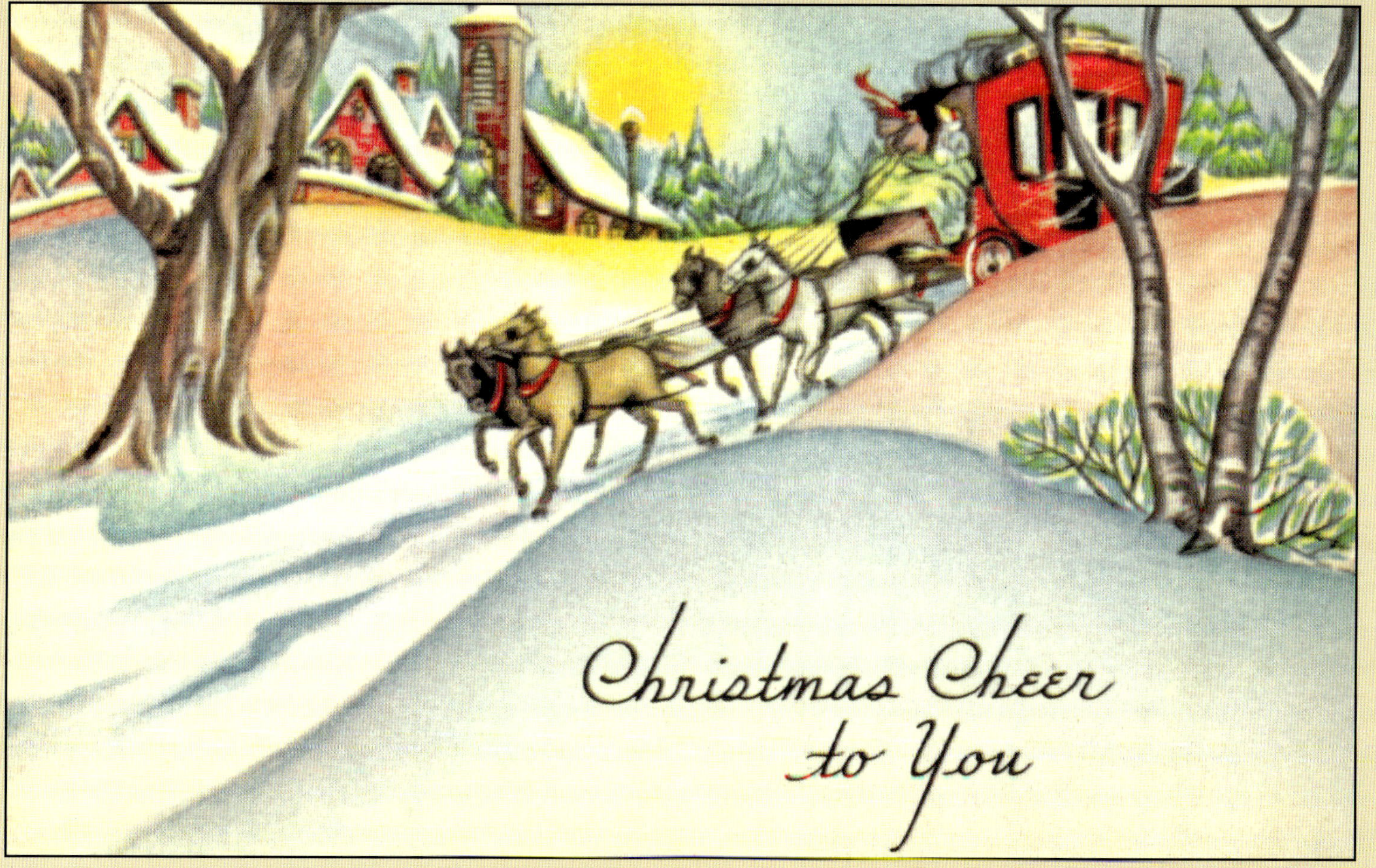
Christmas Cheer
to You

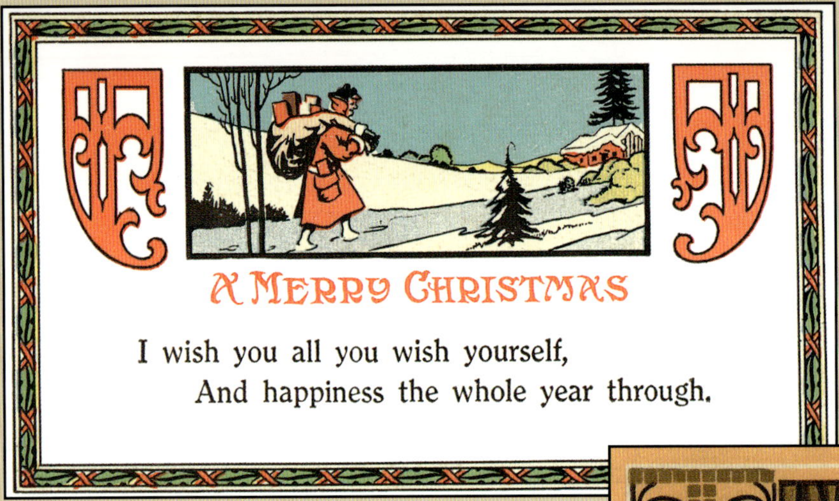
A MERRY CHRISTMAS
I wish you all you wish yourself,
And happiness the whole year through.

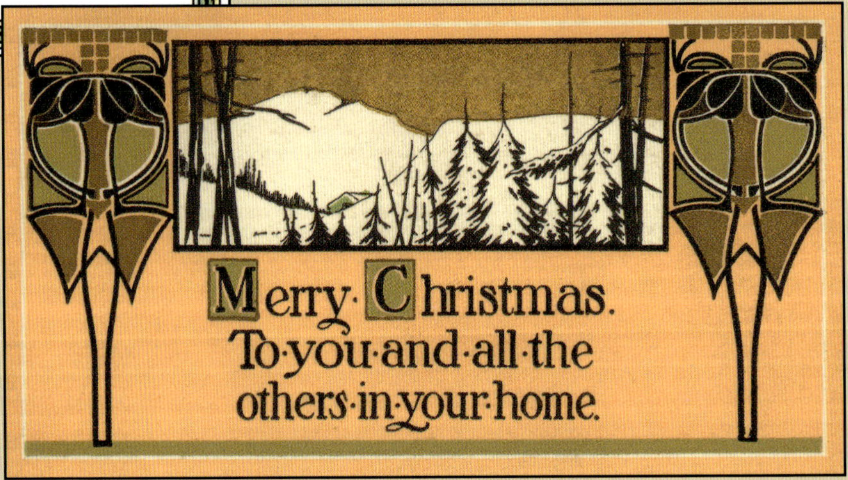
Merry·Christmas.
To·you·and·all·the
others·in·your·home.

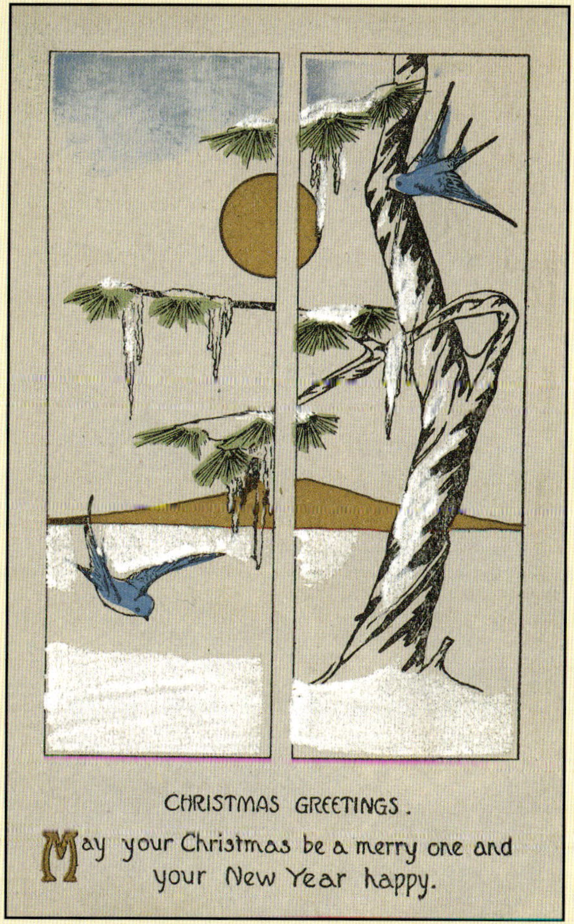
CHRISTMAS GREETINGS.
May your Christmas be a merry one and your New Year happy.

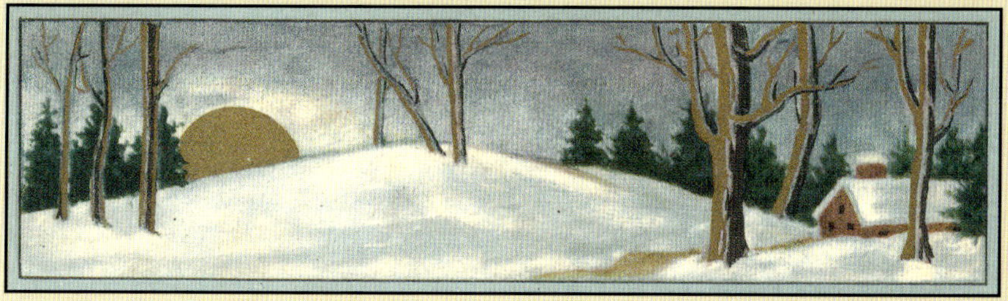

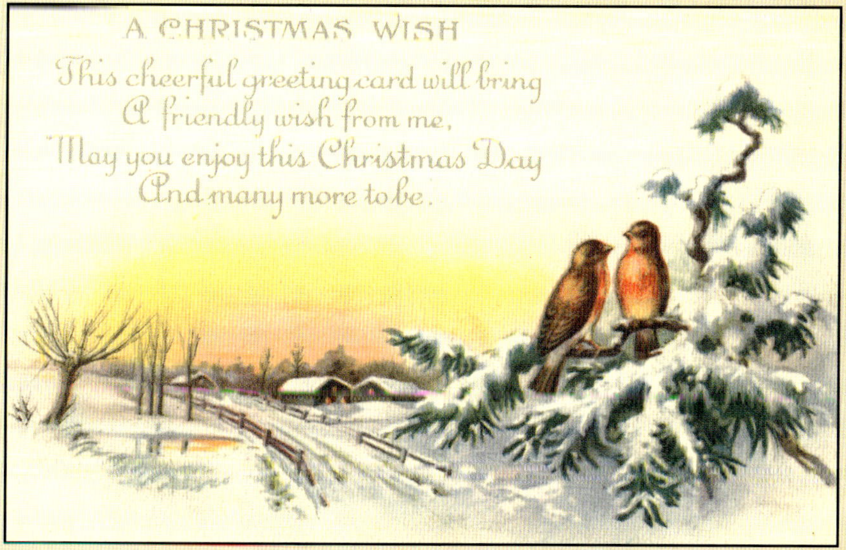
A CHRISTMAS WISH
This cheerful greeting card will bring
A friendly wish from me,
May you enjoy this Christmas Day
And many more to be.

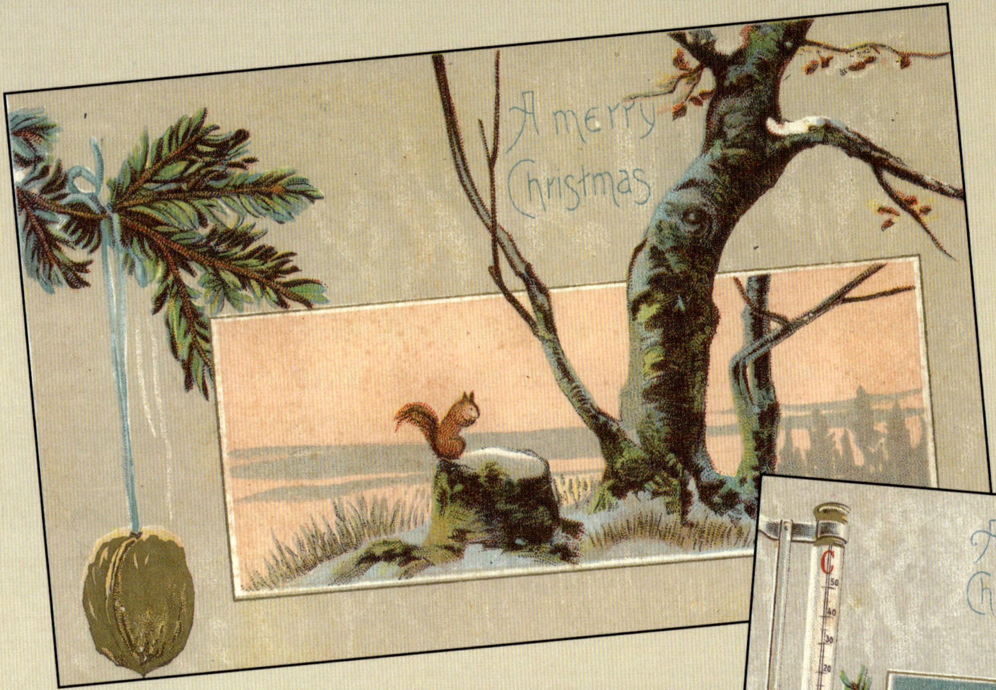
A merry Christmas

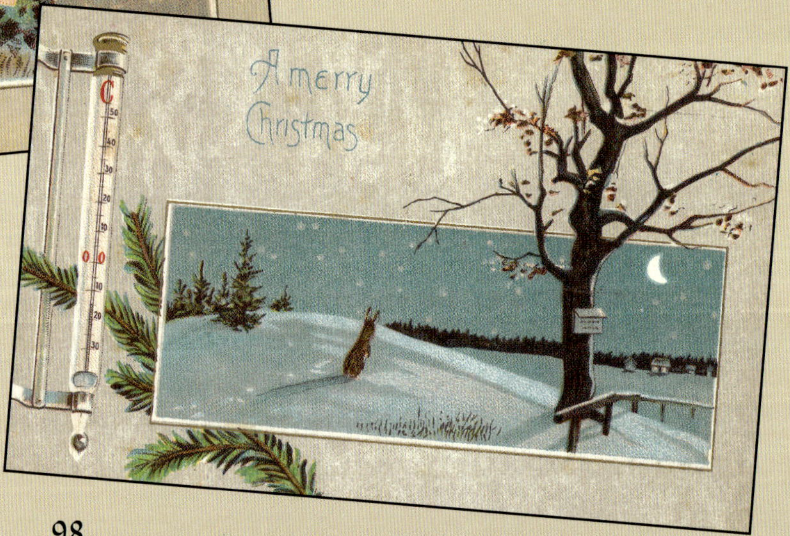
A merry Christmas

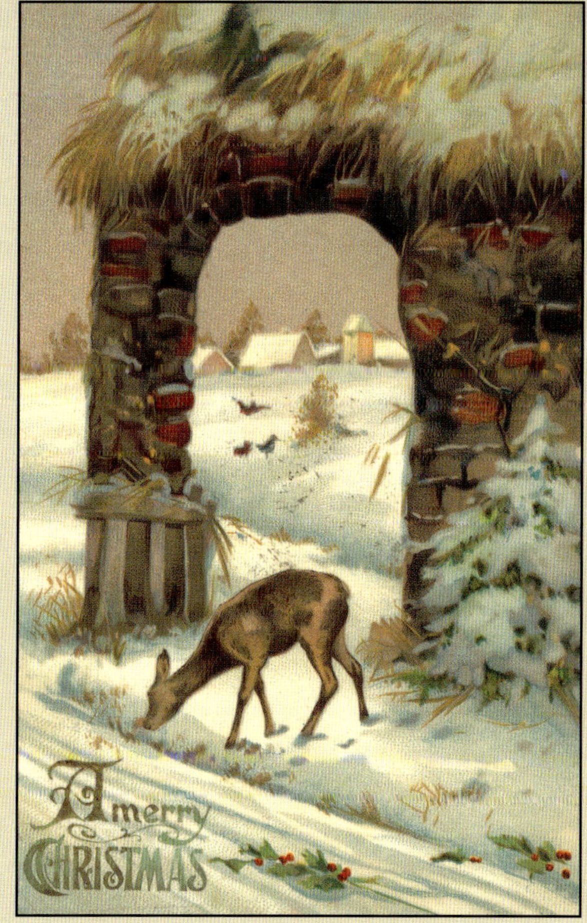
A merry
CHRISTMAS
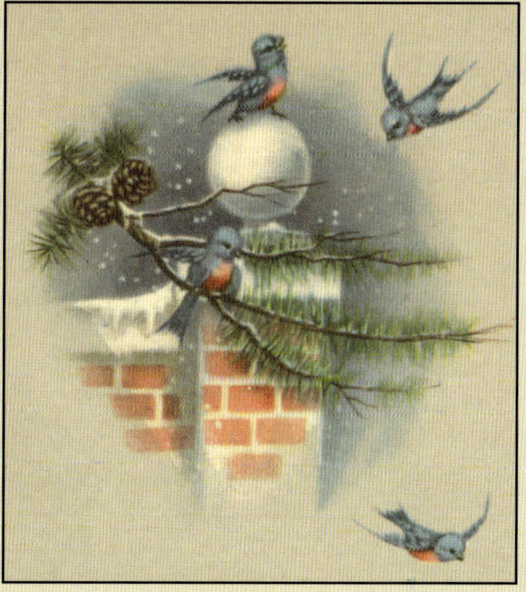
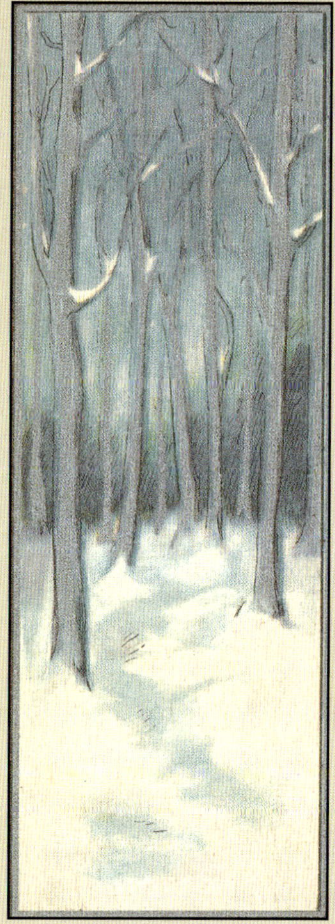

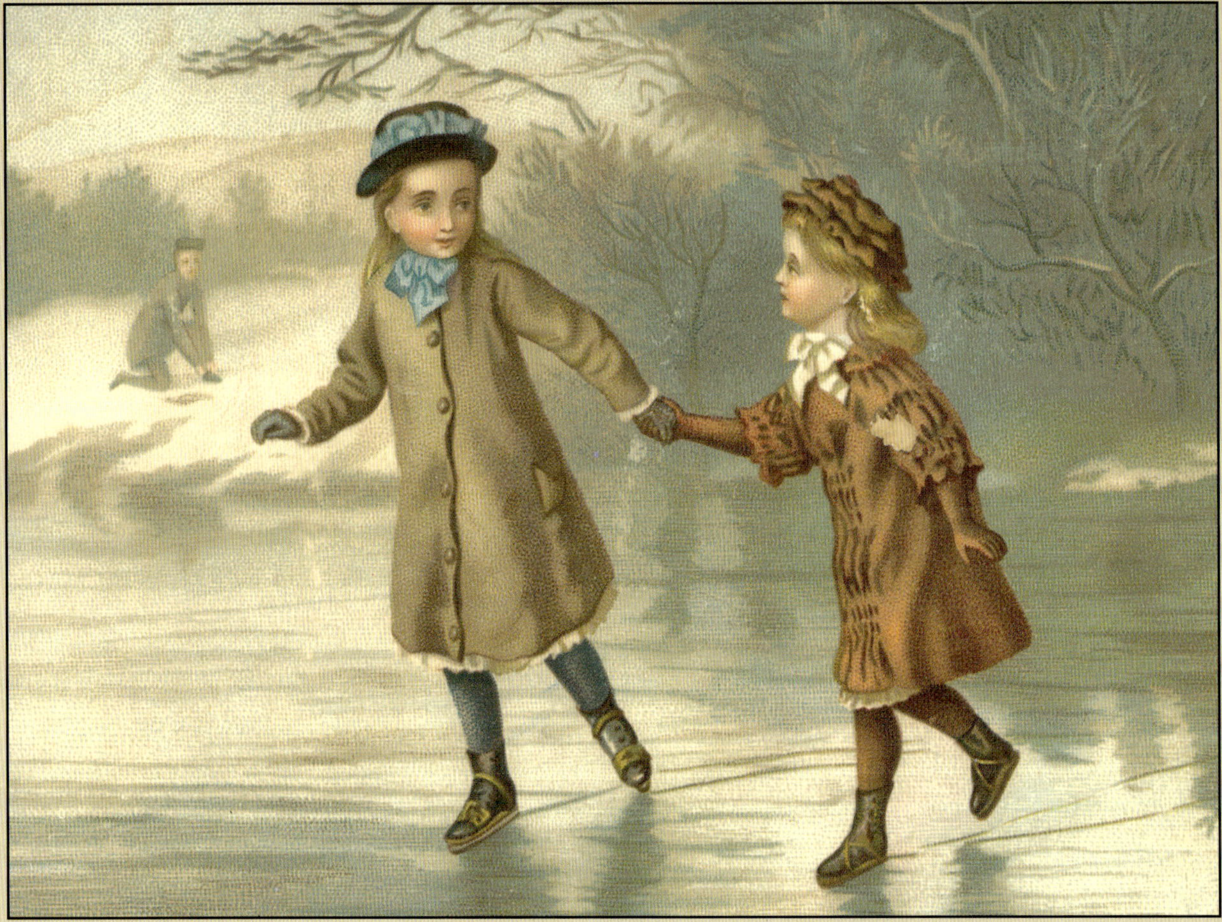

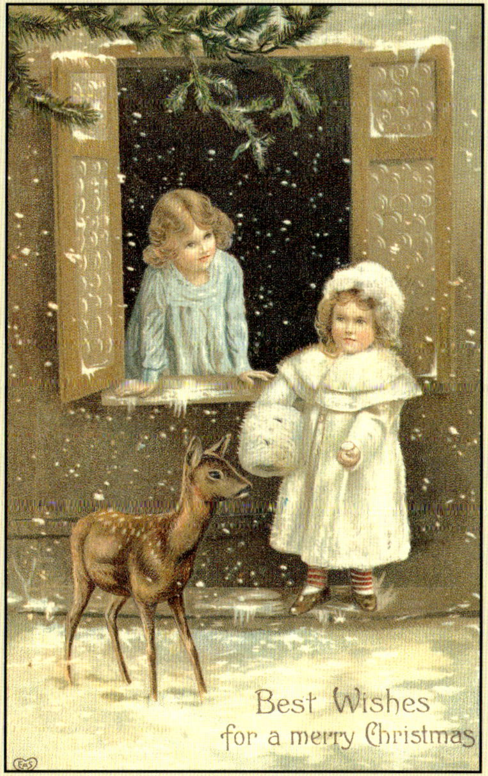
Best Wishes
for a merry Christmas

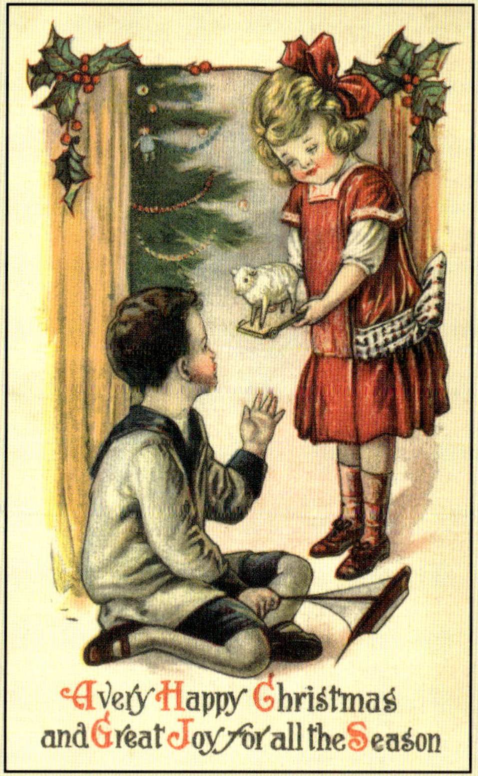
A very Happy Christmas
and Great Joy for all the Season

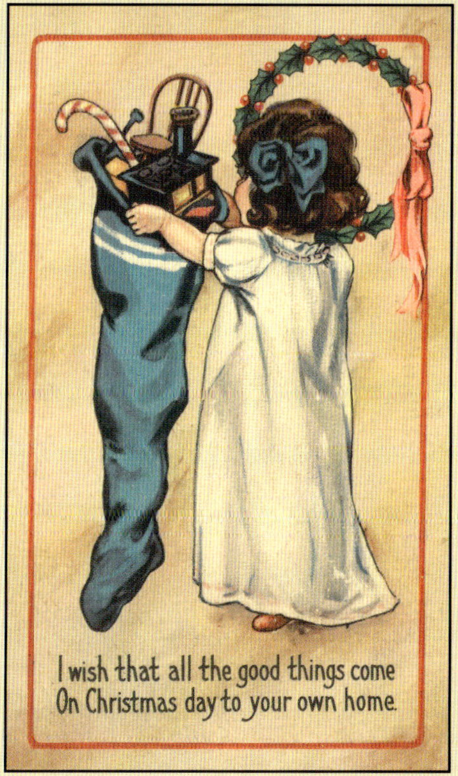
I wish that all the good things come
On Christmas day to your own home.

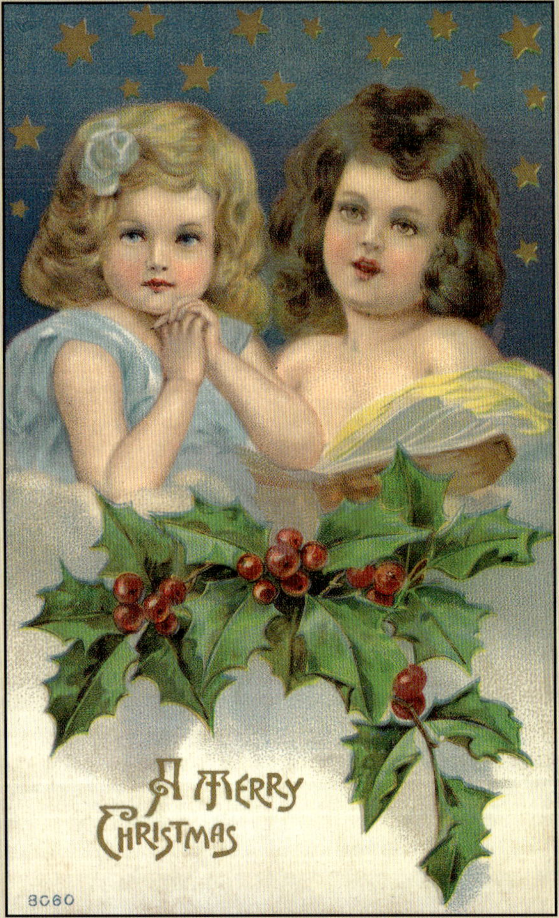
A Merry
Christmas
8060

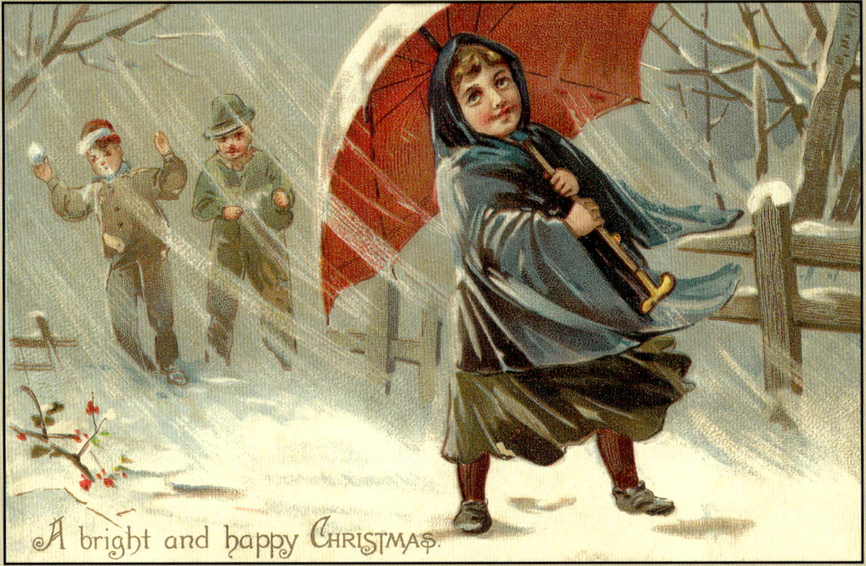
A bright and happy Christmas.

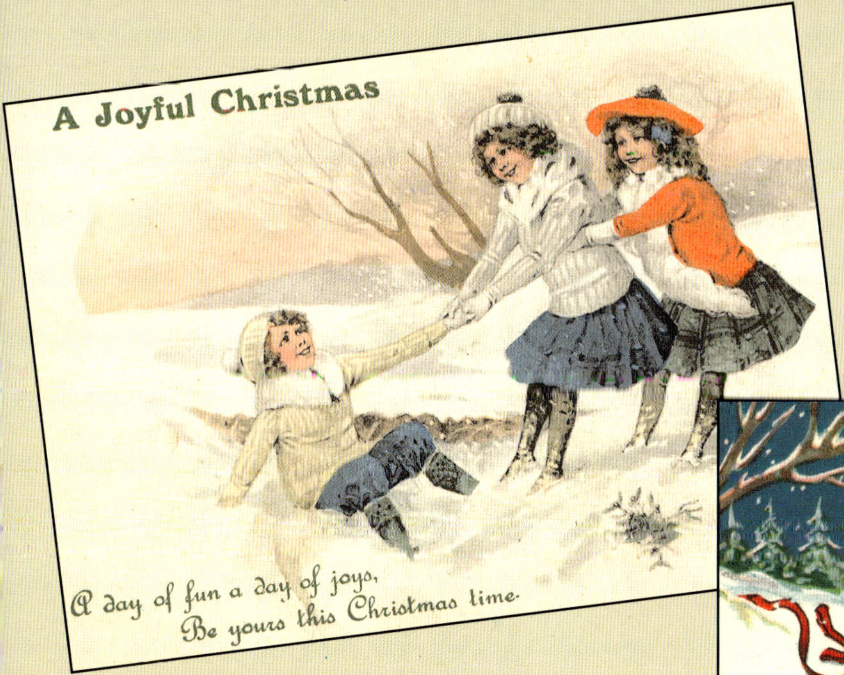
A Joyful Christmas
A day of fun a day of joys,
Be yours this Christmas time.

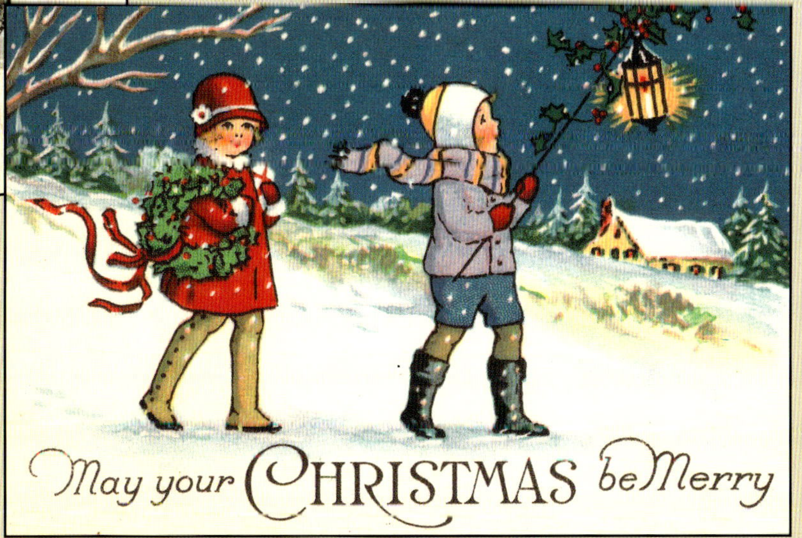
May your CHRISTMAS be Merry

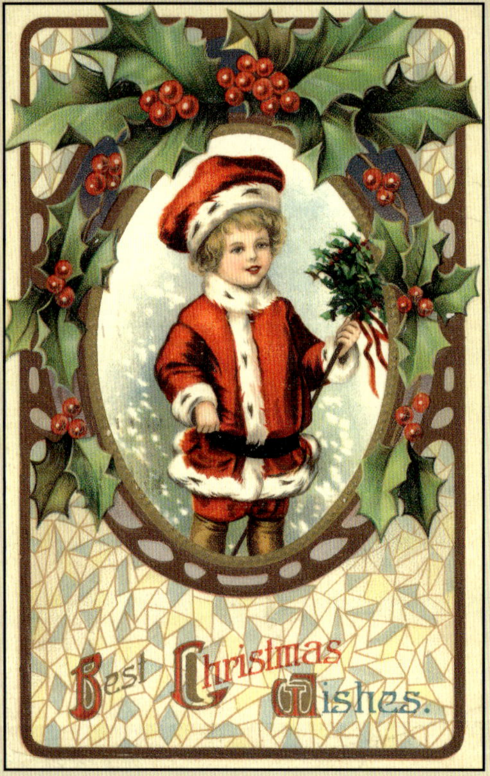
Best Christmas Wishes.

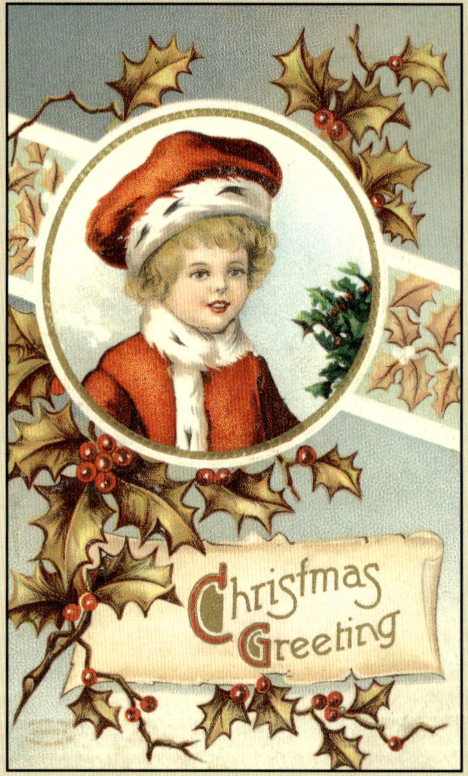
Christmas Greeting

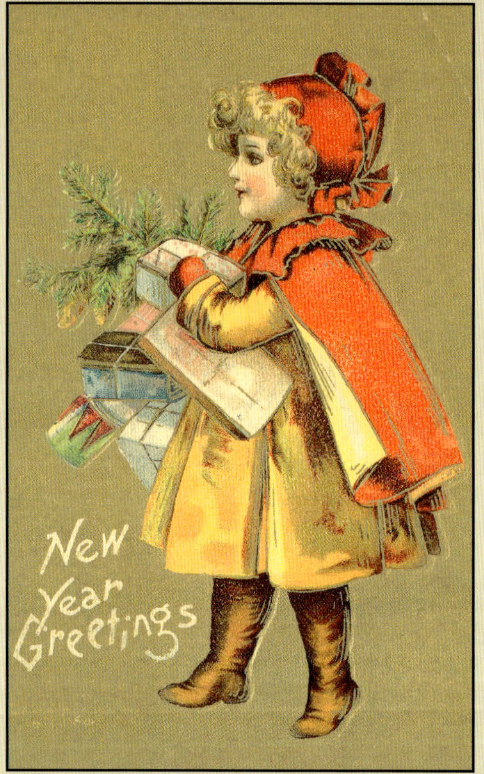
New Year Greetings

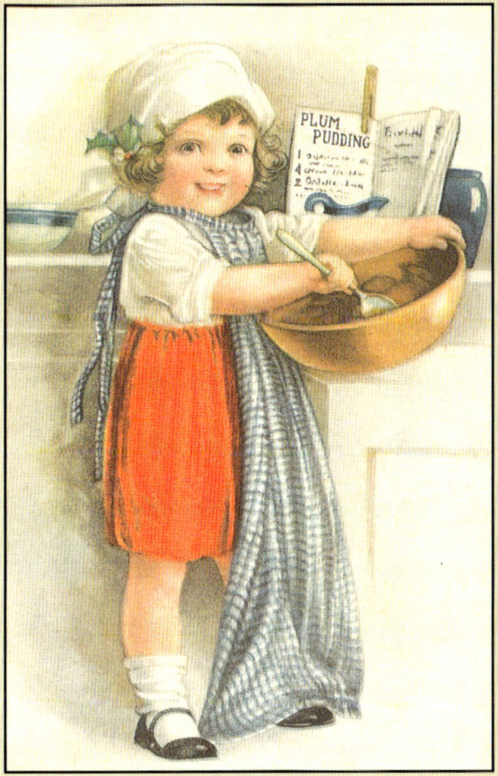
PLUM
PUDDING

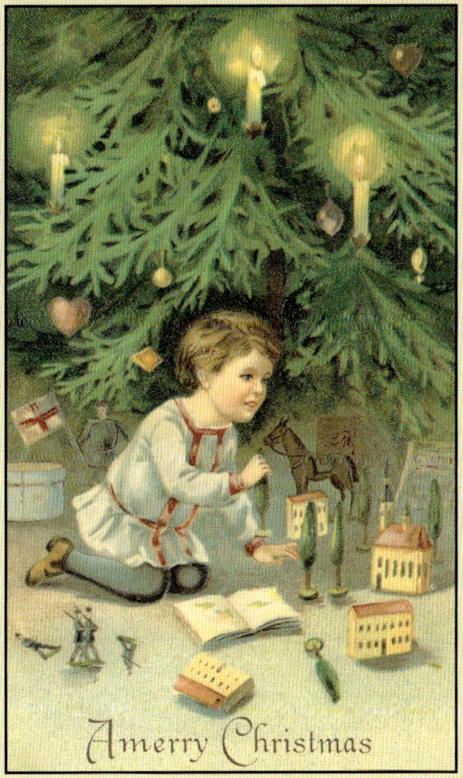
Amerry Christmas

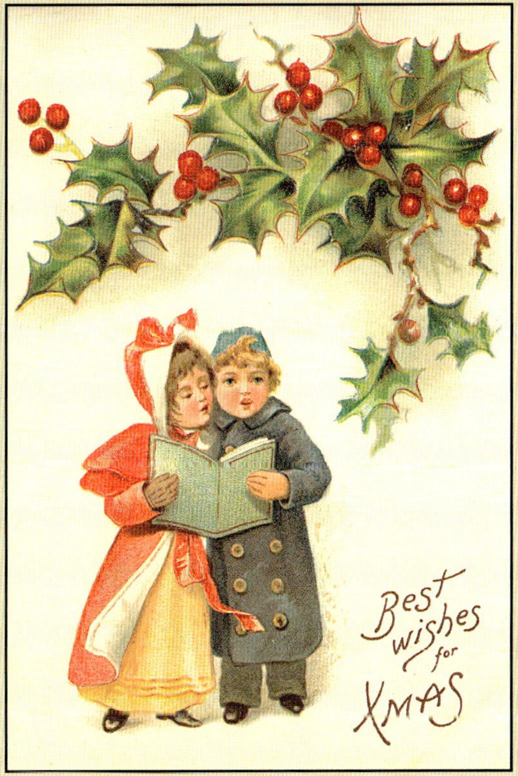
Best
wishes
for
XMAS

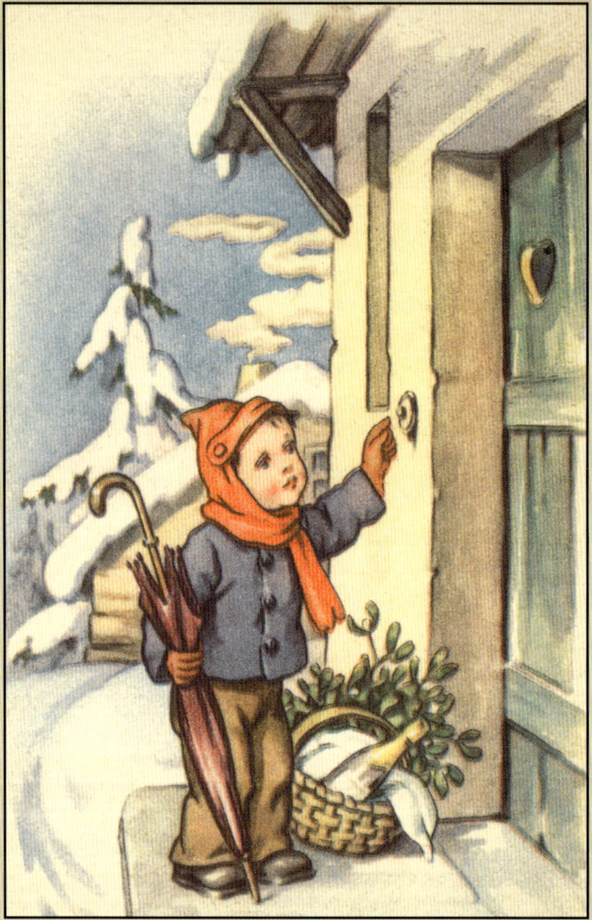

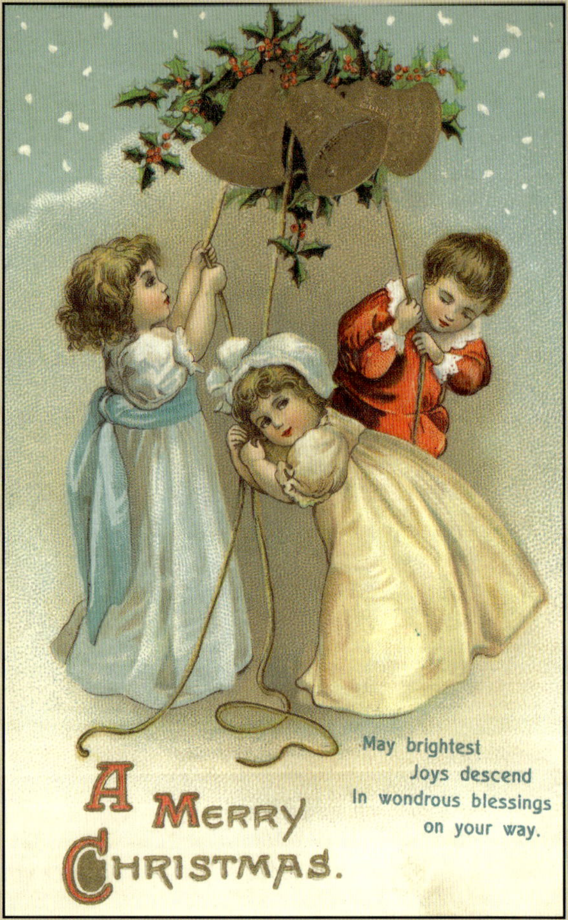
May brightest
Joys descend
In wondrous blessings
on your way.
A Merry
Christmas.

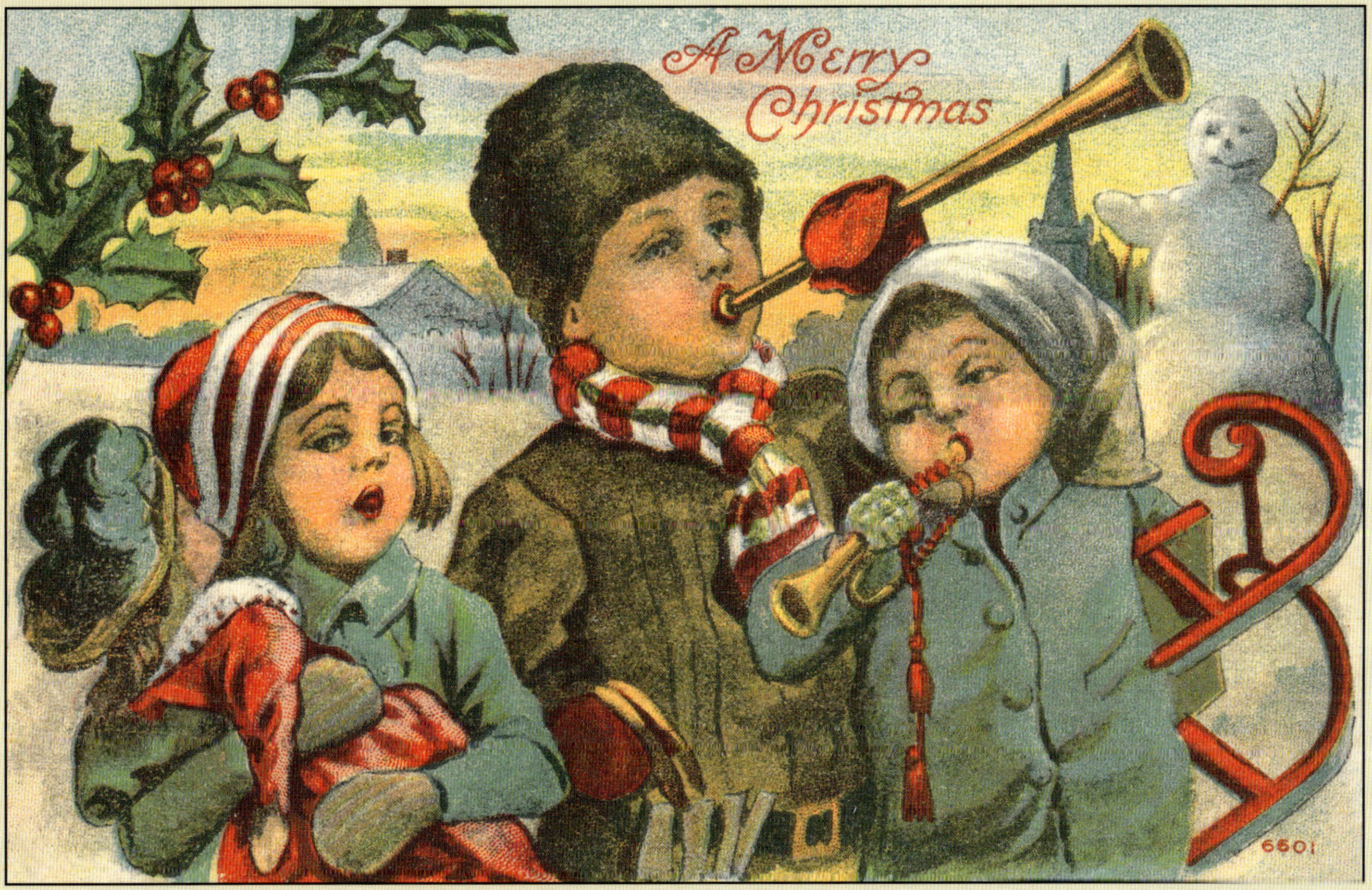
A Merry Christmas
6501

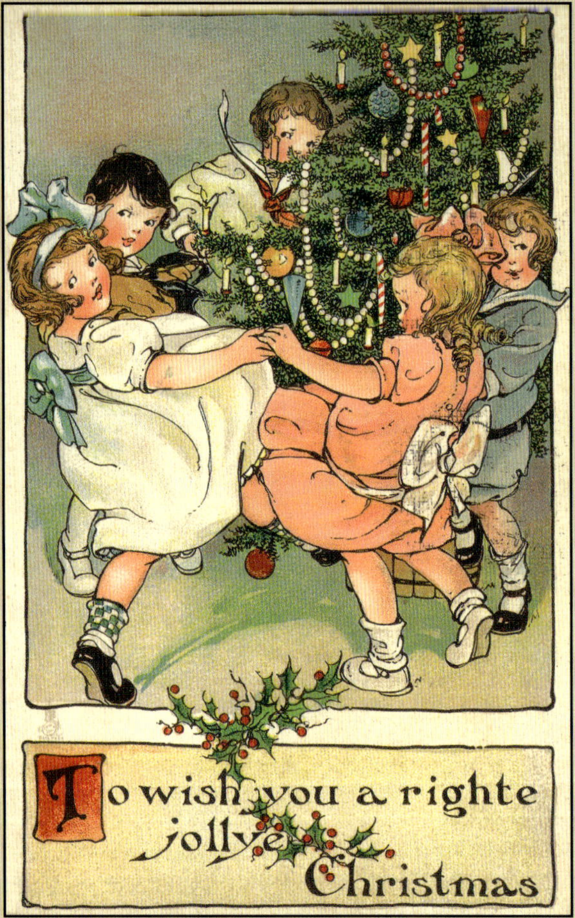
To wish you a righte jollye Christmas

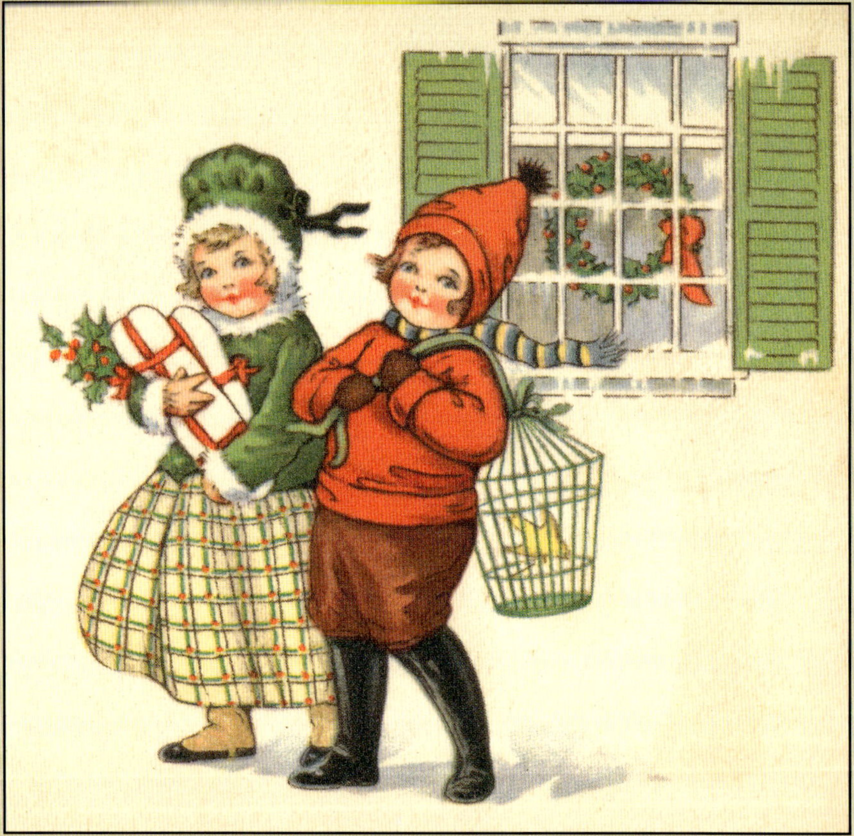

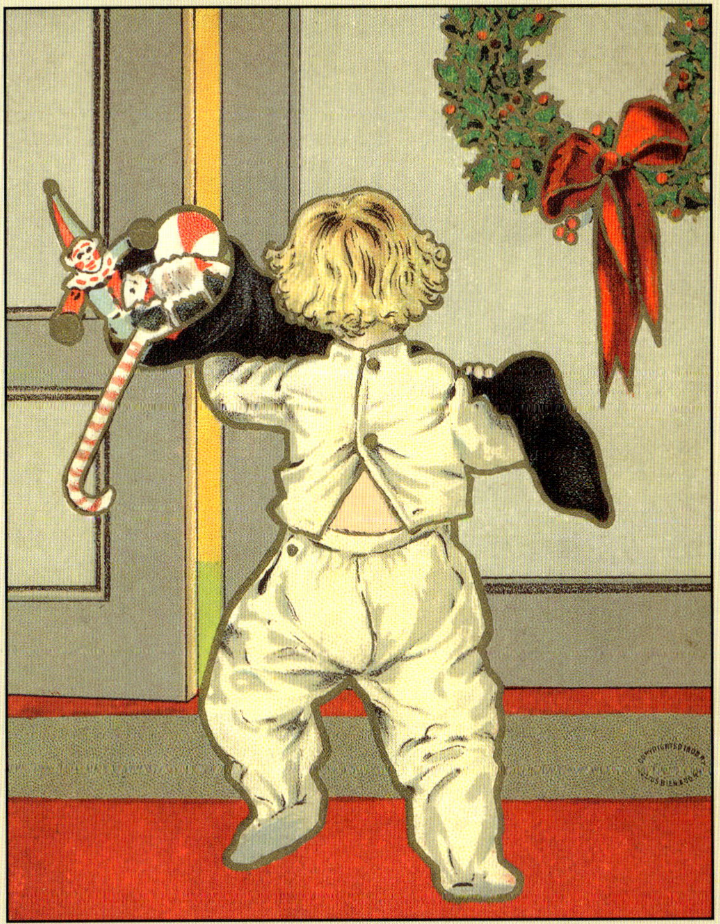

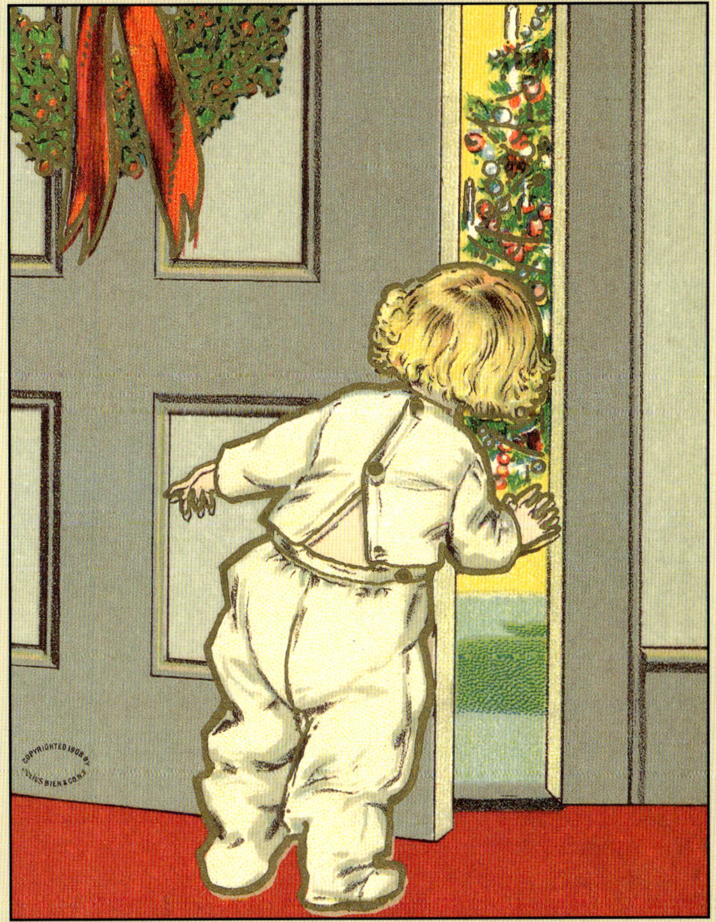

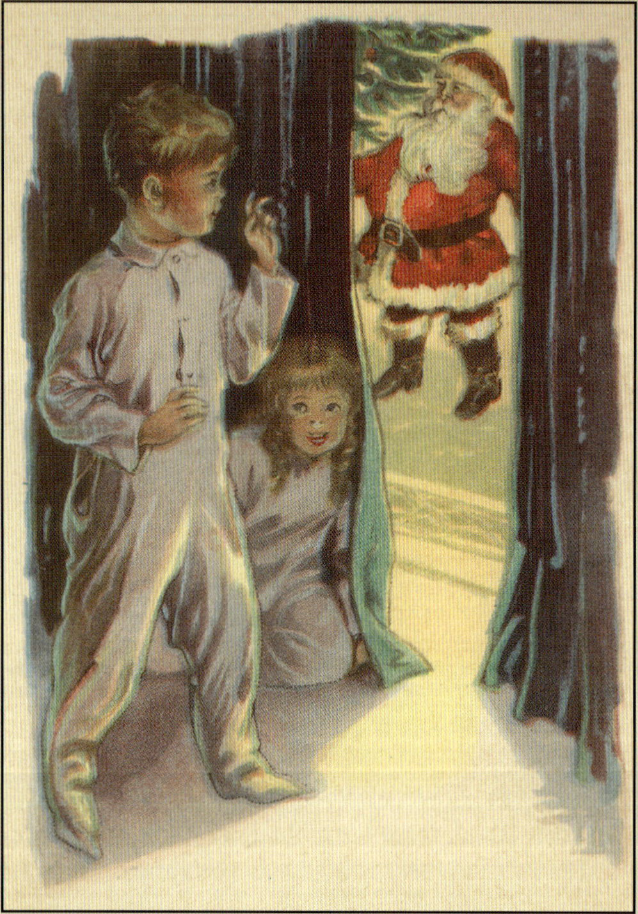

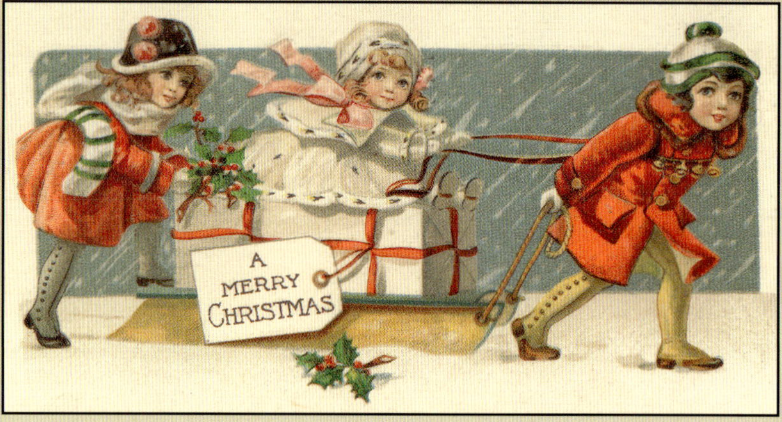
A
MERRY
CHRISTMAS

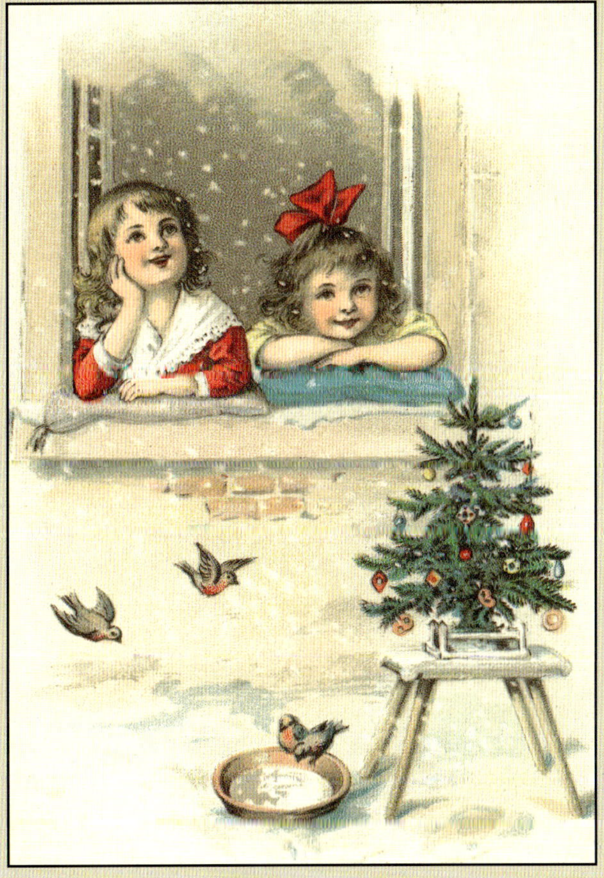

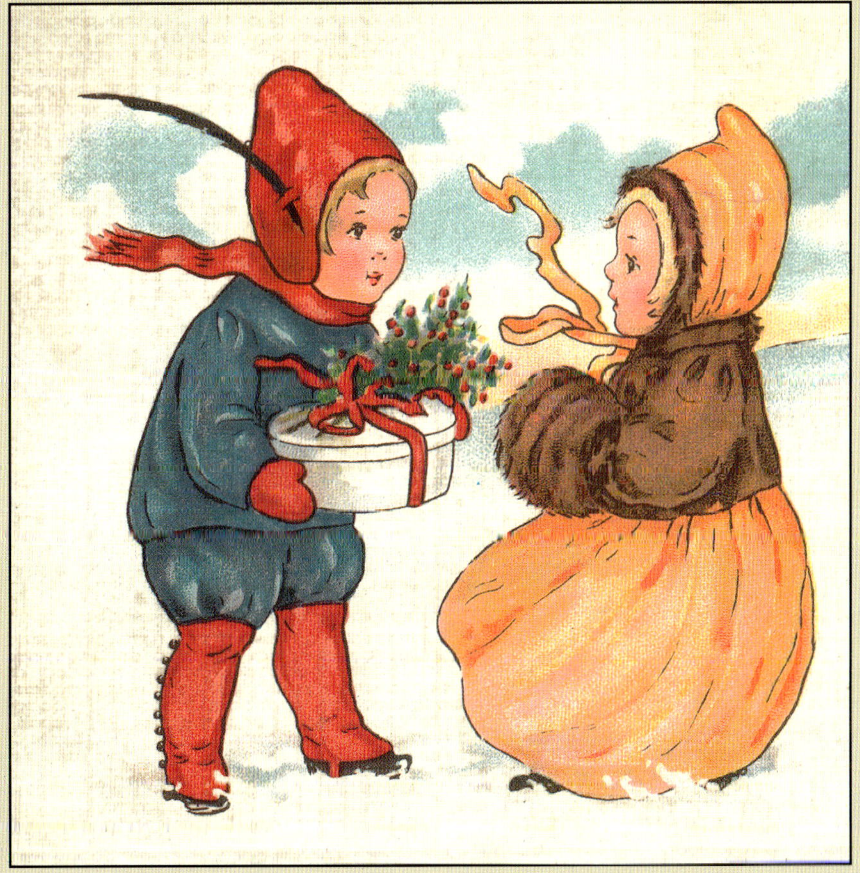

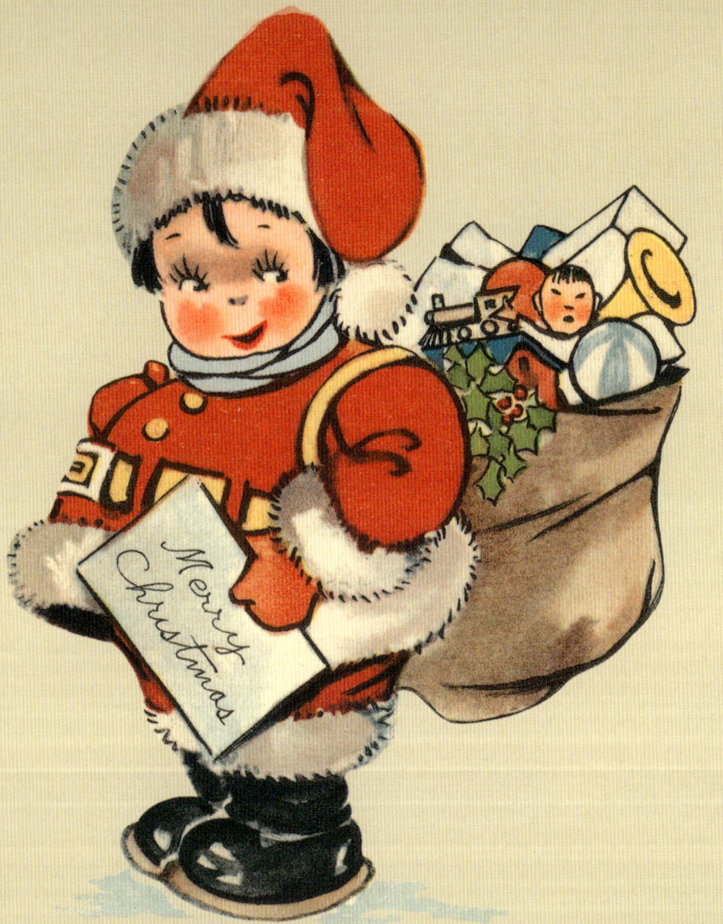
Merry Christmas

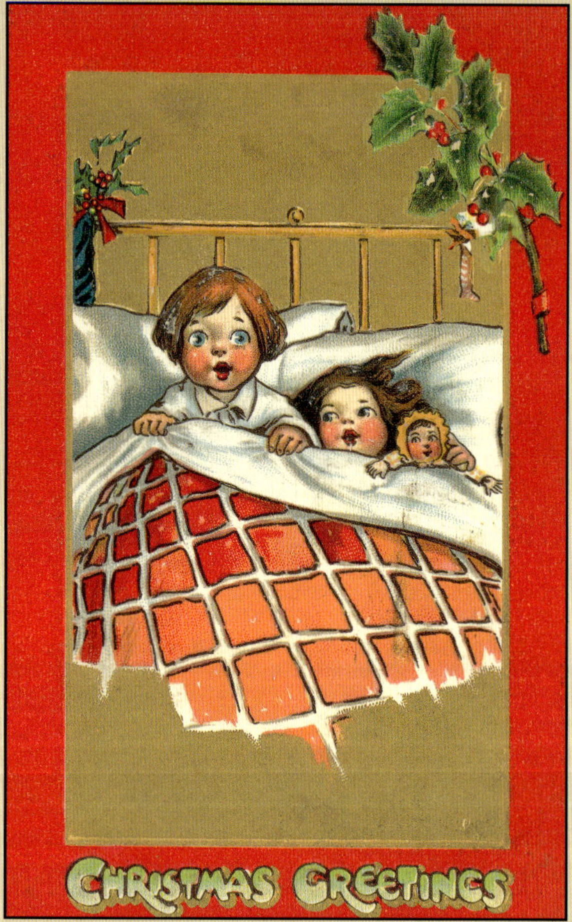
CHRISTMAS GREETINGS

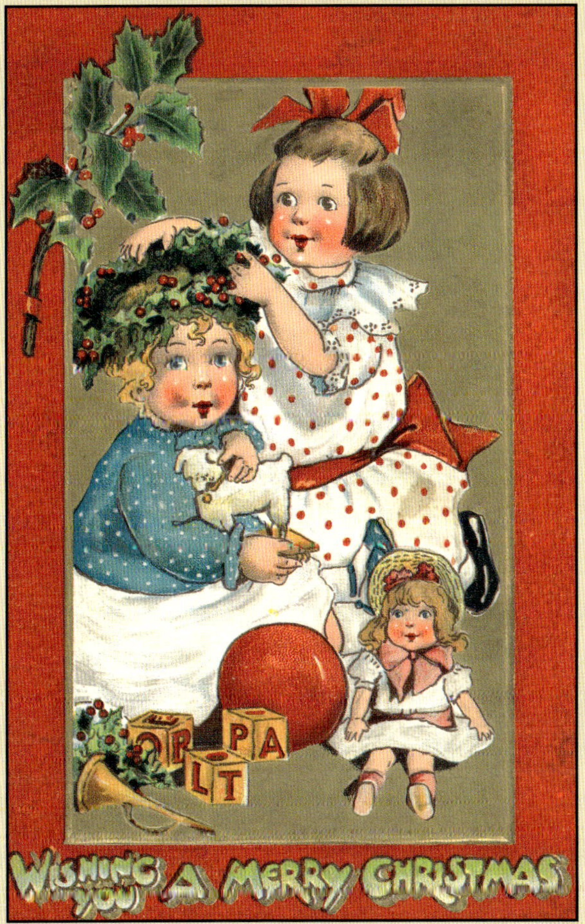
WISHING YOU A MERRY CHRISTMAS

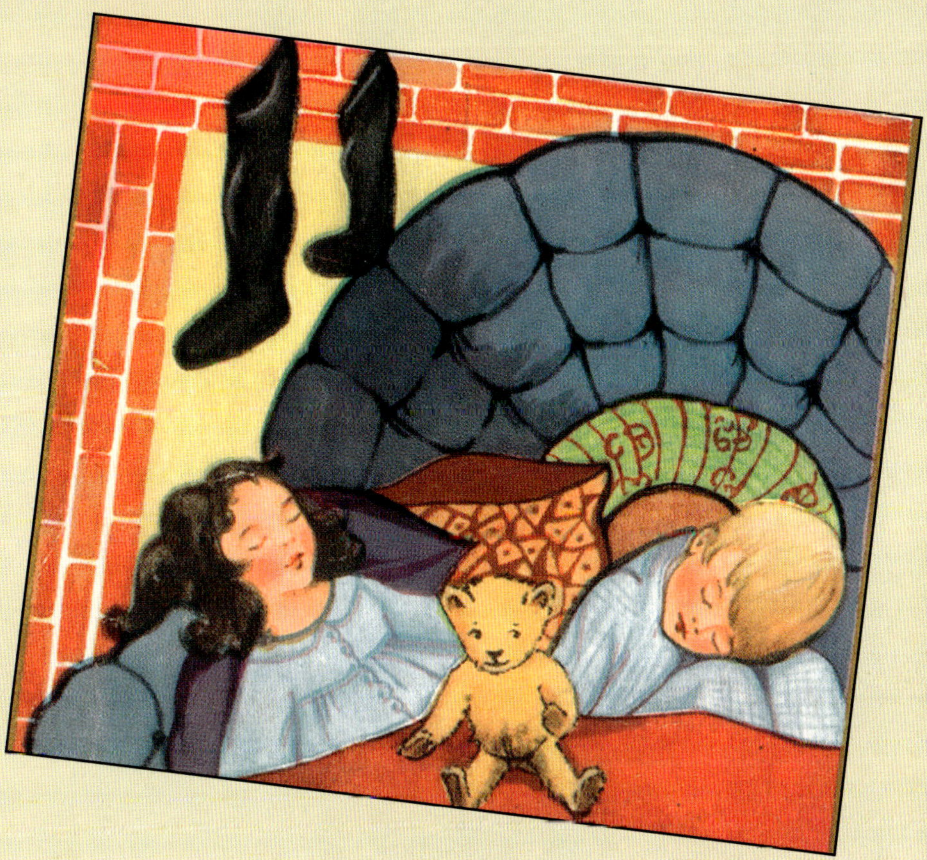

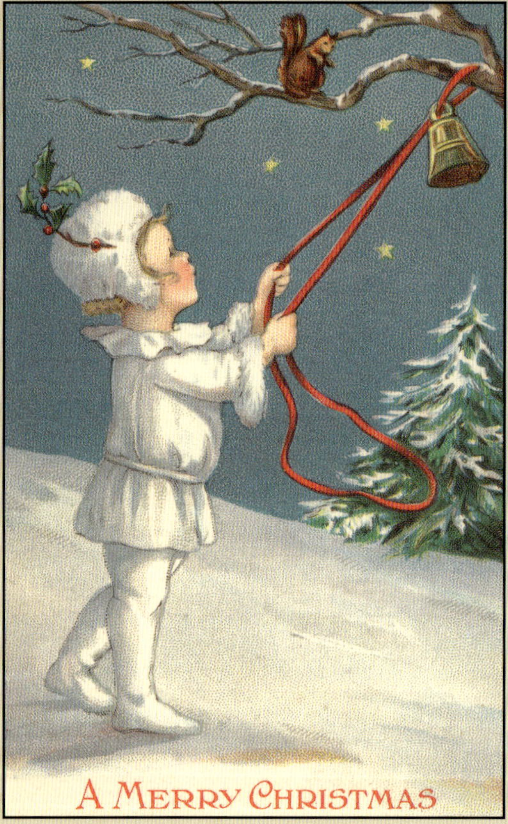
A Merry Christmas

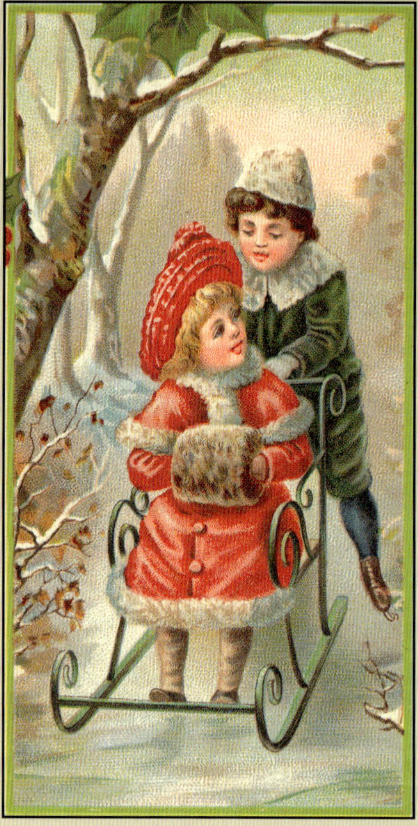

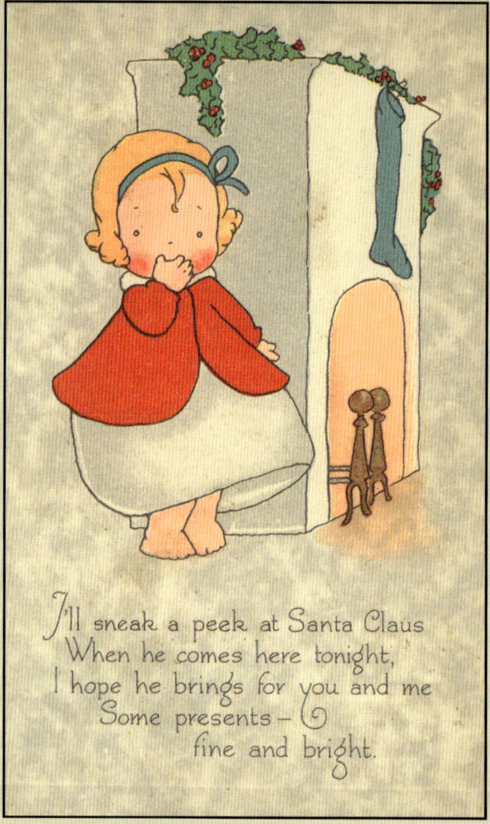
I'll sneak a peek at Santa Claus
When he comes here tonight,
I hope he brings for you and me
Some presents –
fine and bright.

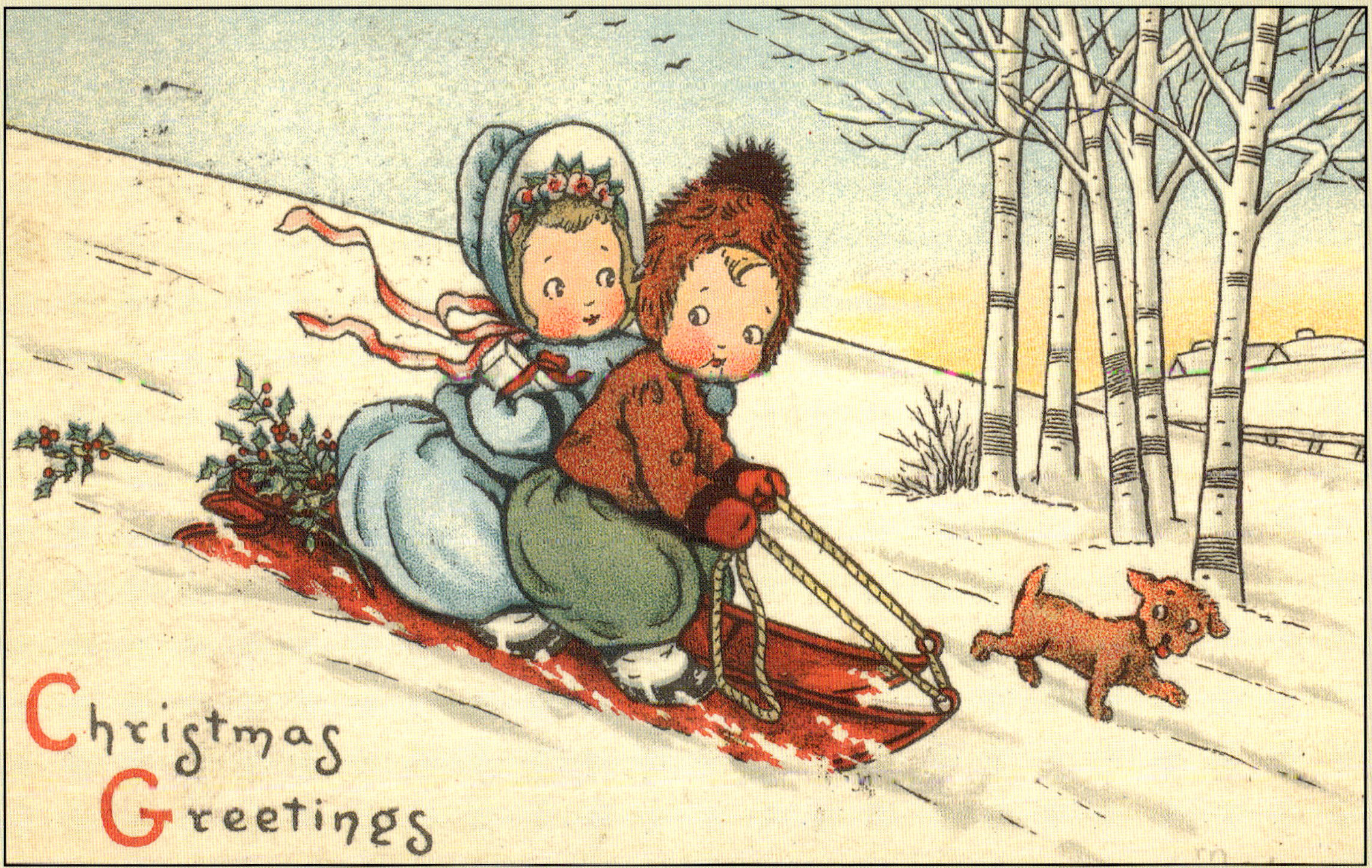
Christmas
Greetings

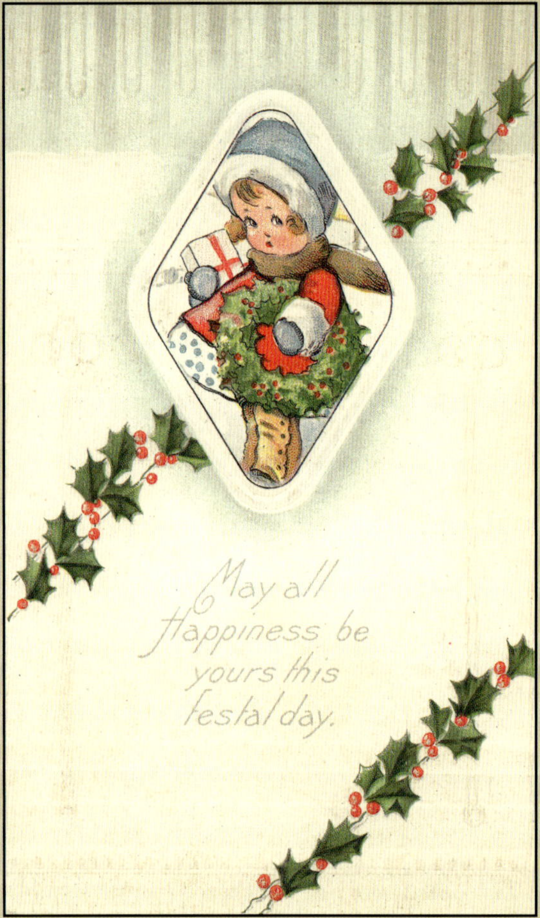
May all
Happiness be
yours this
festal day.

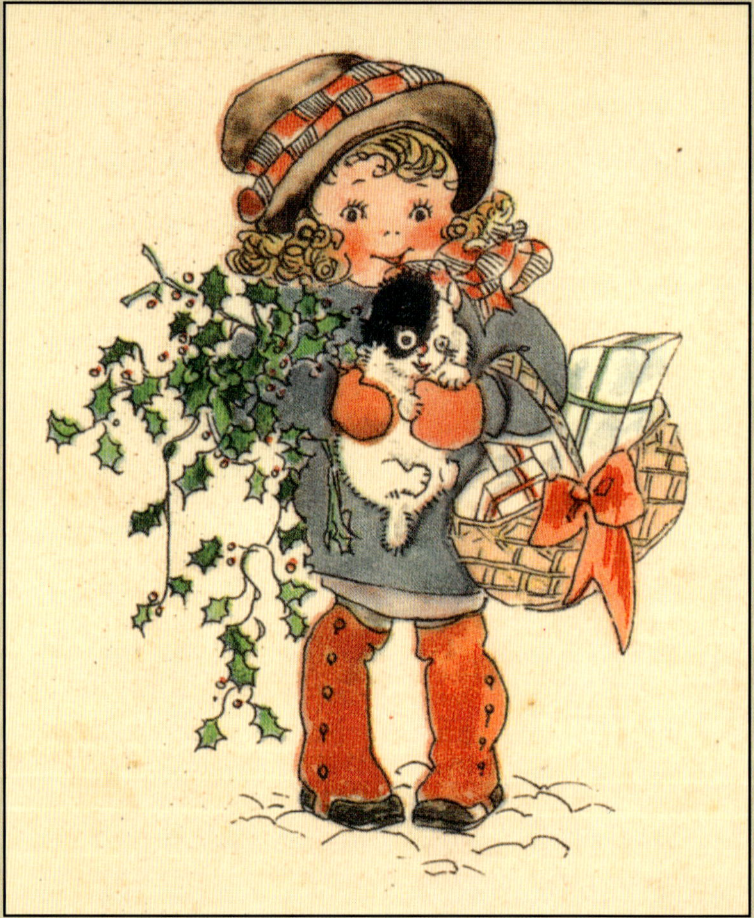

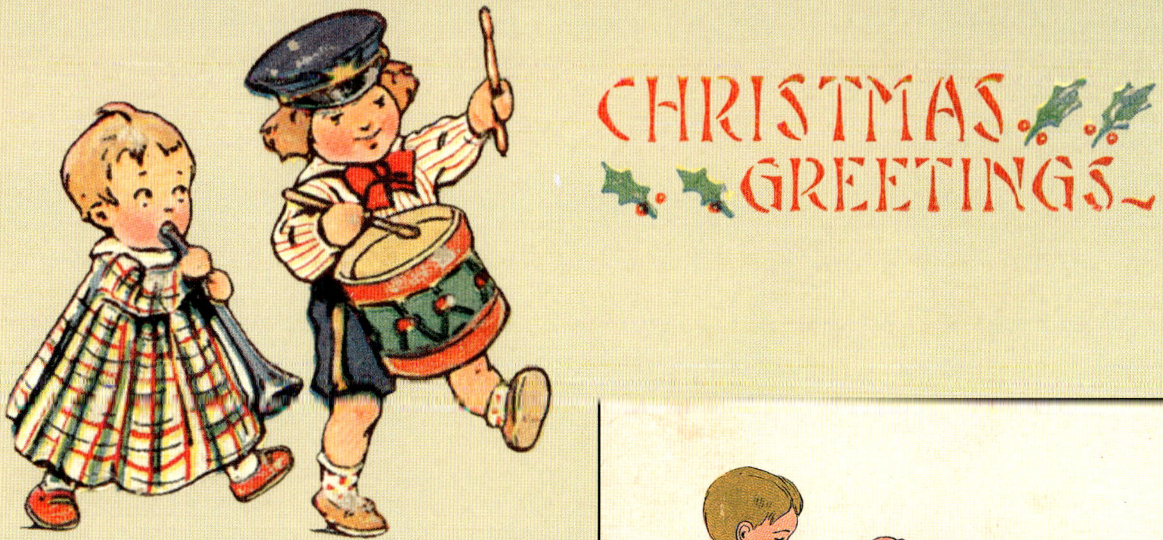
CHRISTMAS
GREETINGS

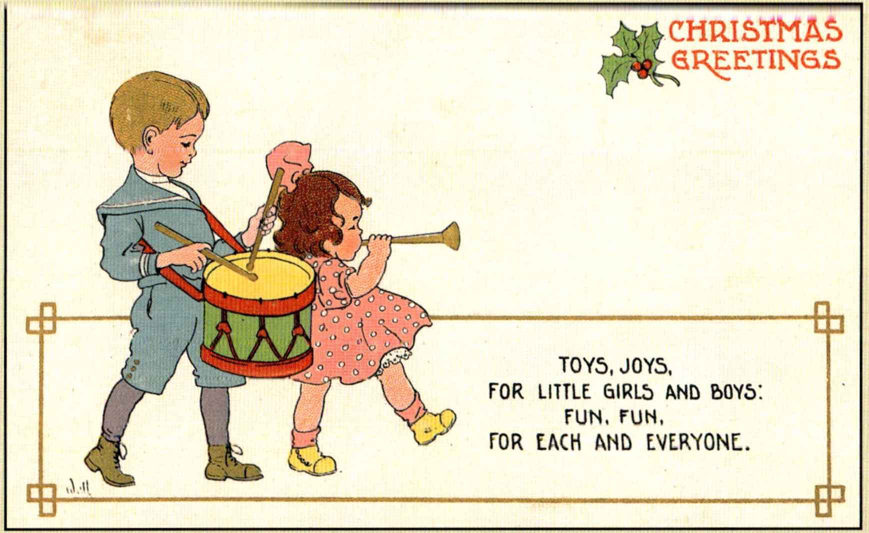
CHRISTMAS
GREETINGS
TOYS, JOYS,
FOR LITTLE GIRLS AND BOYS:
FUN, FUN,
FOR EACH AND EVERYONE.

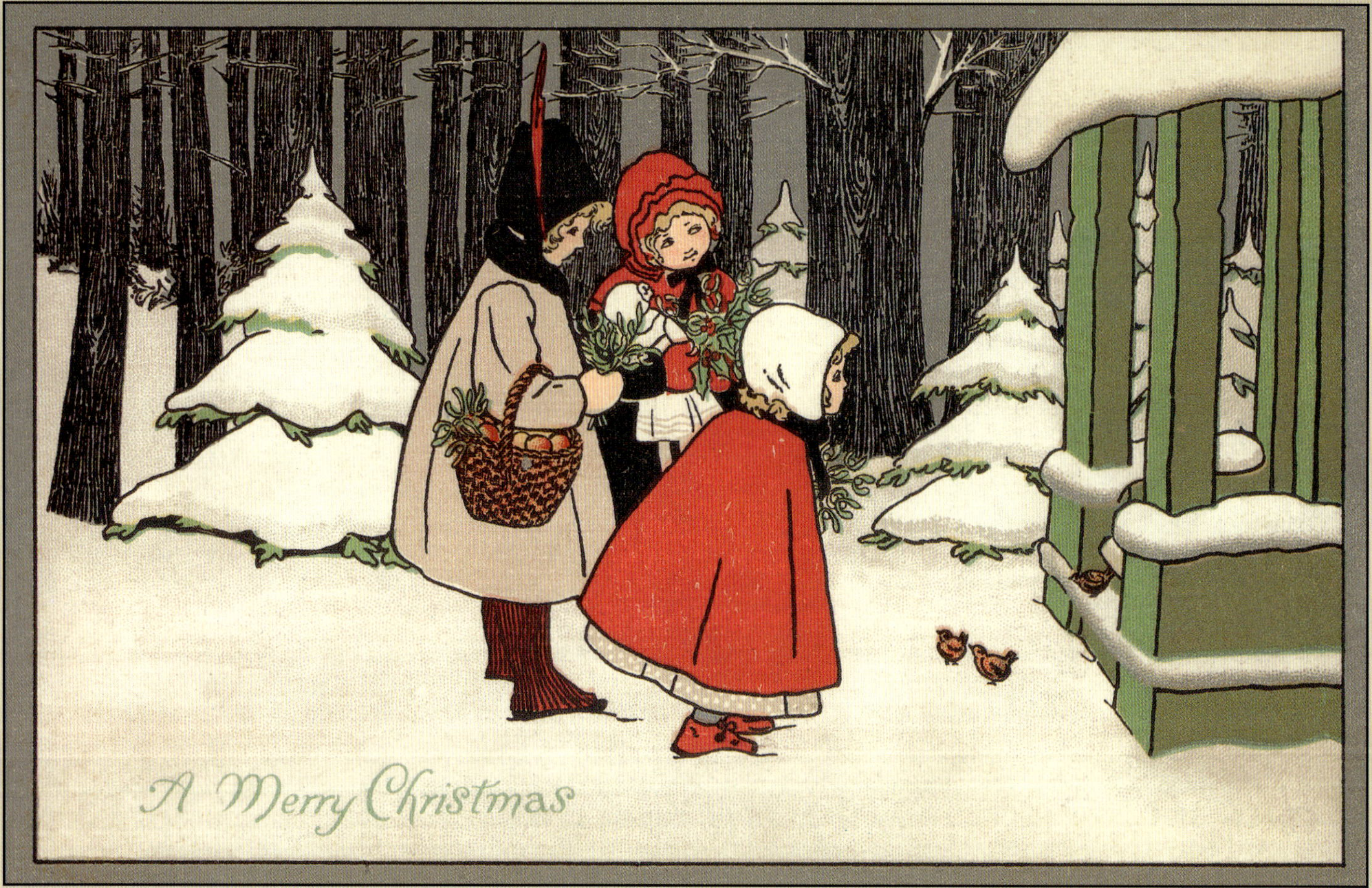
A Merry Christmas

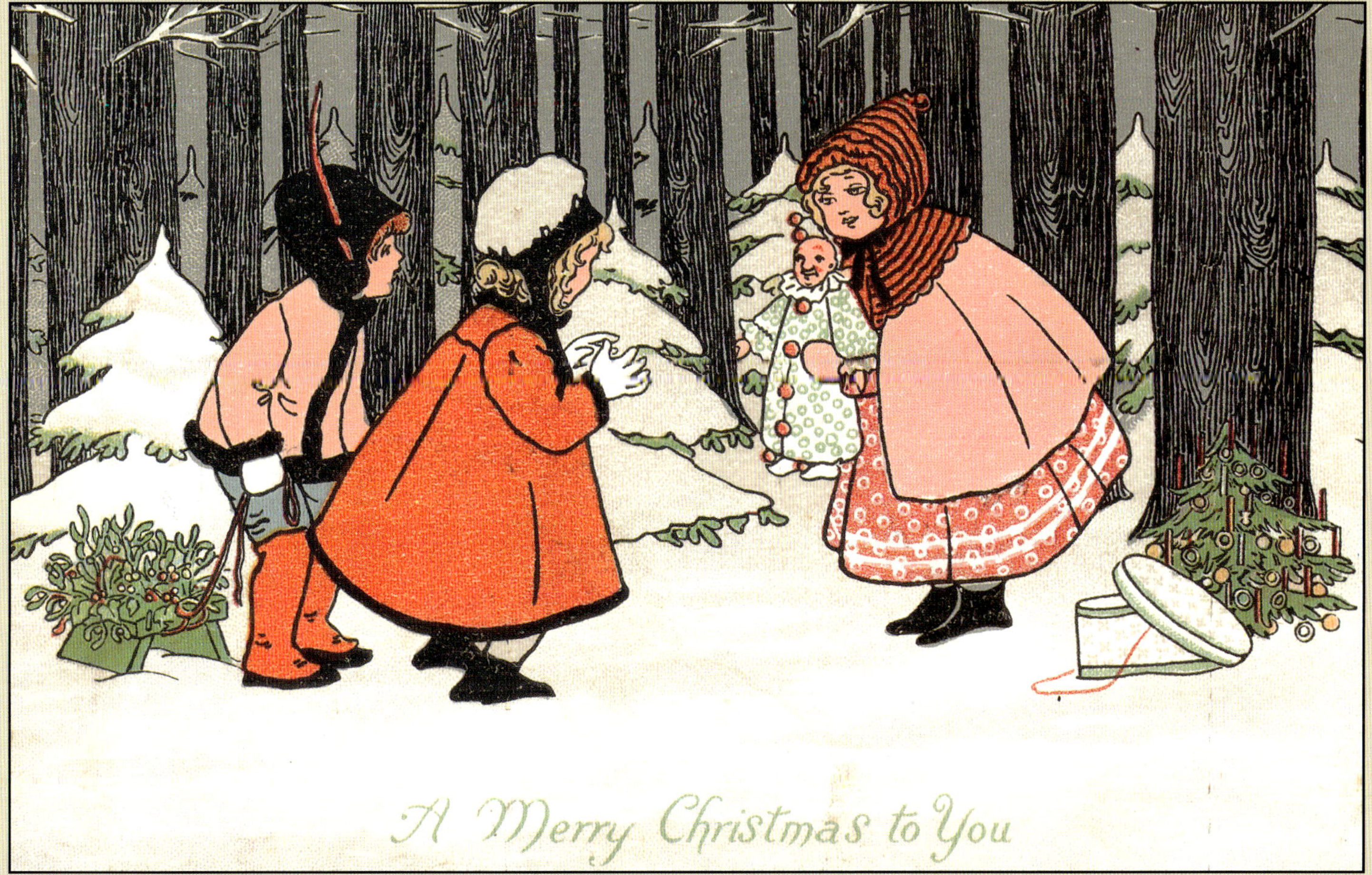
A Merry Christmas to You

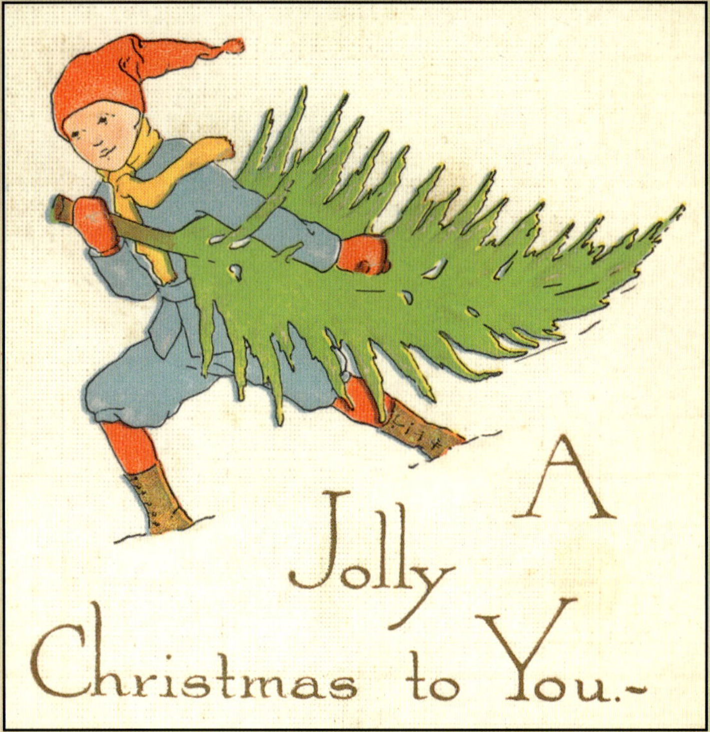
A
Jolly
Christmas to You.-

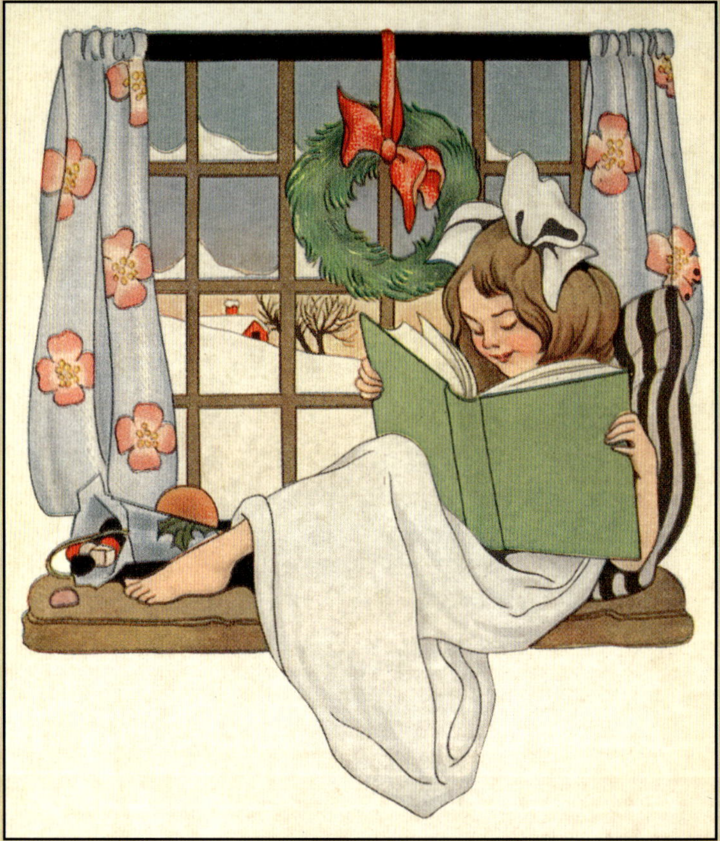

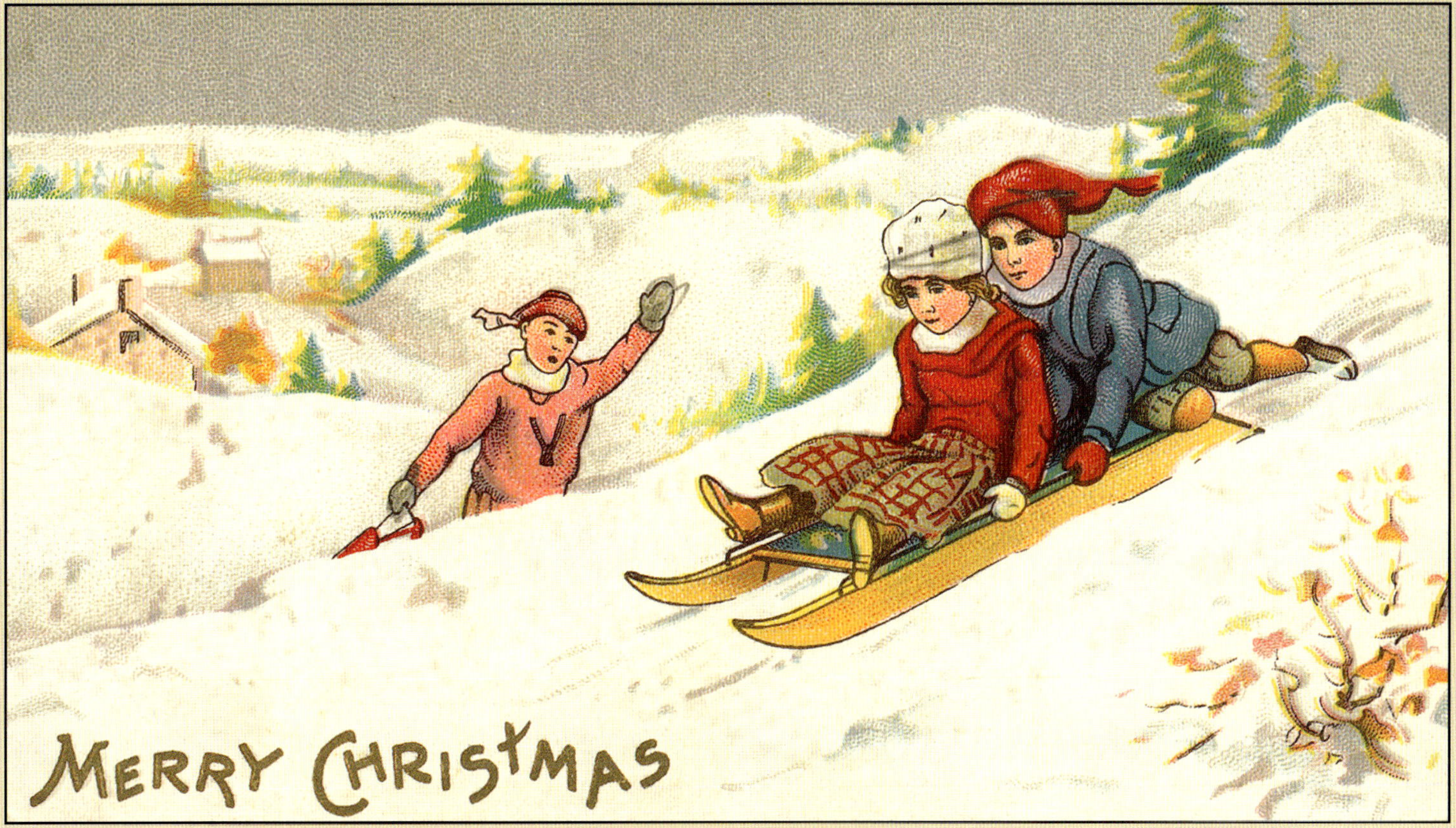
MERRY CHRISTMAS

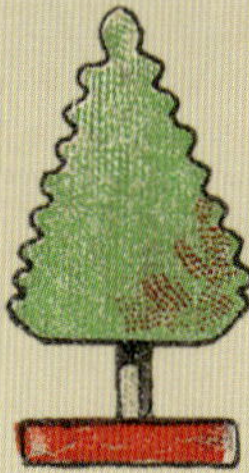

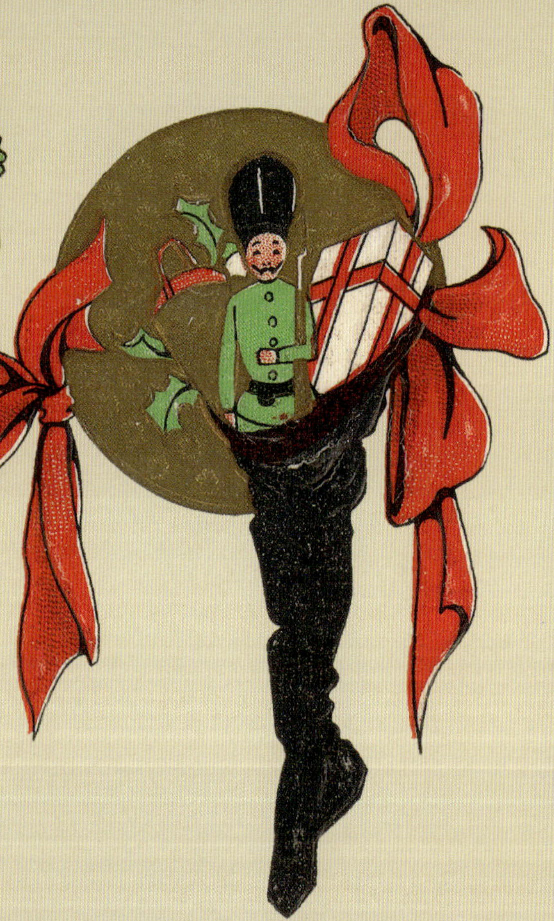

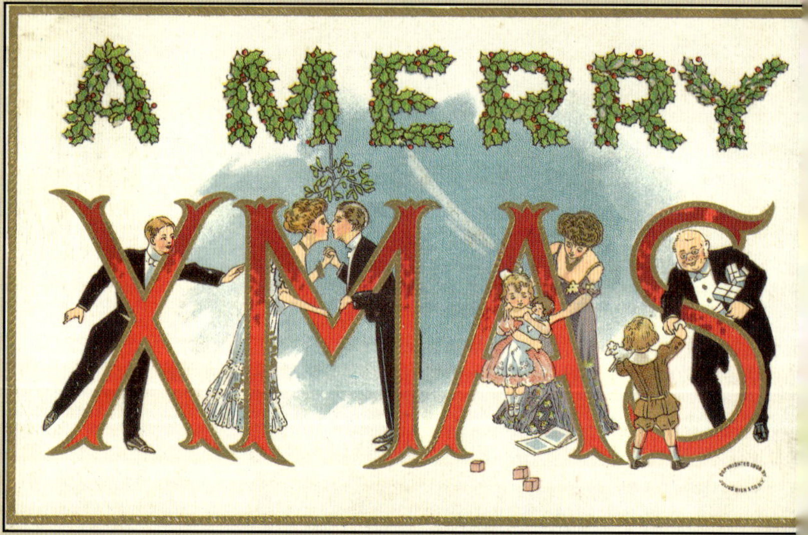
A MERRY
XMAS

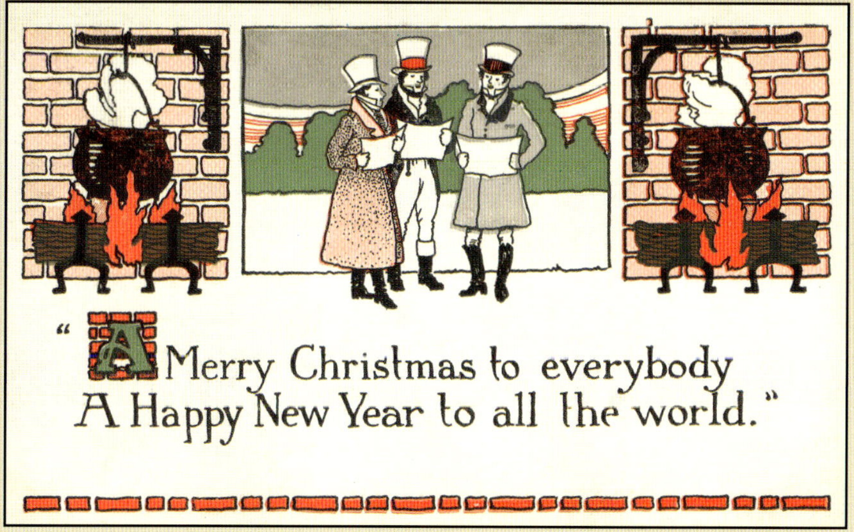
"A Merry Christmas to everybody
A Happy New Year to all the world."

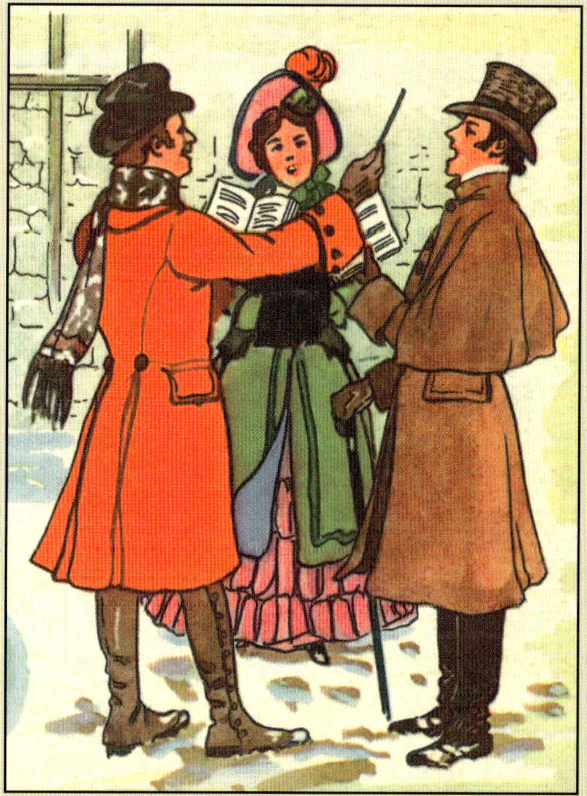

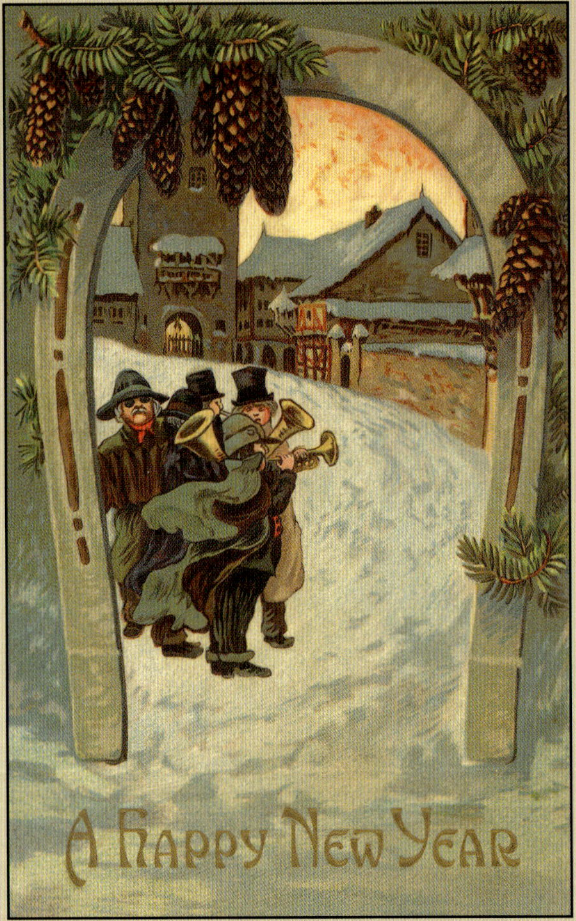
A Happy New Year

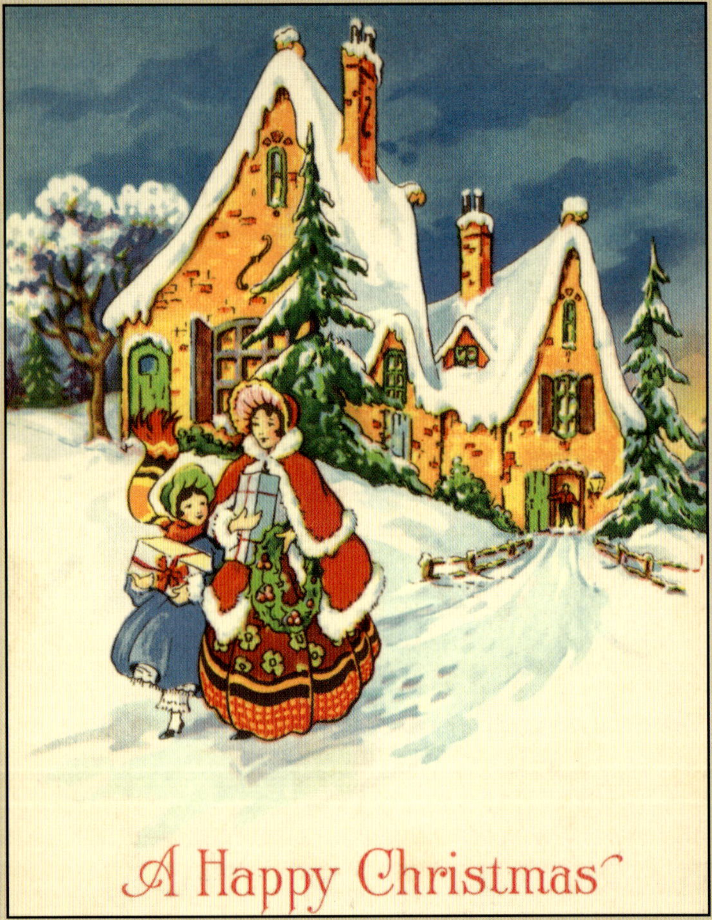
A Happy Christmas

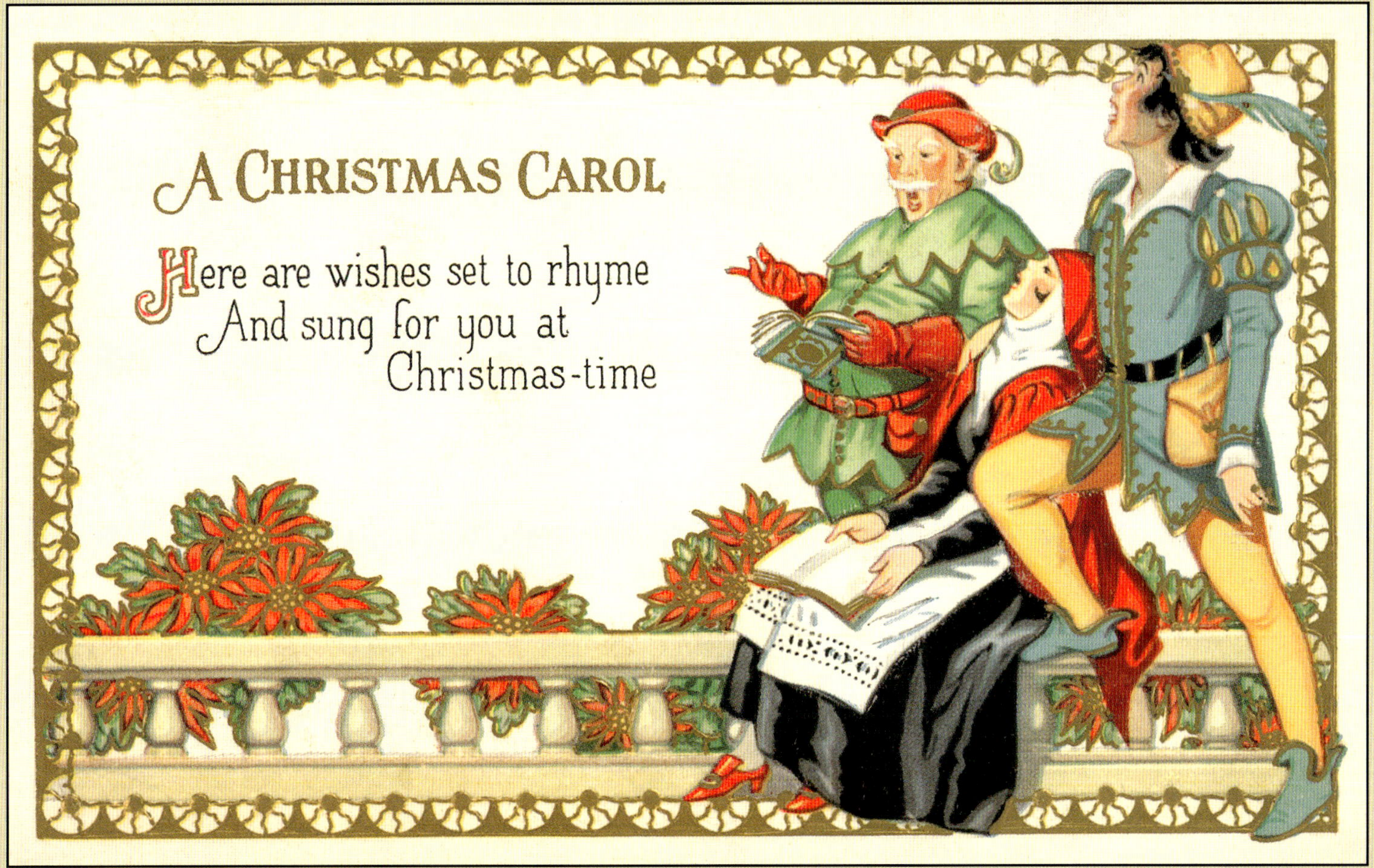
A CHRISTMAS CAROL
Here are wishes set to rhyme
And sung for you at
Christmas-time

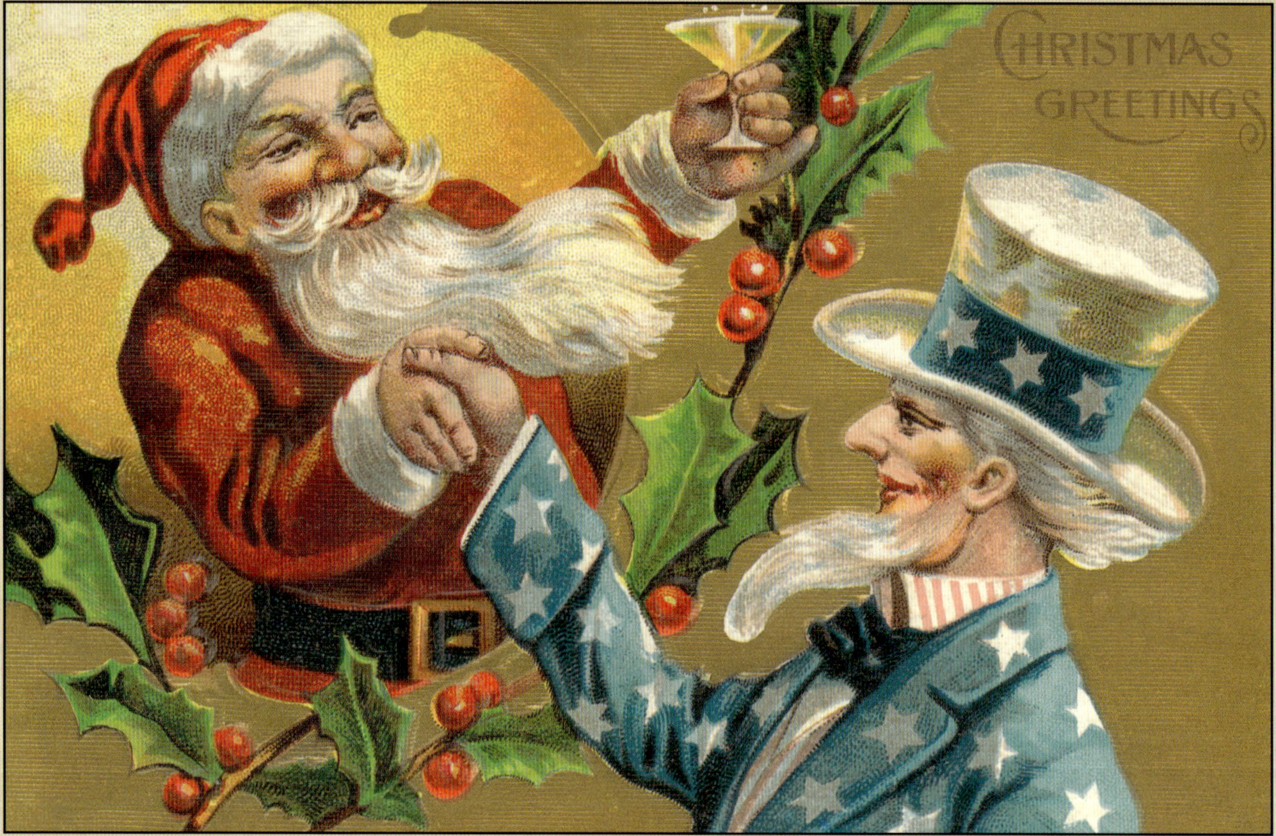
CHRISTMAS
GREETINGS

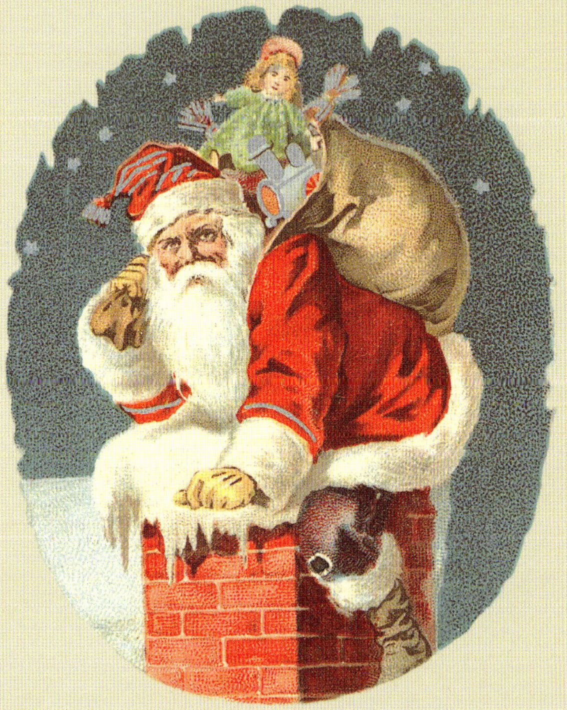

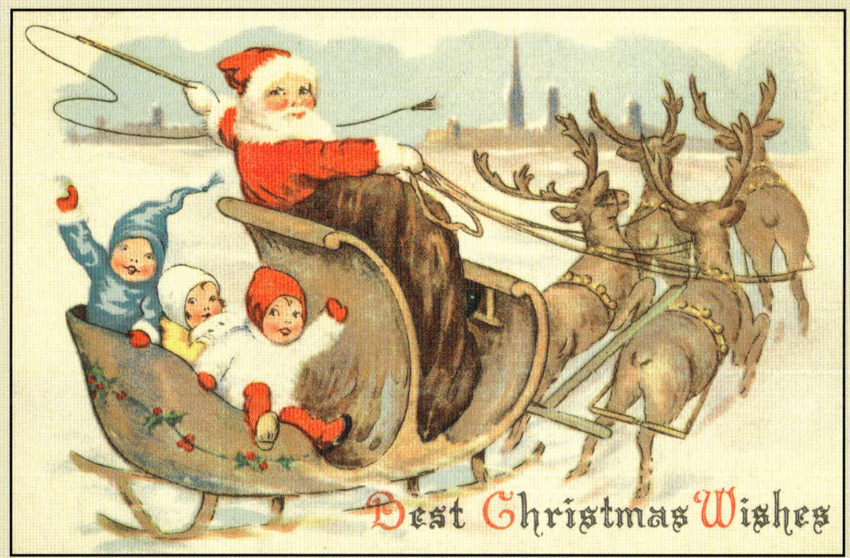
Best Christmas Wishes

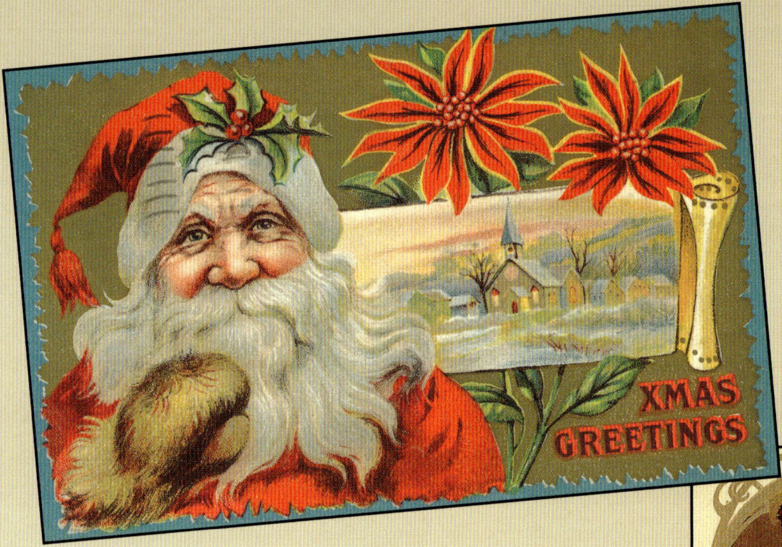
XMAS
GREETINGS

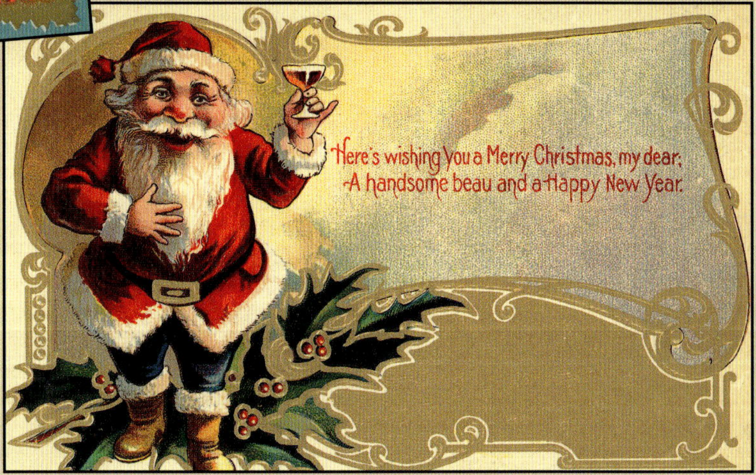
Here's wishing you a Merry Christmas, my dear;
A handsome beau and a Happy New Year.

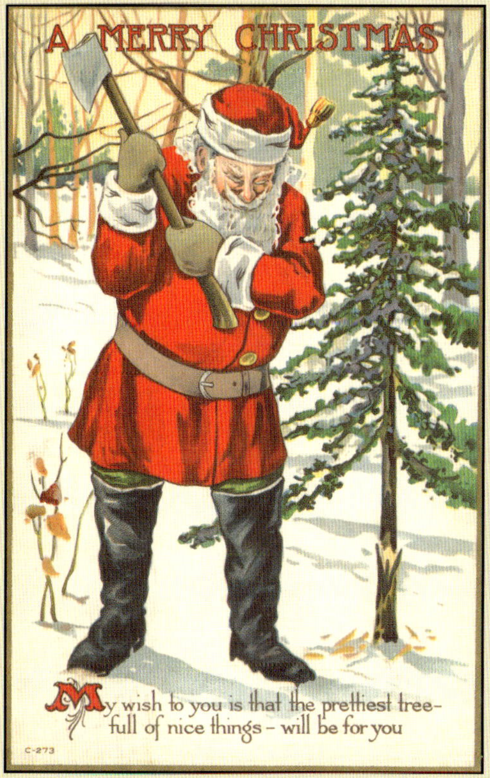
A MERRY CHRISTMAS
My wish to you is that the prettiest tree-
full of nice things - will be for you
C-273

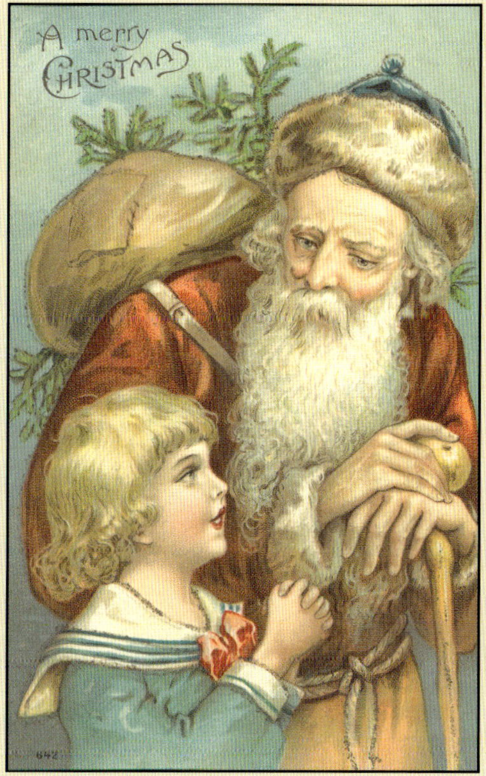
A merry
CHRISTMAS
642

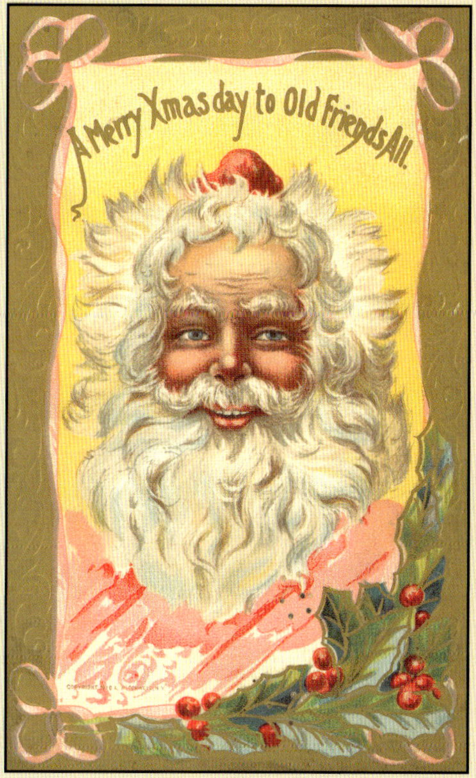
A Merry Xmas day to Old Friends All.

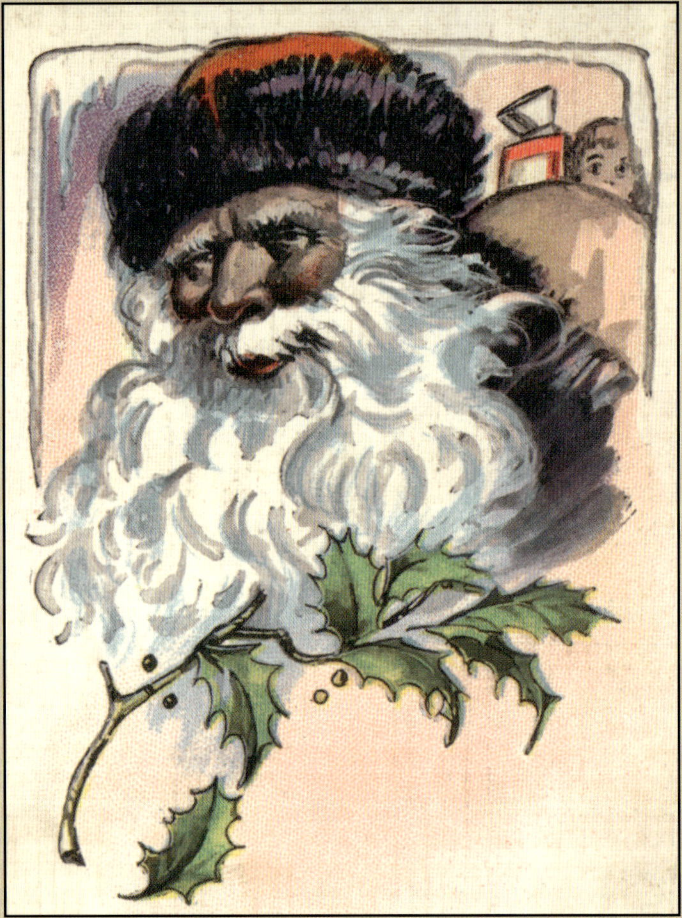

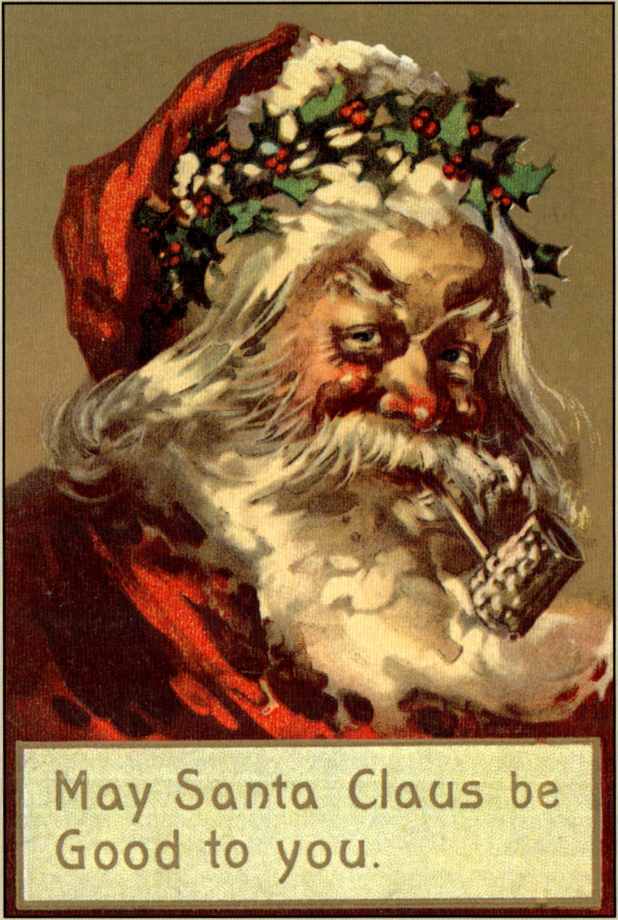
May Santa Claus be
Good to you.

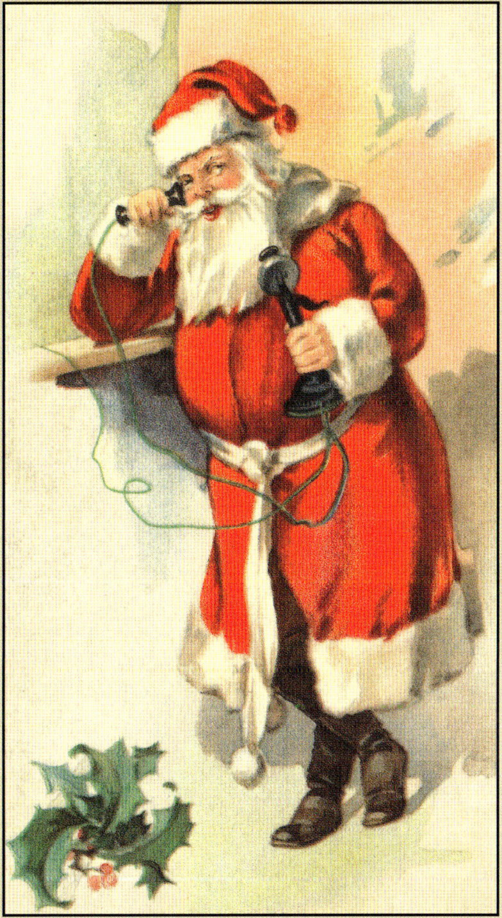

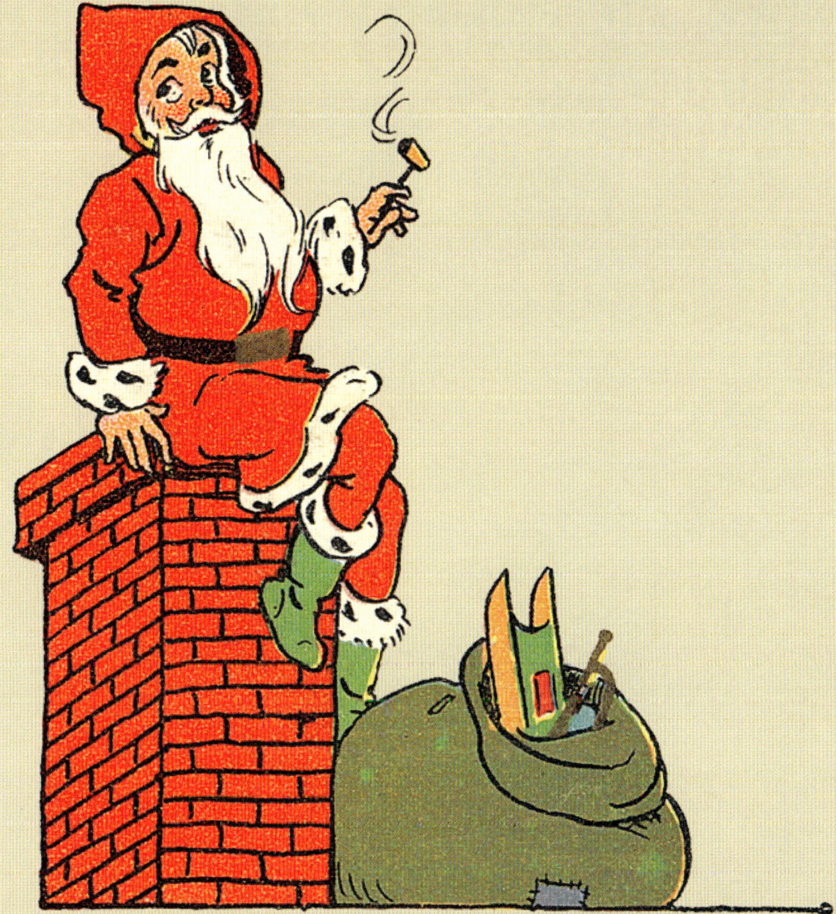

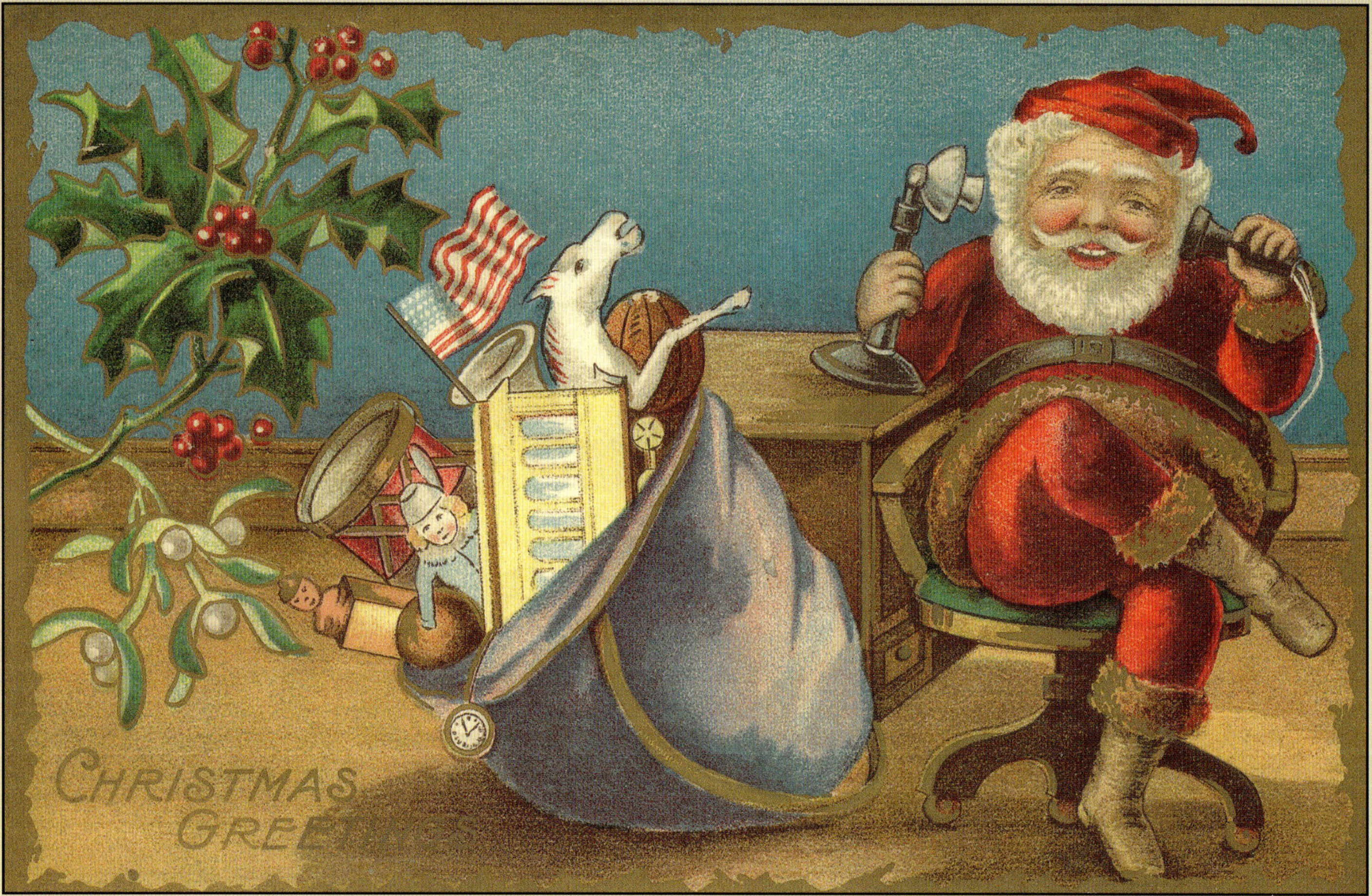
CHRISTMAS

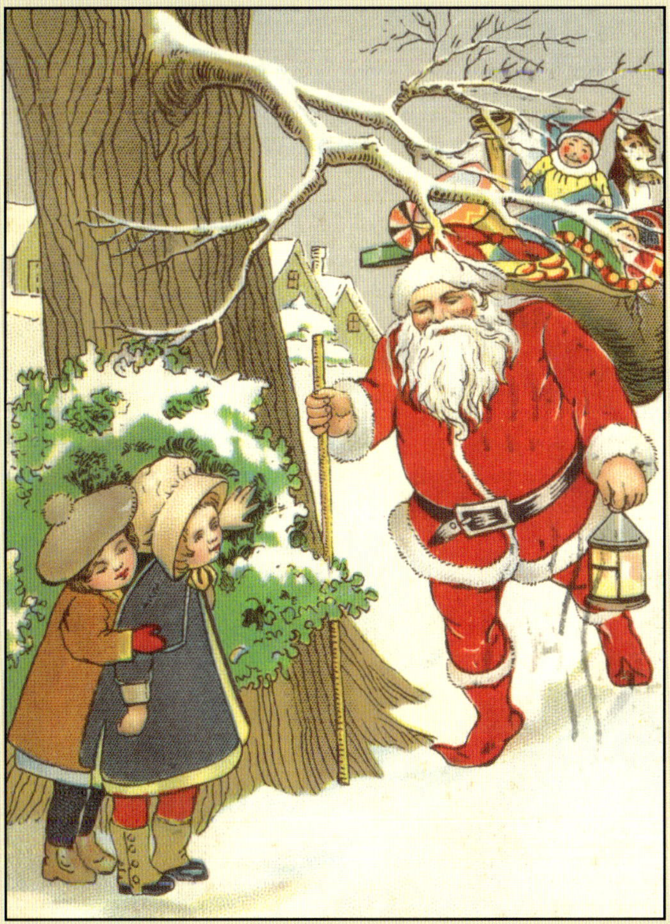

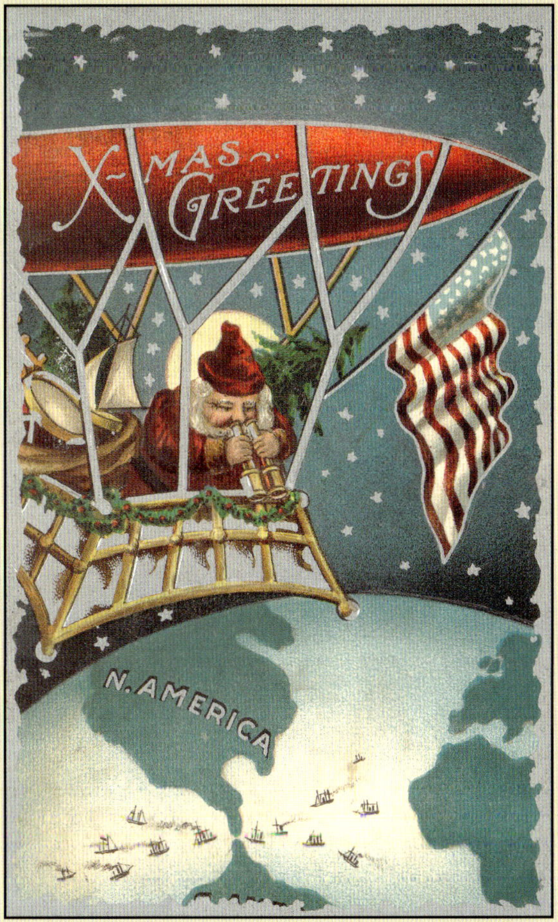
X-MAS GREETINGS
N. AMERICA

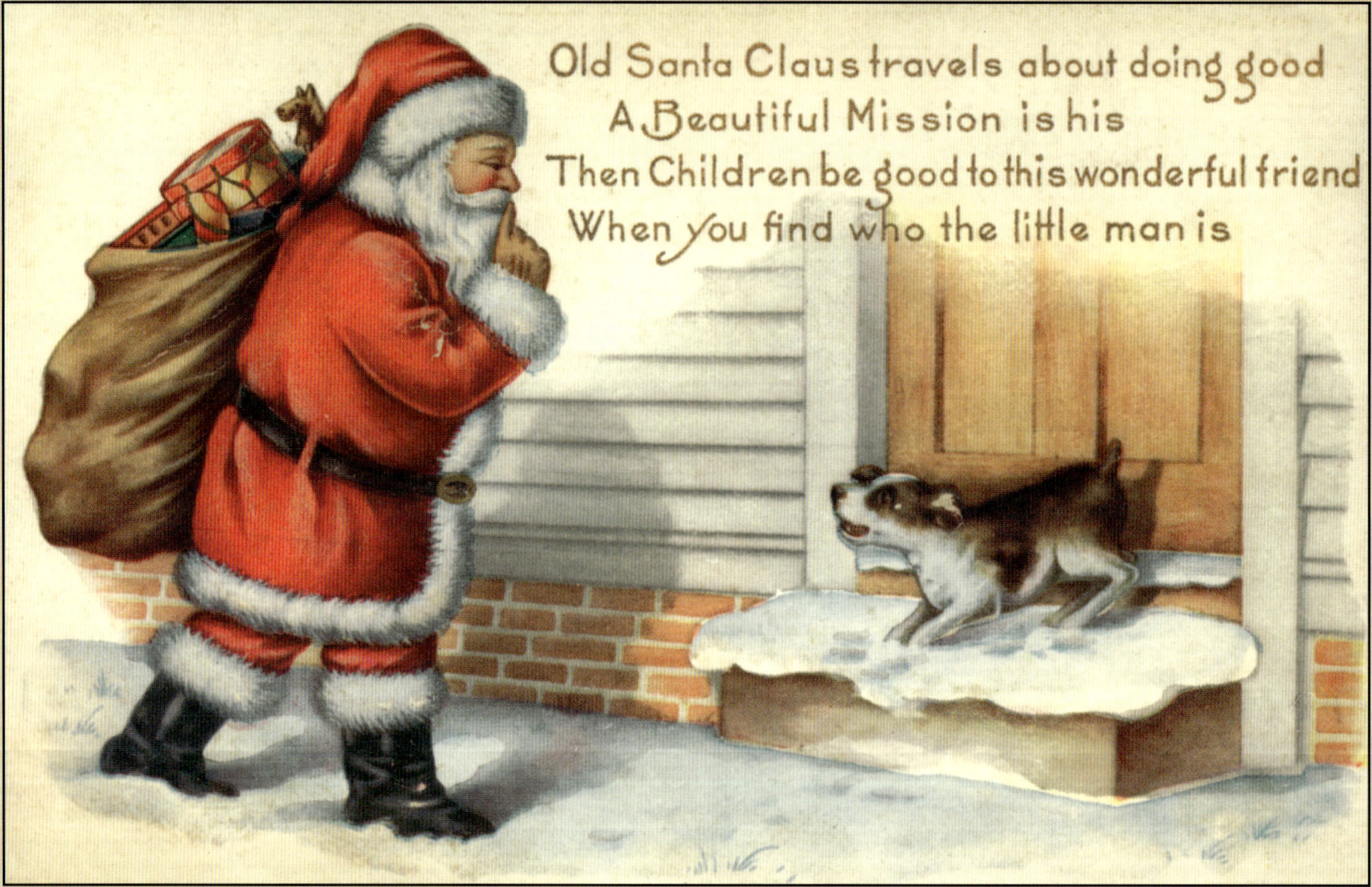
Old Santa Claus travels about doing good
A Beautiful Mission is his
Then Children be good to this wonderful friend
When you find who the little man is

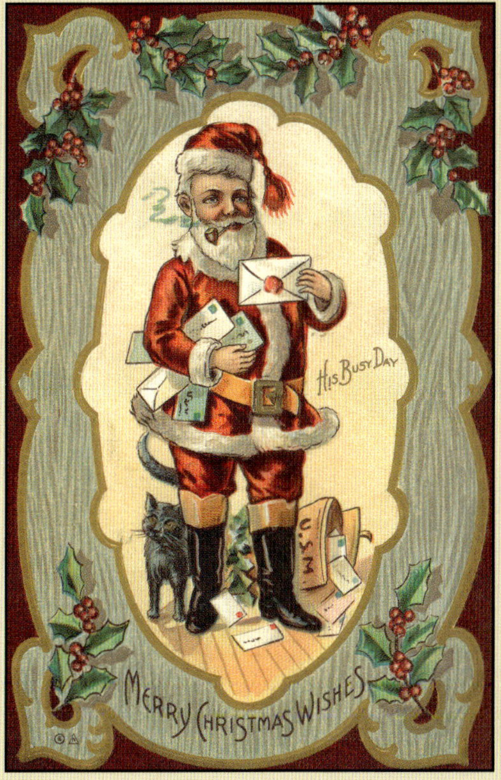
His Busy Day
Merry Christmas Wishes

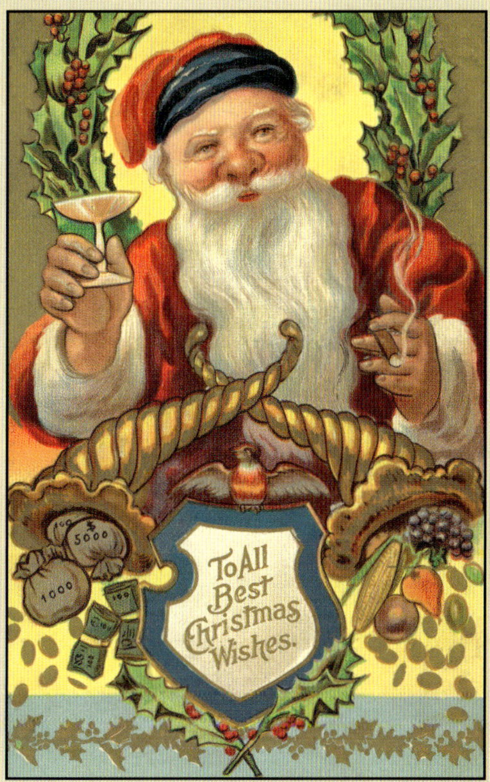
To All Best Christmas Wishes.

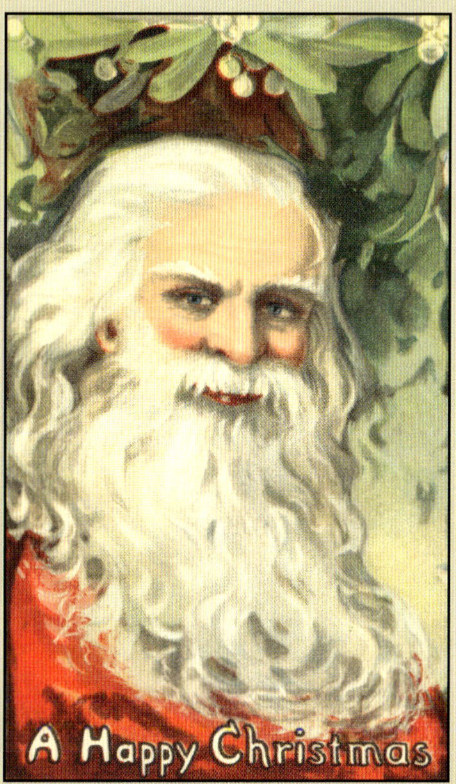
A Happy Christmas

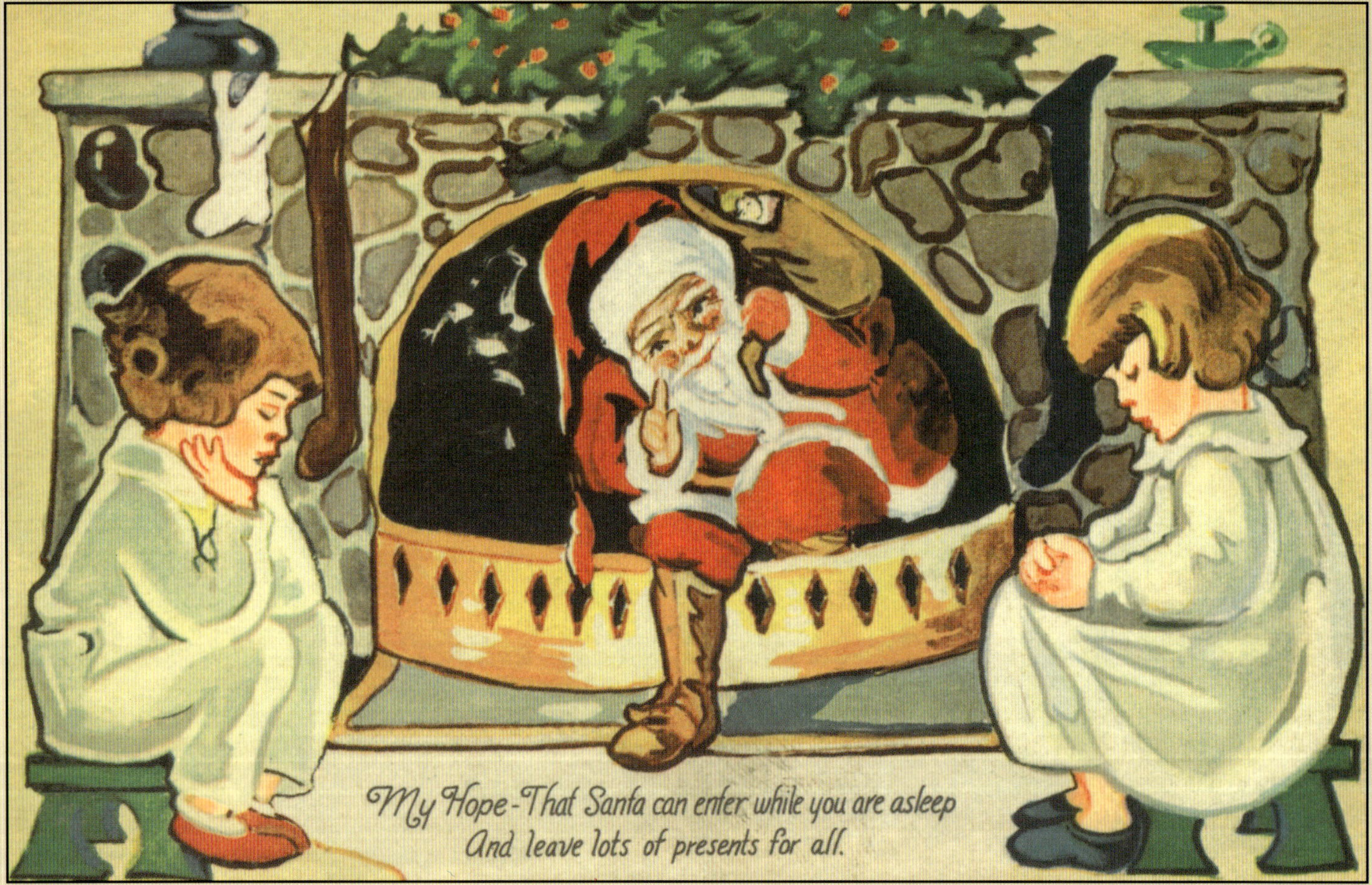
My Hope-That Santa can enter while you are asleep
And leave lots of presents for all.

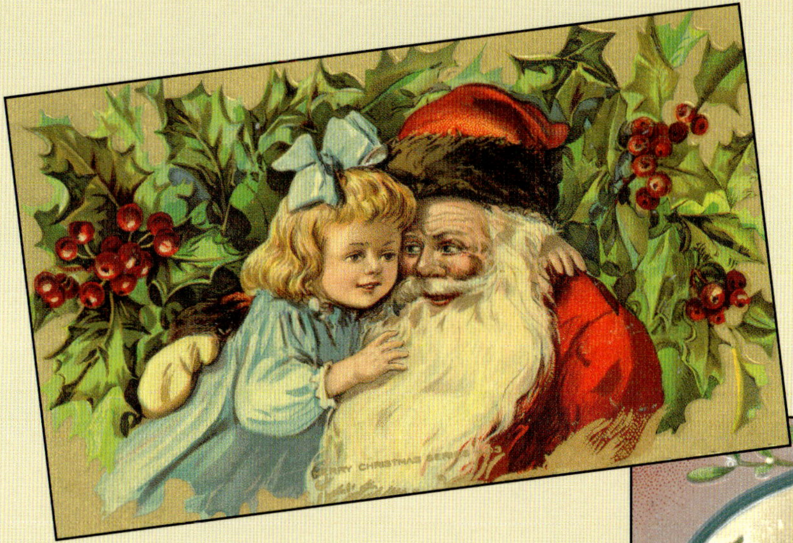

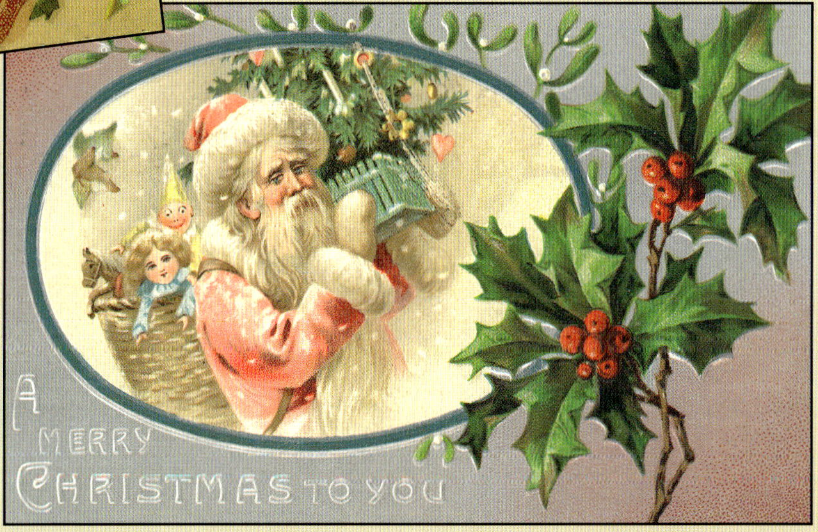
A MERRY CHRISTMAS TO YOU

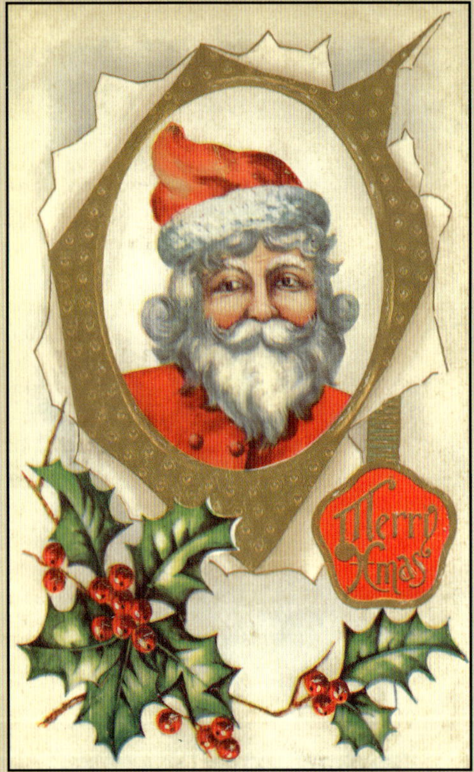
Merry Xmas

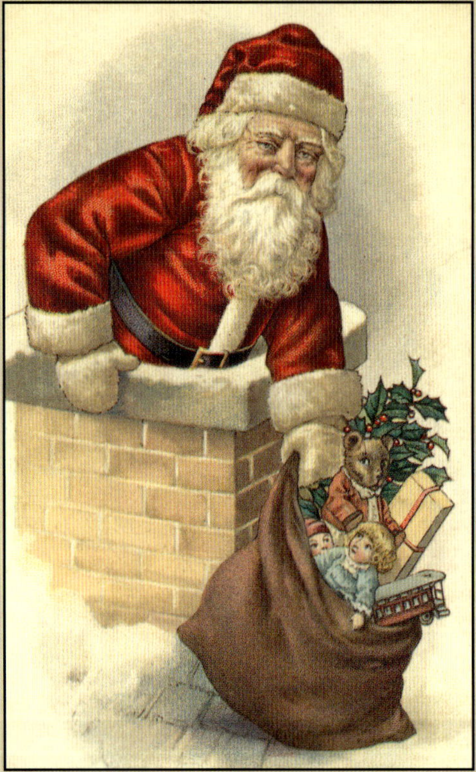

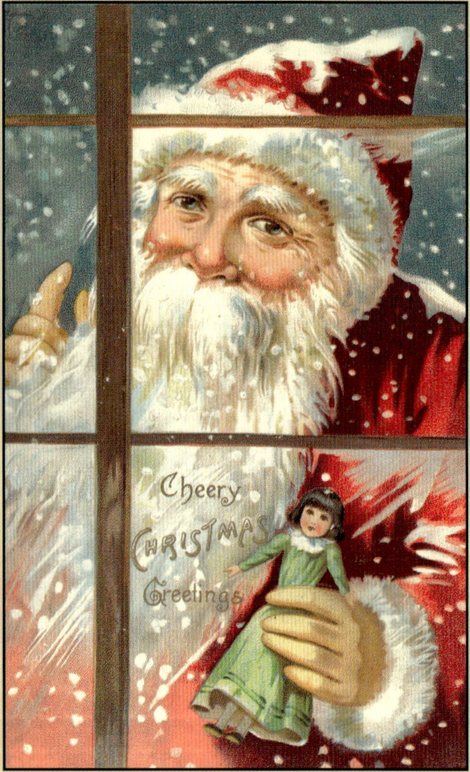
Cheery
CHRISTMAS
Greetings

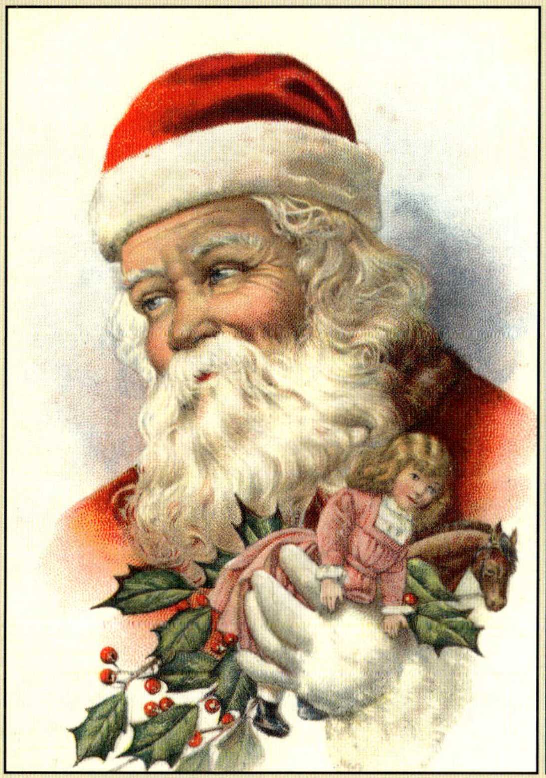

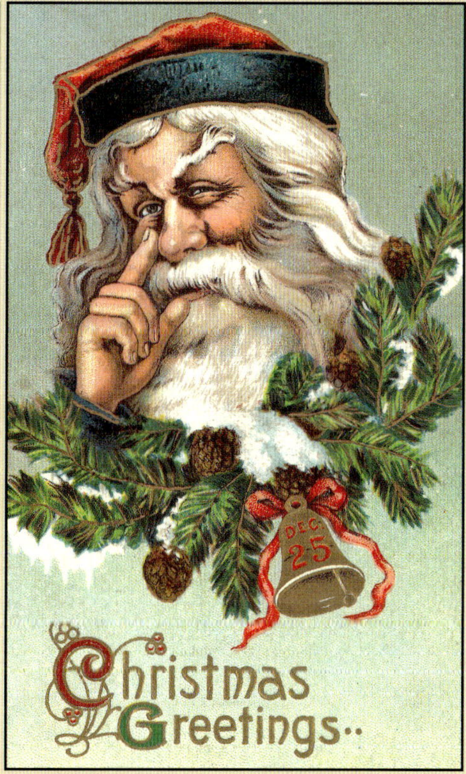
DEC
25
Christmas
Greetings..

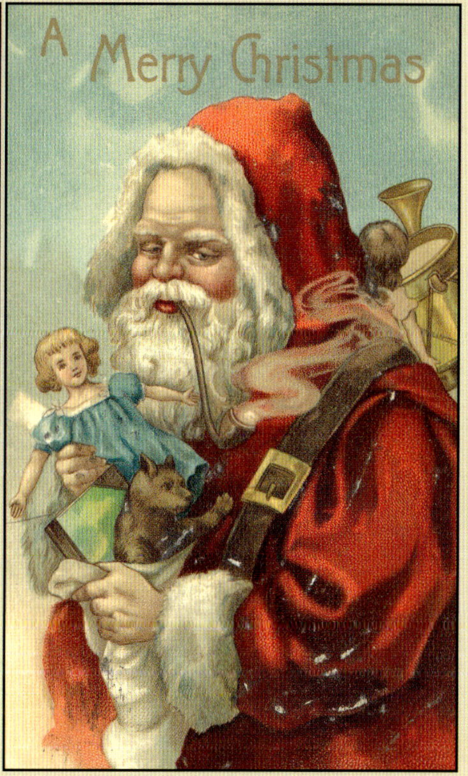
A Merry Christmas

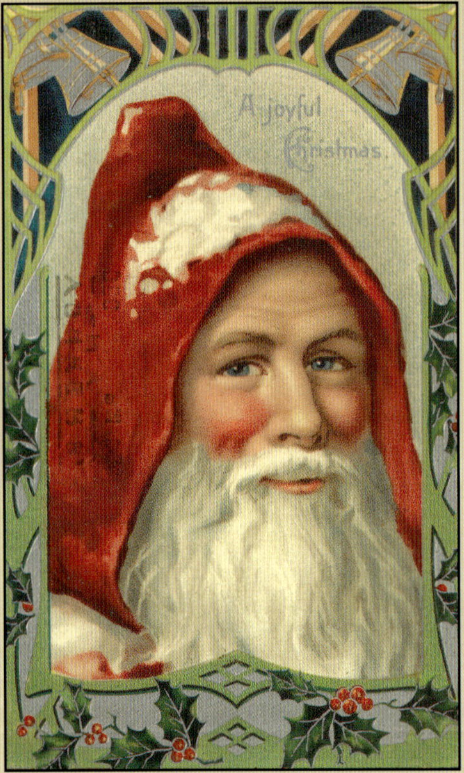
A joyful
Christmas.

Christmas Wishes

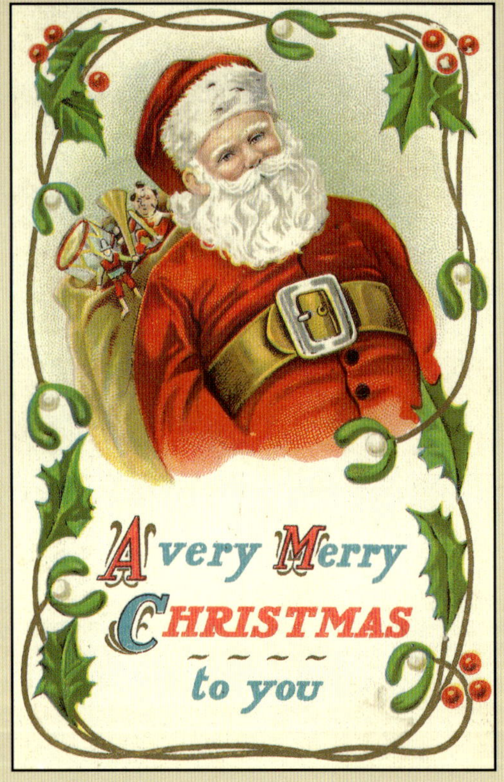
A very Merry
CHRISTMAS
to you

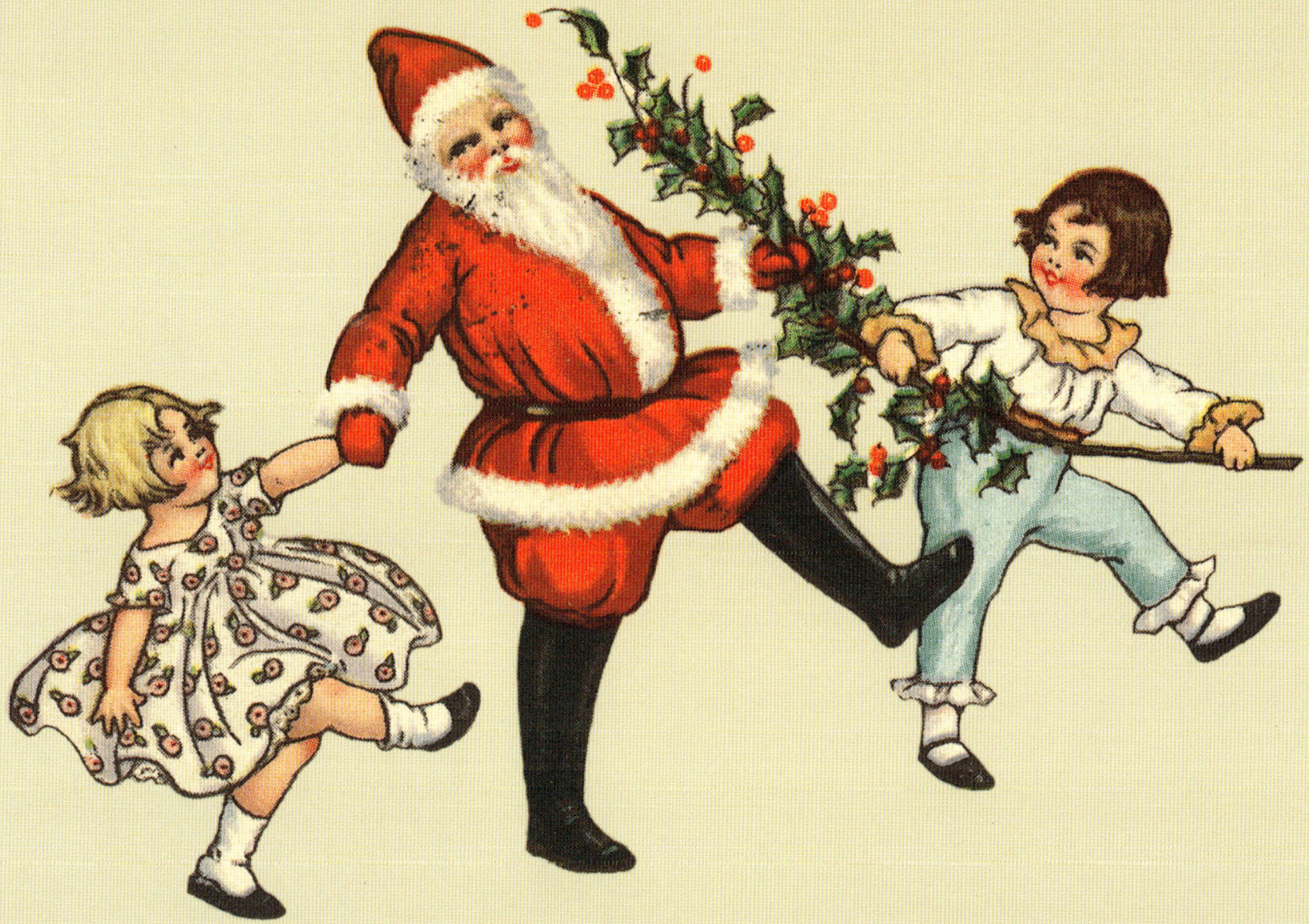

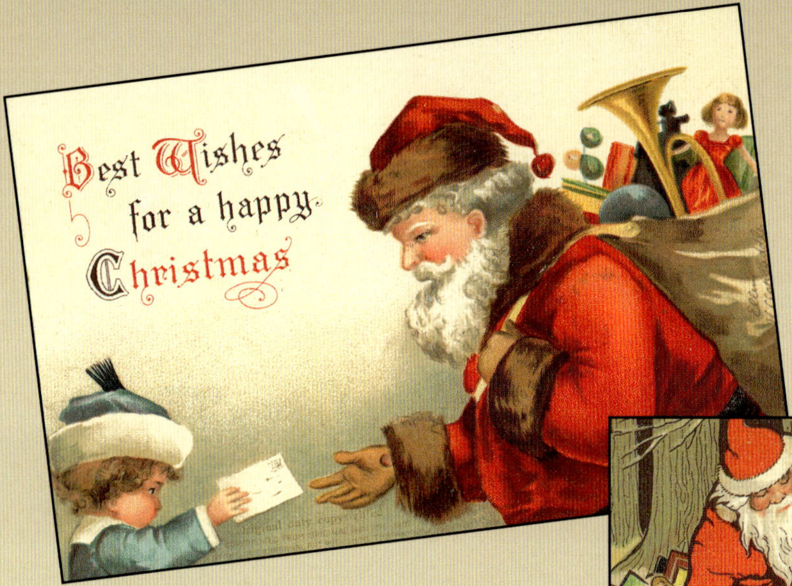
Best Wishes
for a happy
Christmas

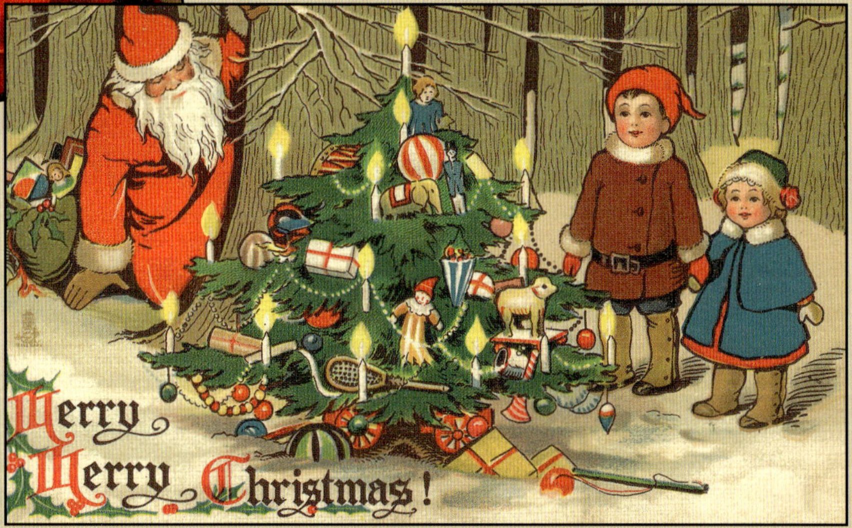
Merry
Merry Christmas!

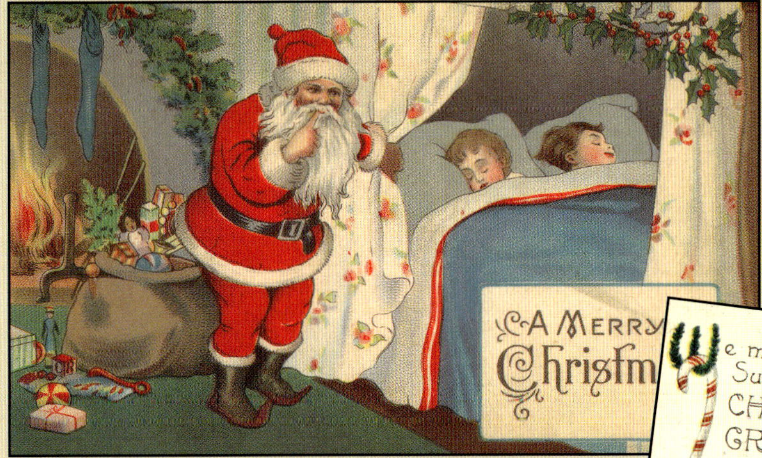
A MERRY

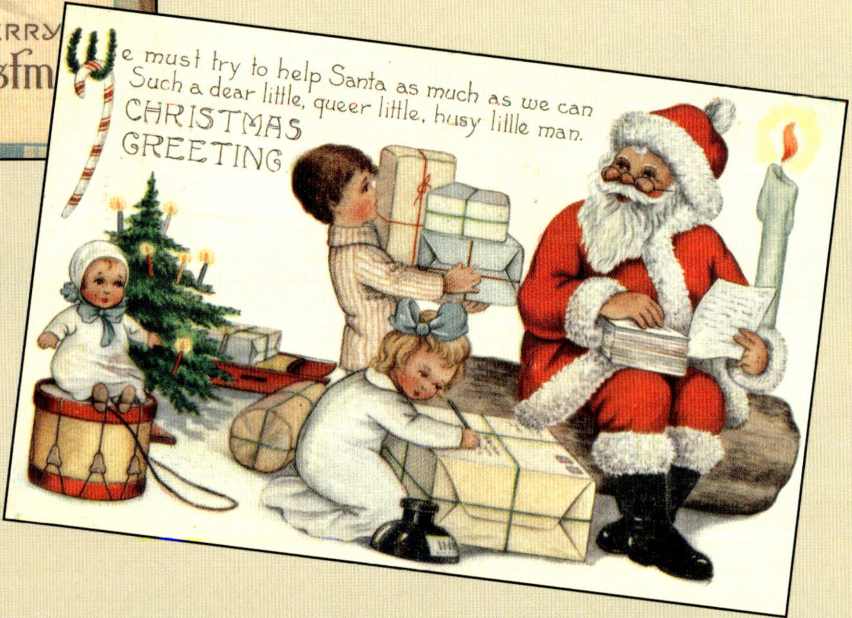
We must try to help Santa as much as we can
Such a dear little, queer little, busy little man.
CHRISTMAS
GREETING

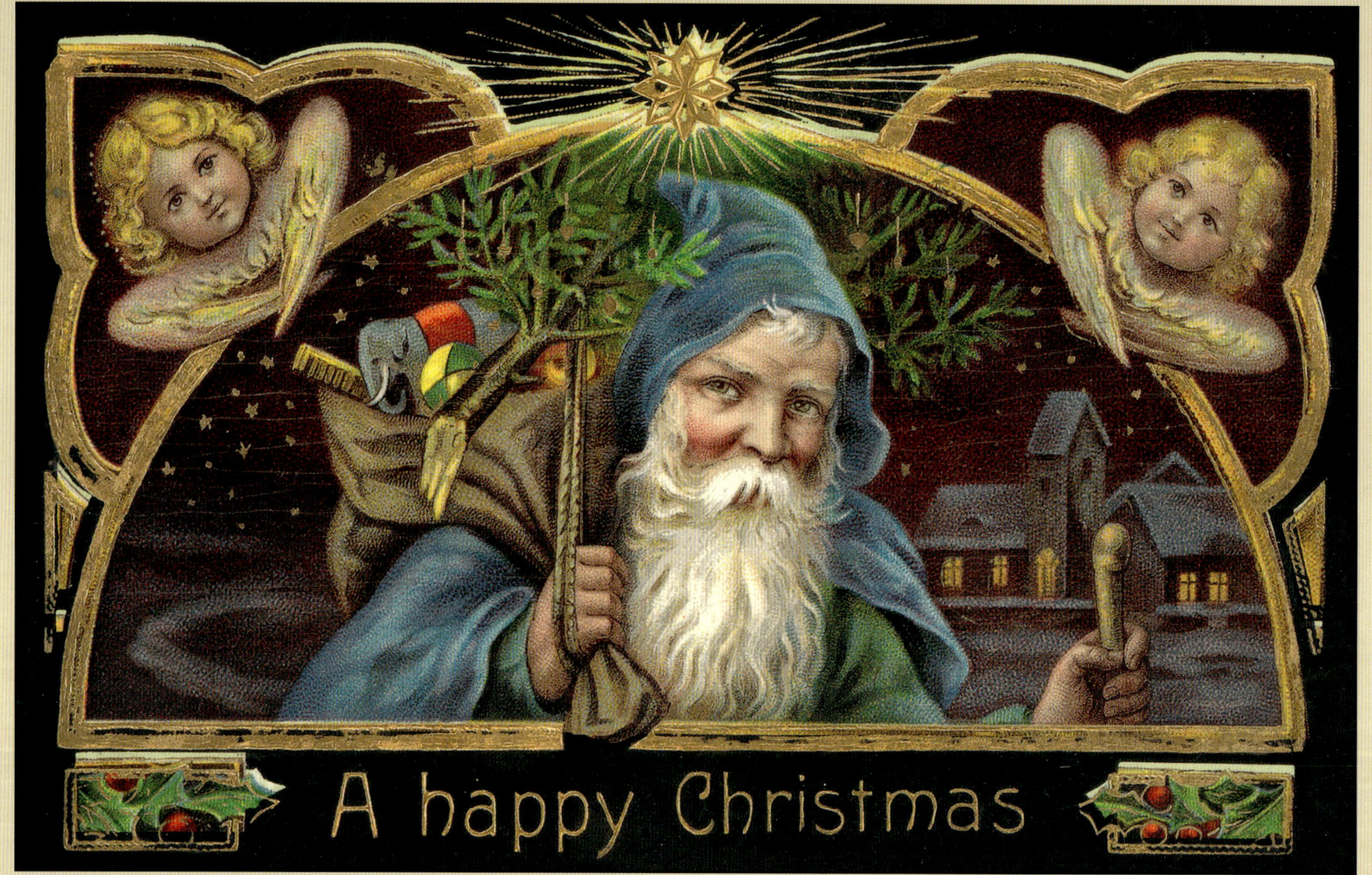
A happy Christmas

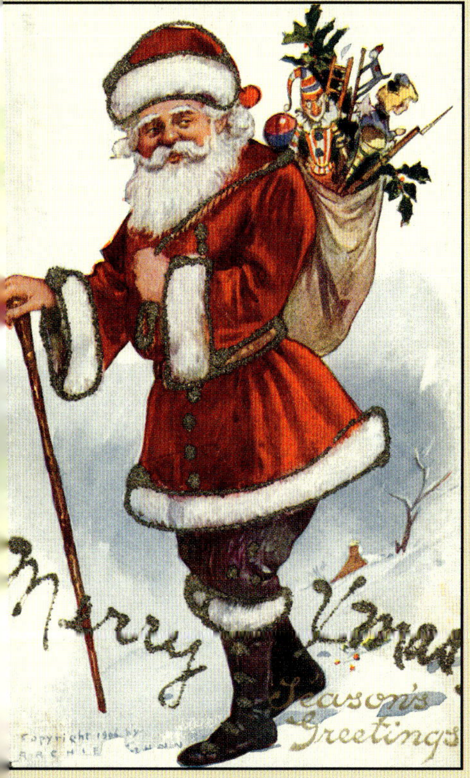
Merry Xmas
Season's Greetings

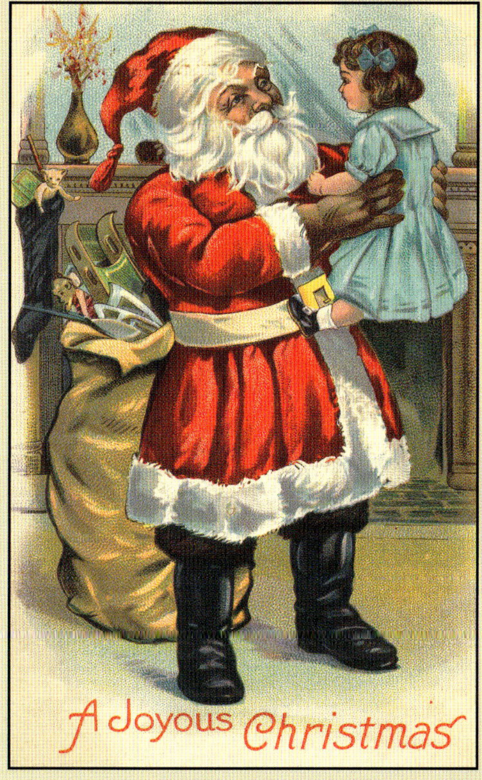
A Joyous Christmas

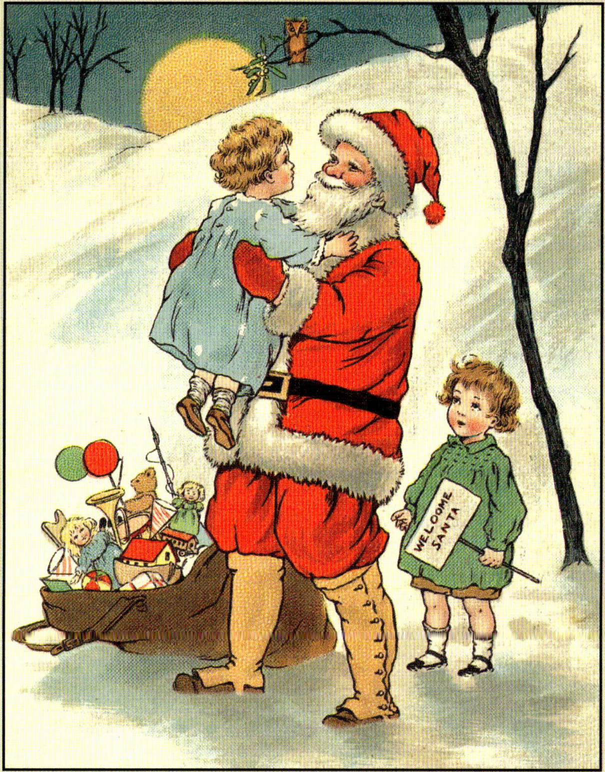
WELCOME SANTA

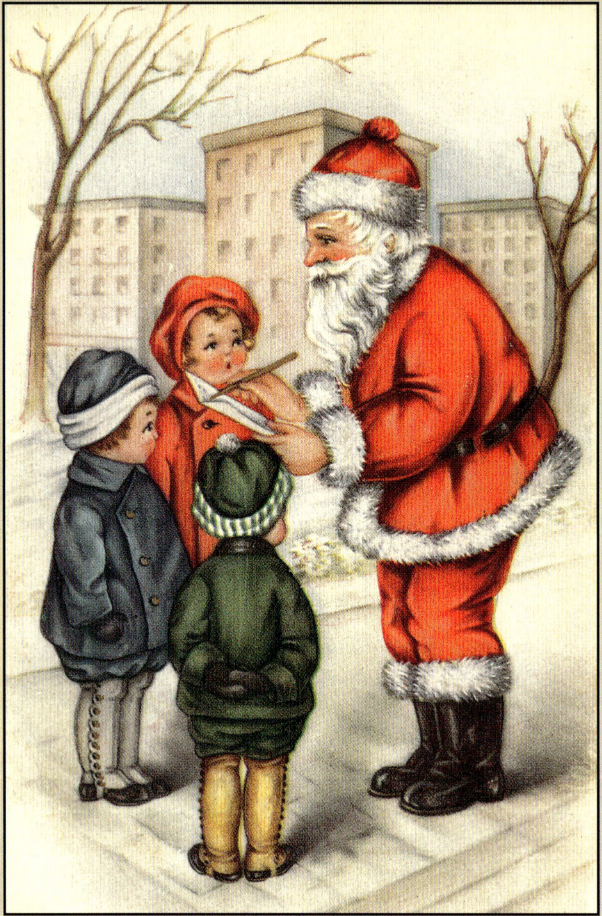

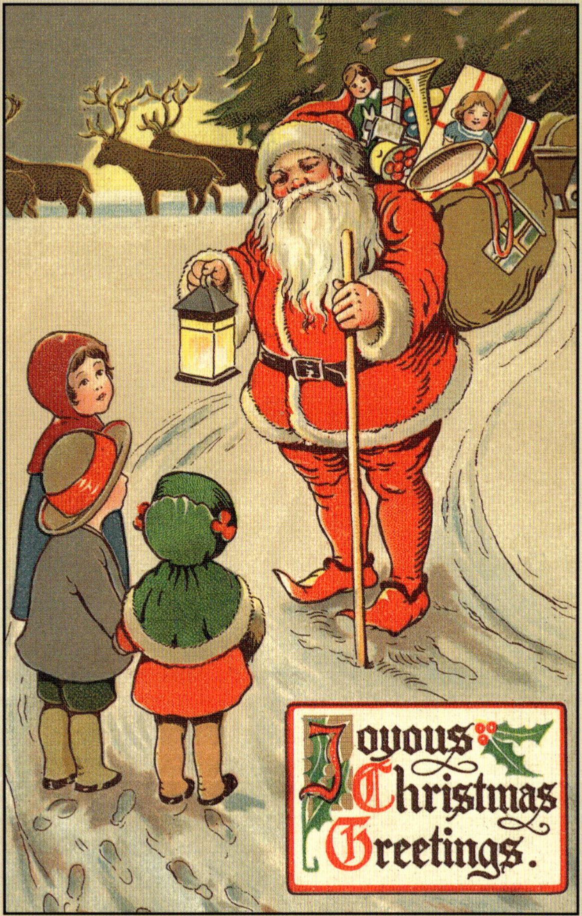
Joyous Christmas Greetings.

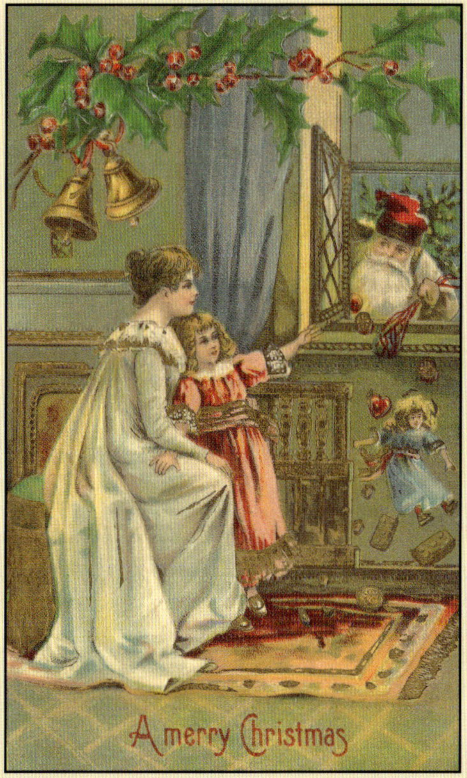
A merry Christmas

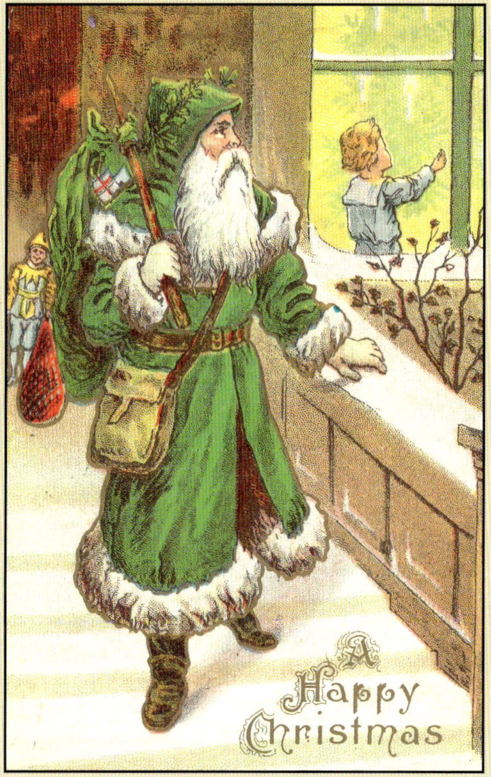
A Happy Christmas

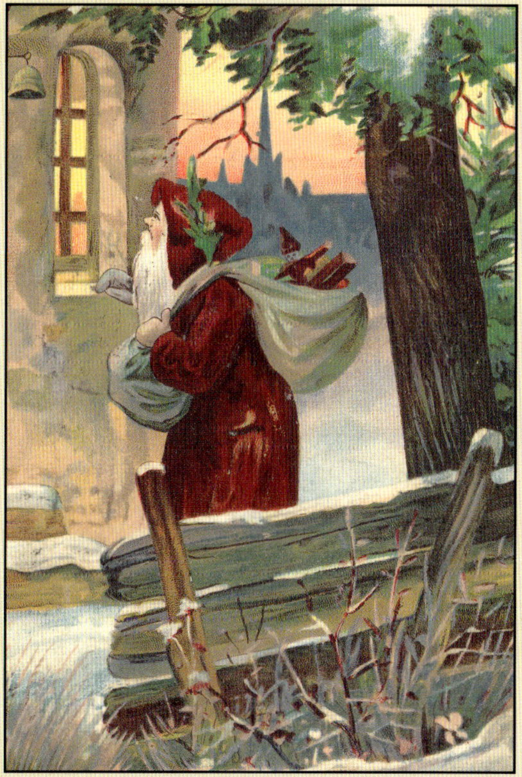

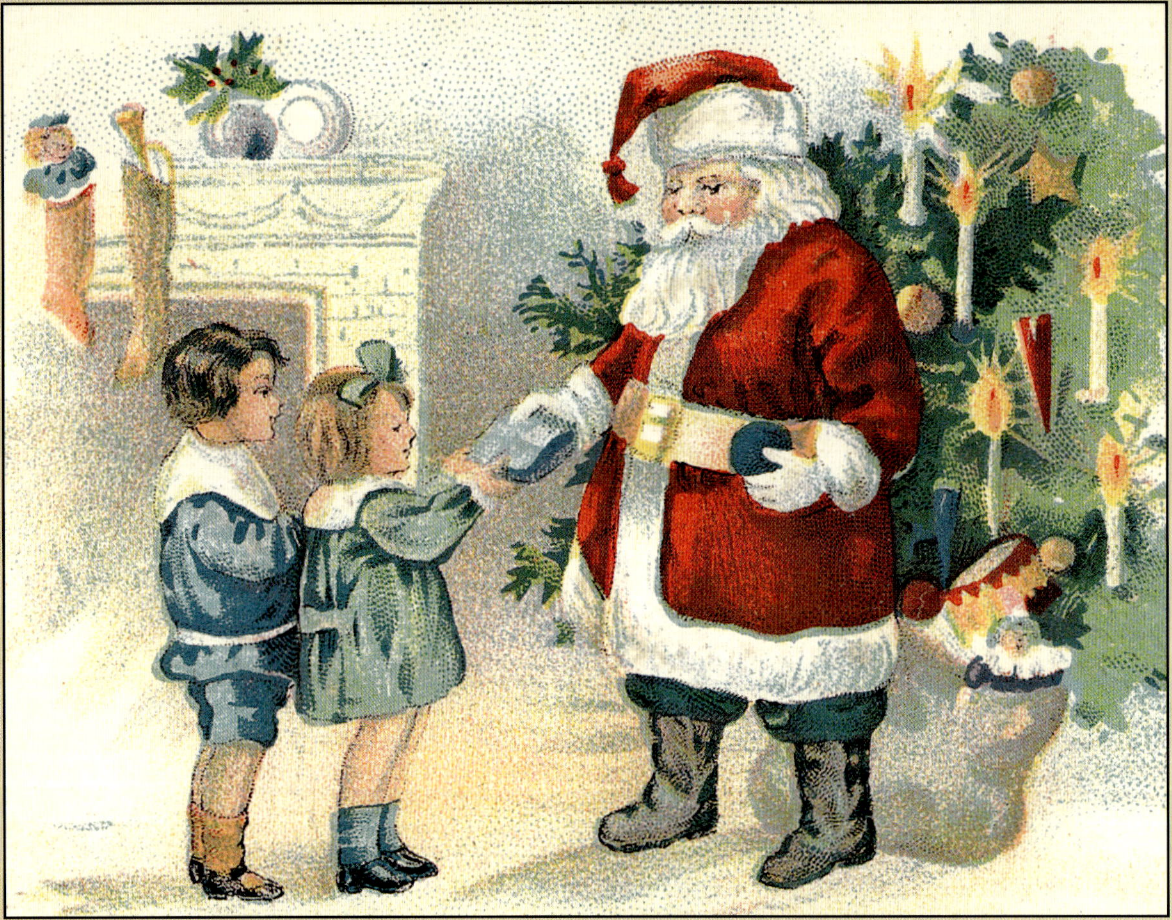

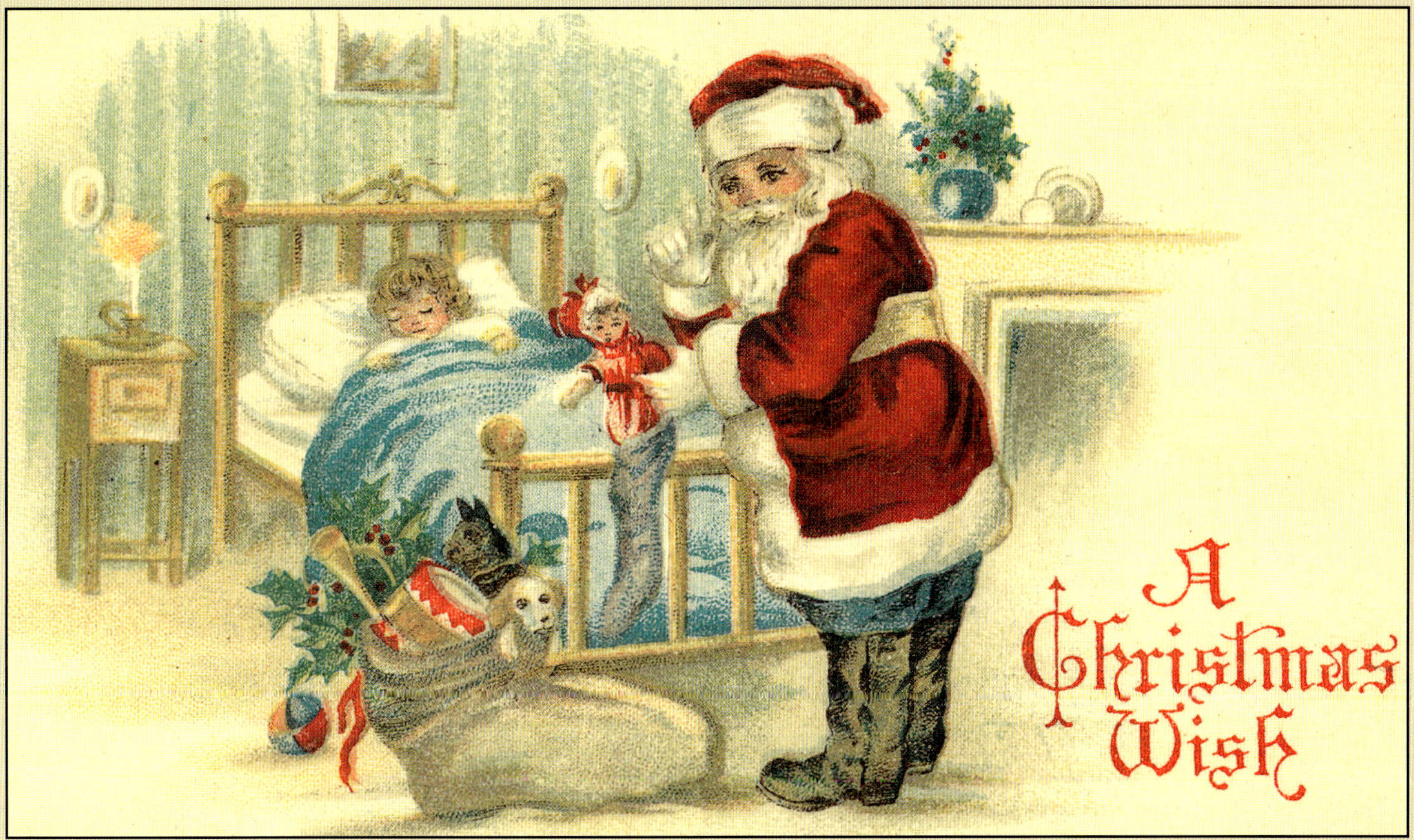
A Christmas Wish

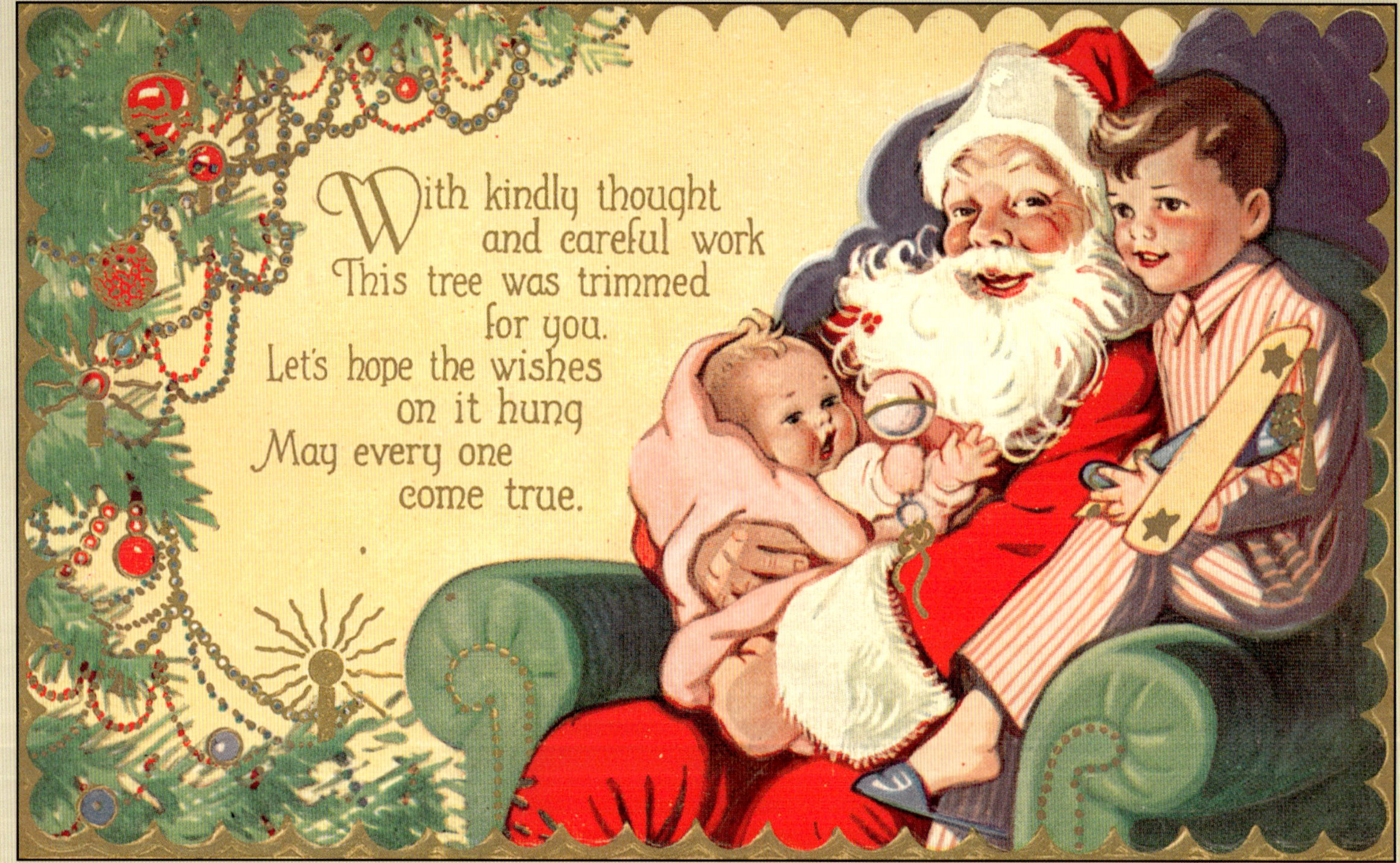
With kindly thought
and careful work
This tree was trimmed
for you.
Let's hope the wishes
on it hung
May every one
come true.

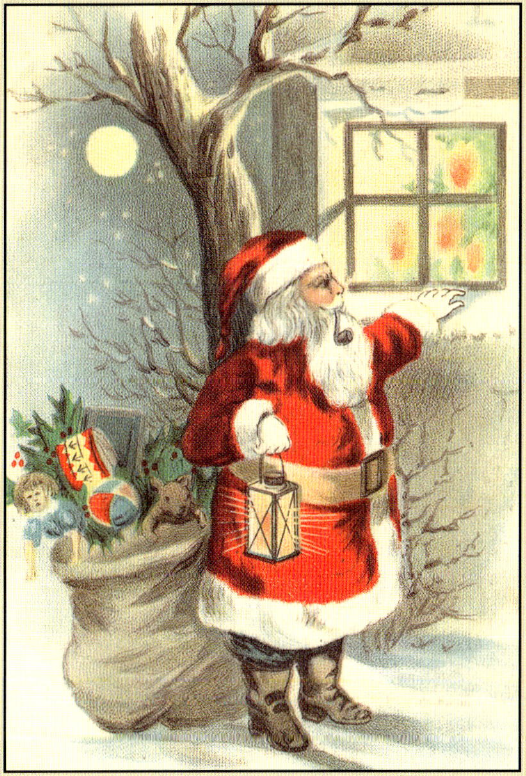

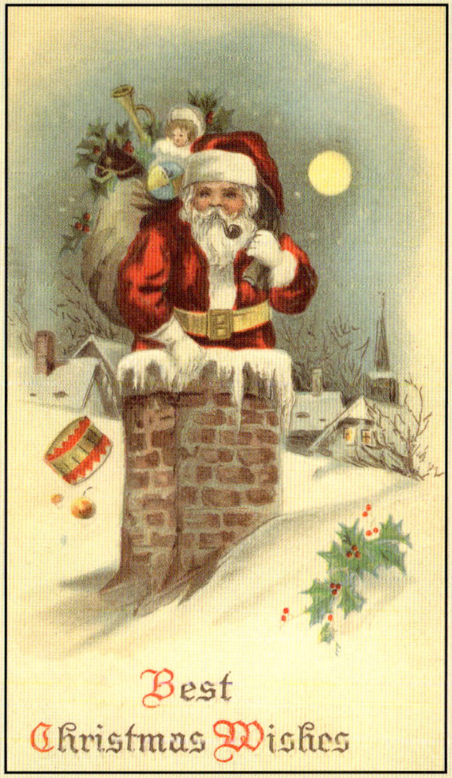
Best
Christmas Wishes

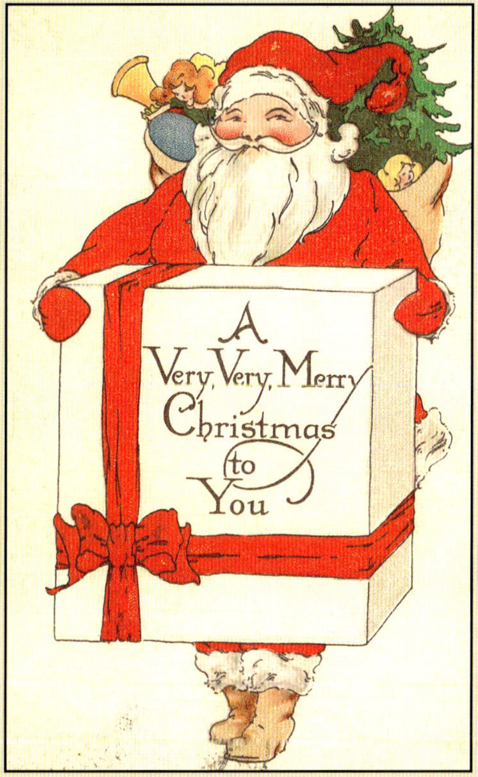
A
Very, Very, Merry
Christmas
to
You

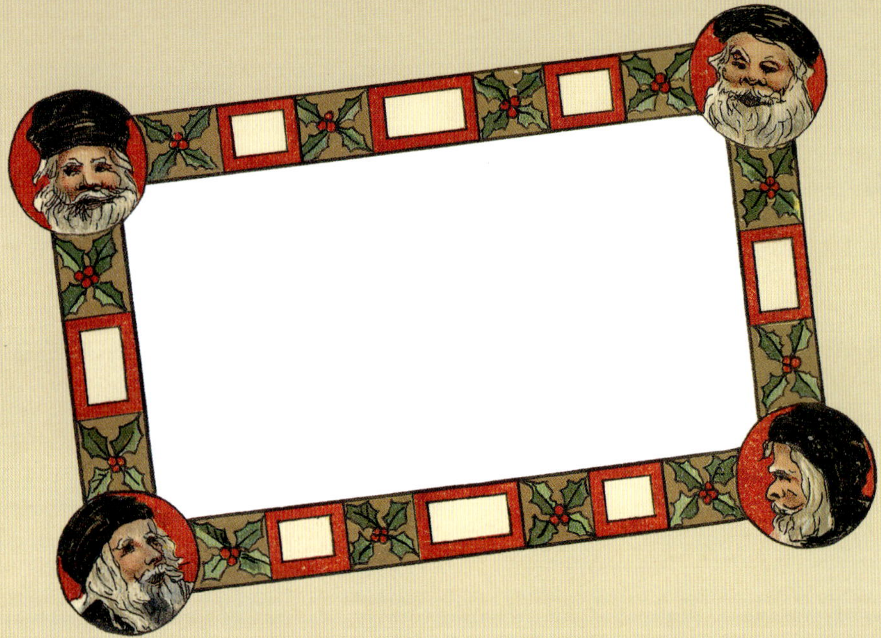

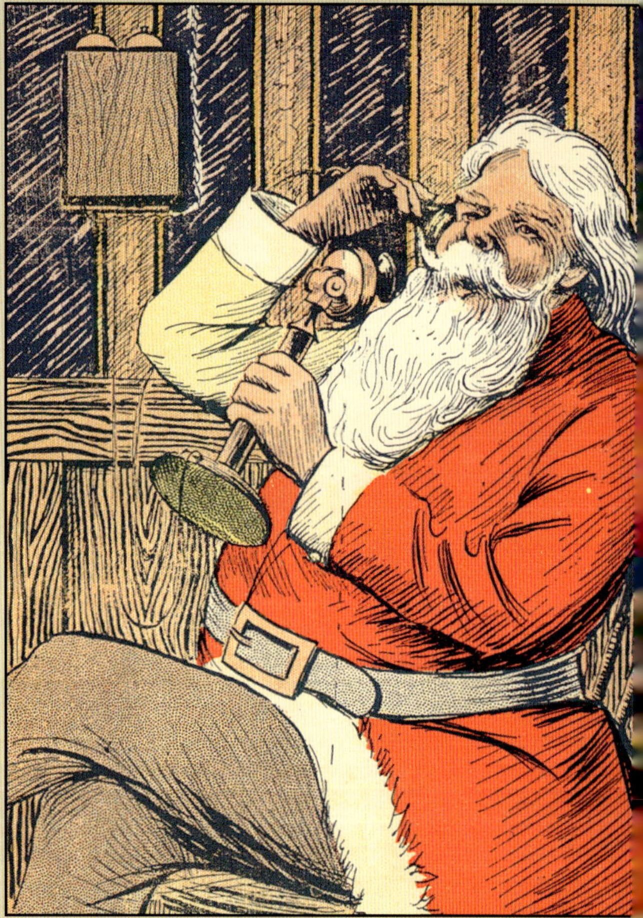

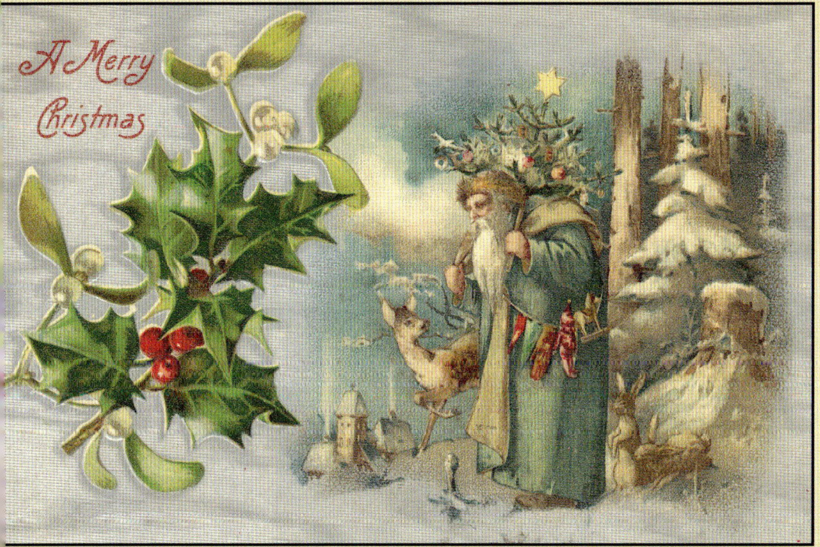
A Merry
Christmas

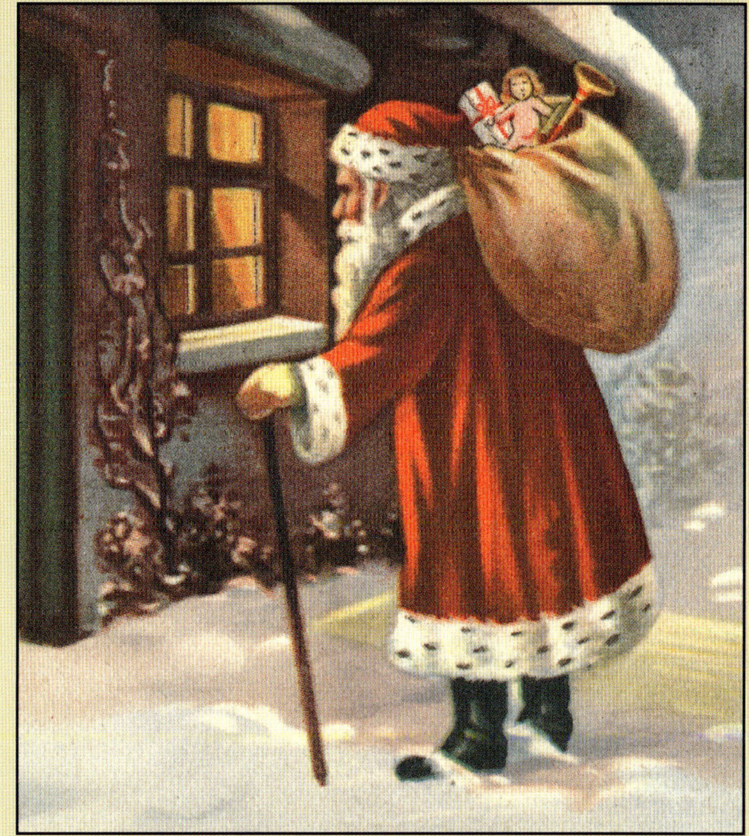

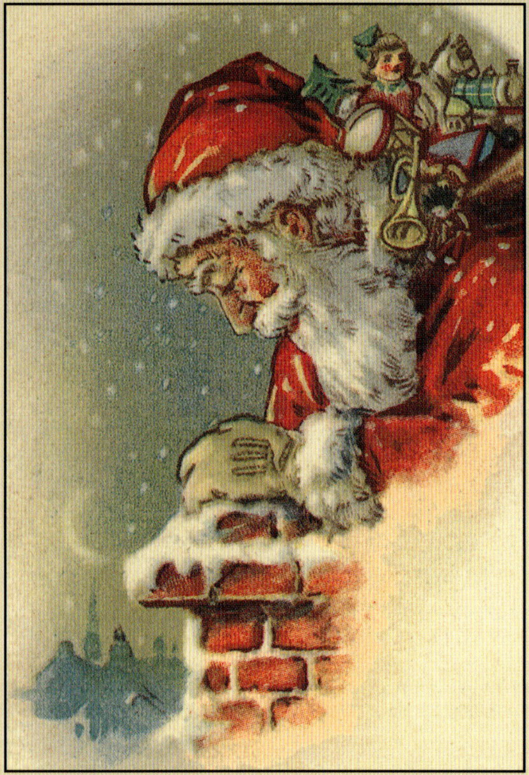

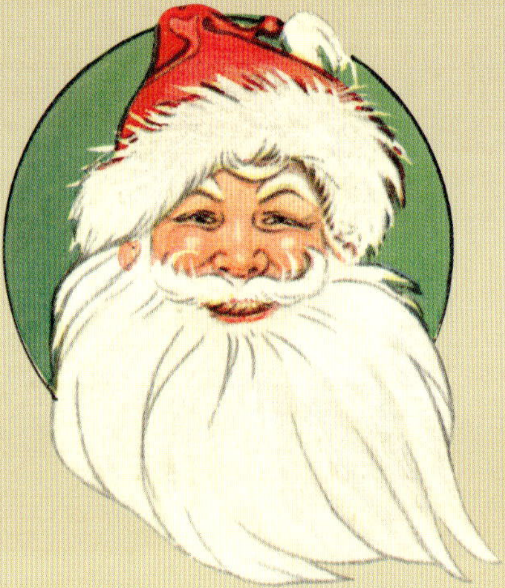

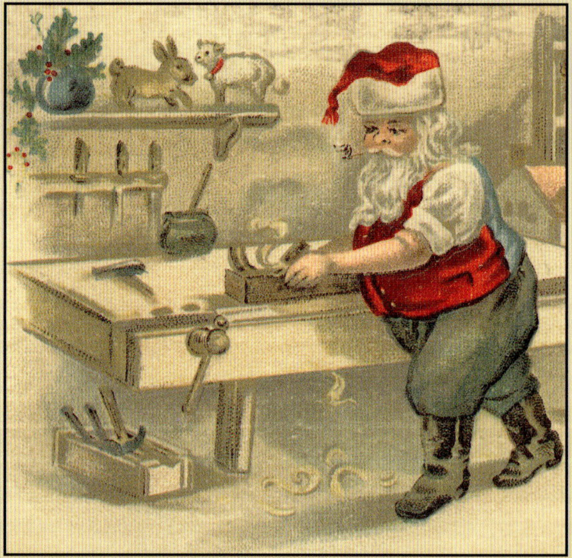

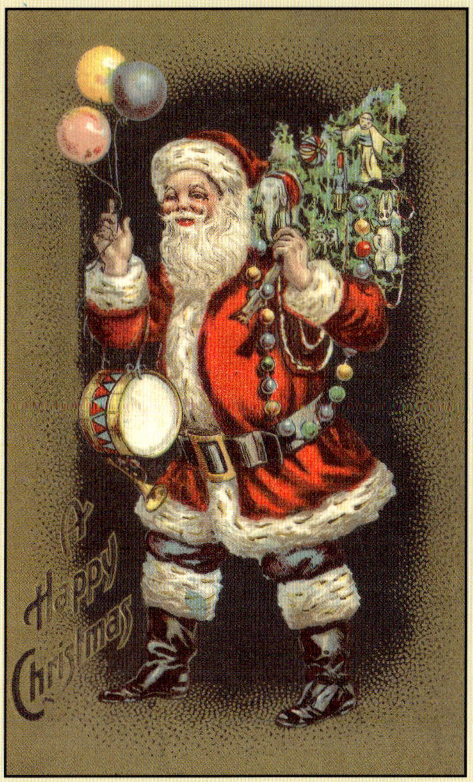
A Happy Christmas

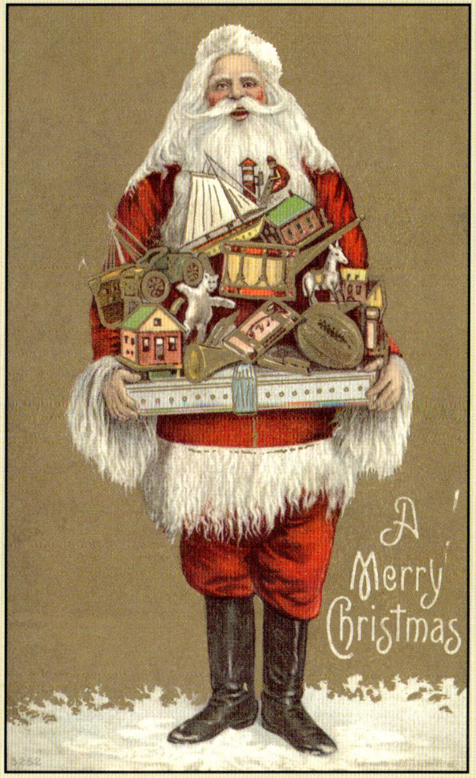
A Merry Christmas

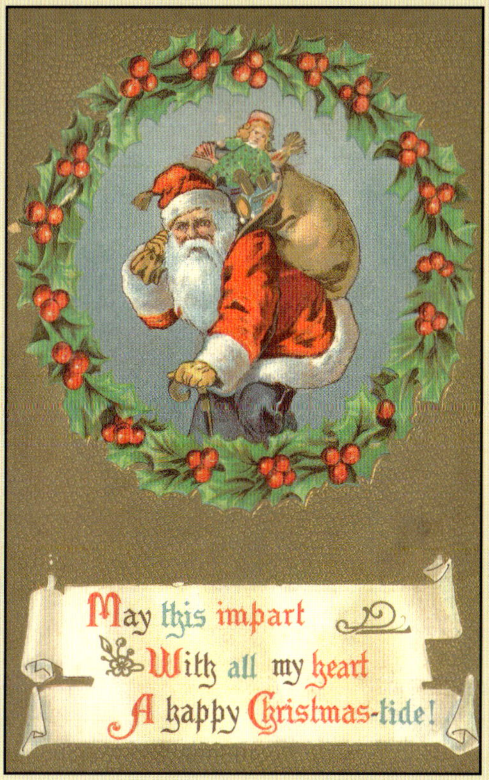
May this impart
With all my heart
A happy Christmas-tide!

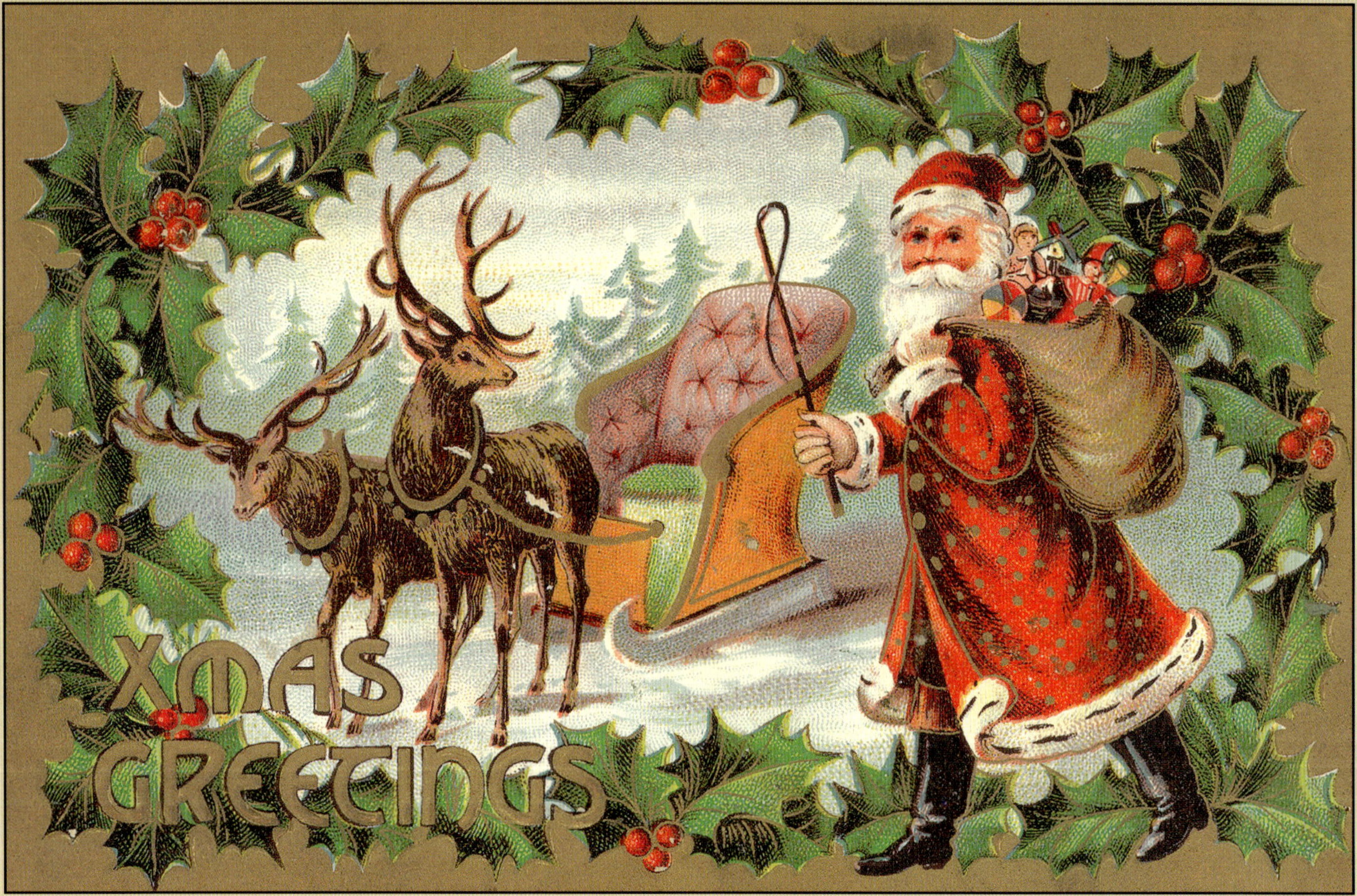
XMAS
GREETINGS

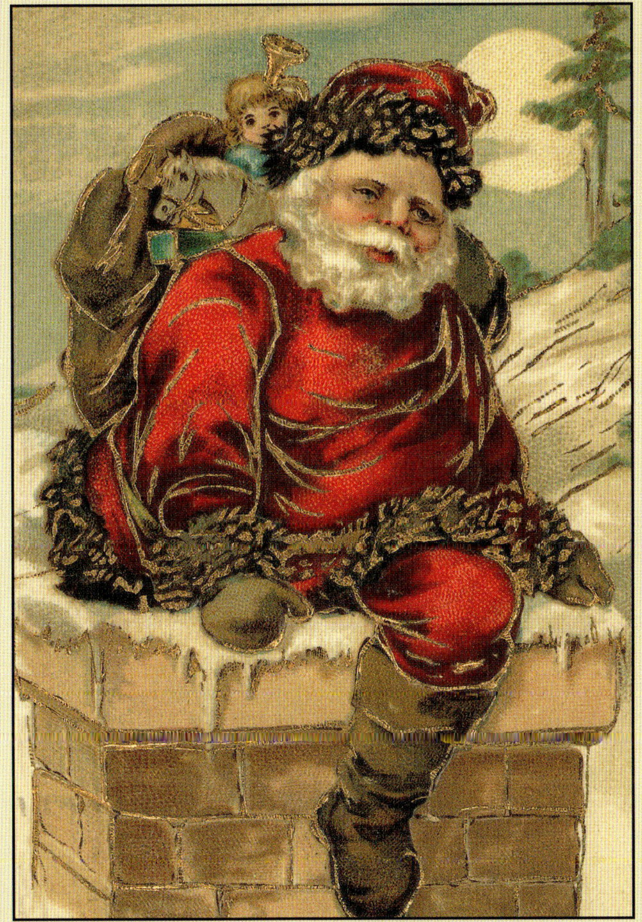

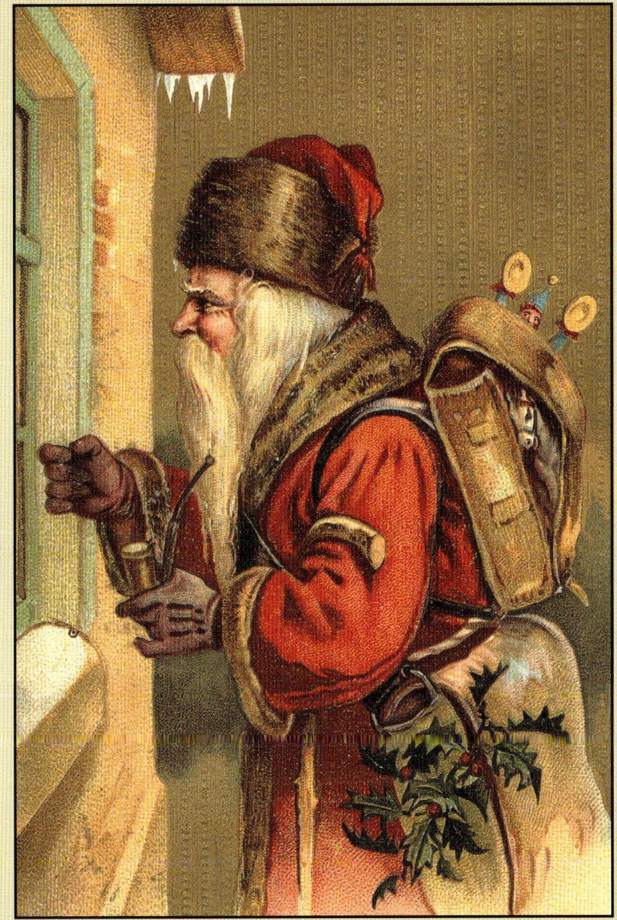

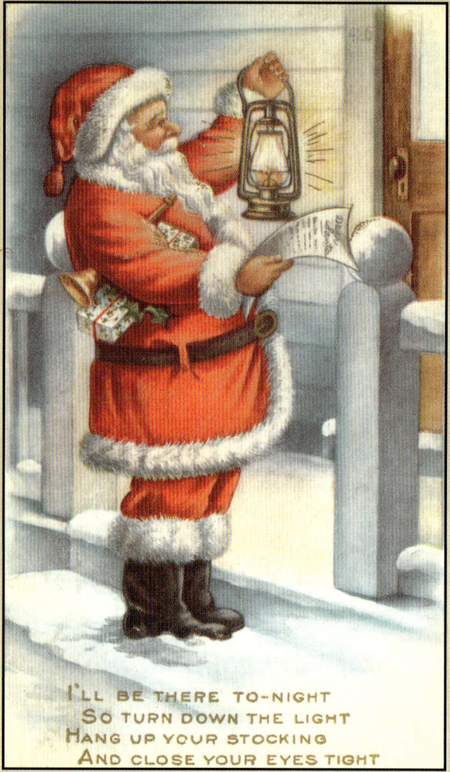
I'll be there to-night
So turn down the light
Hang up your stocking
And close your eyes tight

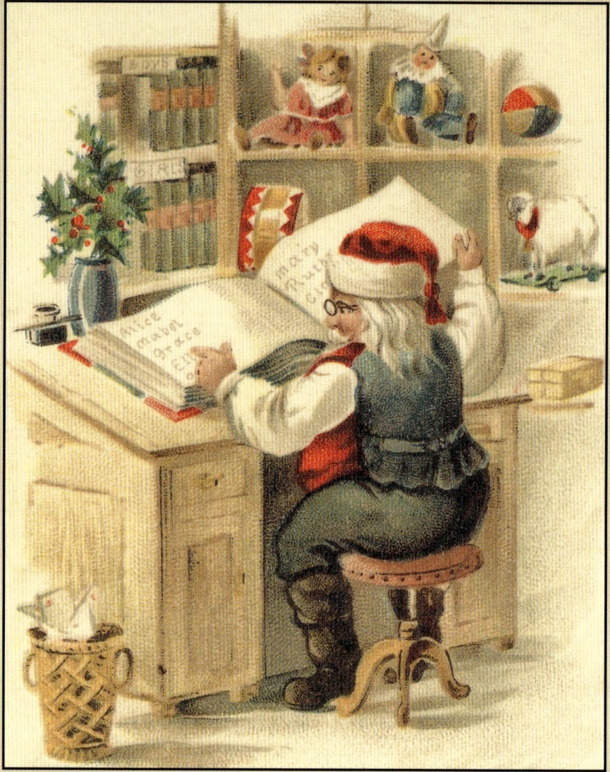

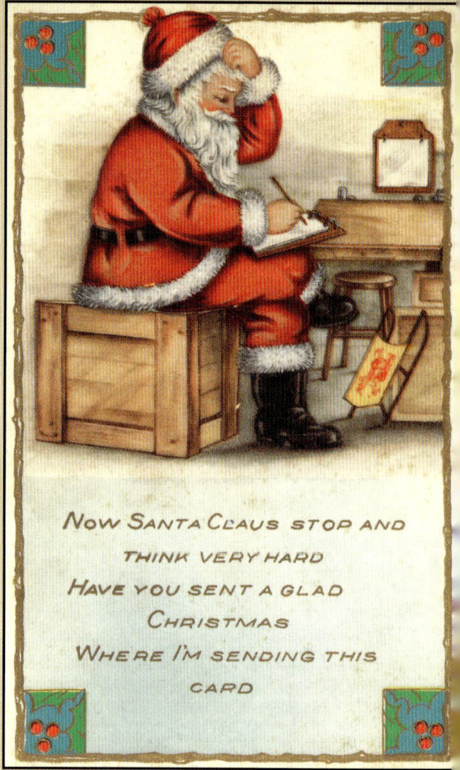
Now Santa Claus stop and
think very hard
Have you sent a glad
Christmas
Where I'm sending this
card

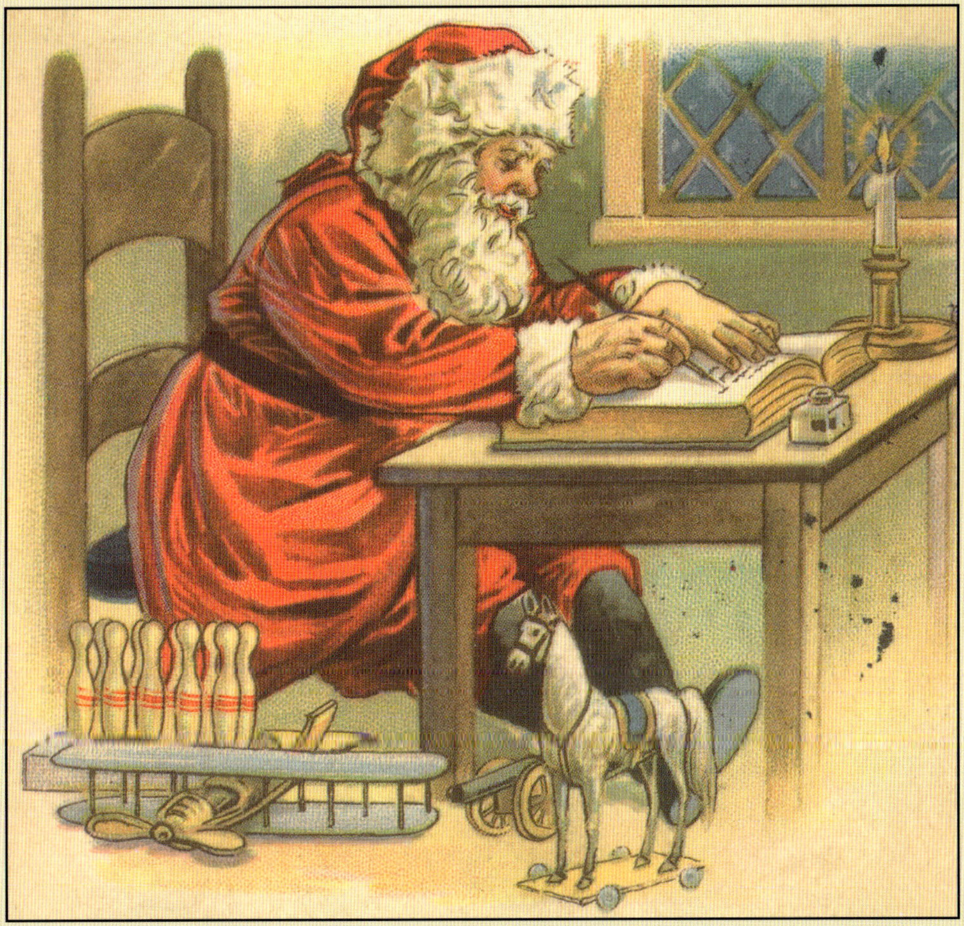

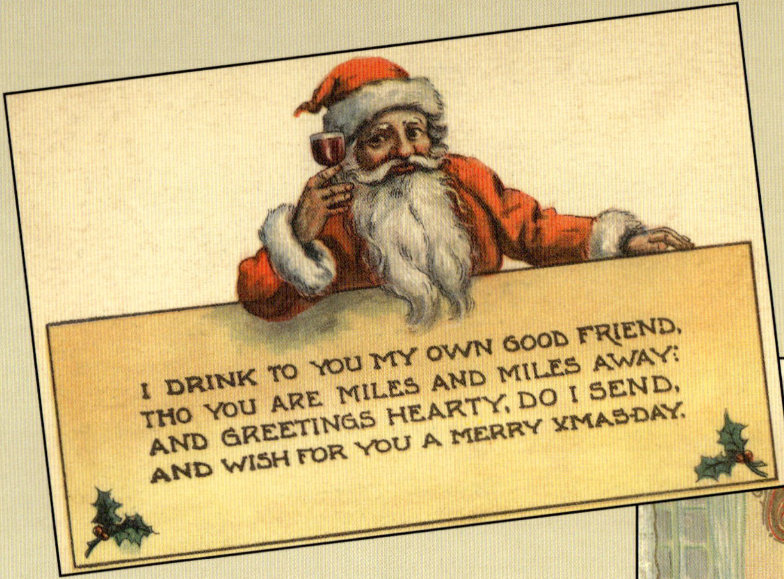
I DRINK TO YOU MY OWN GOOD FRIEND,
THO YOU ARE MILES AND MILES AWAY;
AND GREETINGS HEARTY, DO I SEND,
AND WISH FOR YOU A MERRY XMAS-DAY.

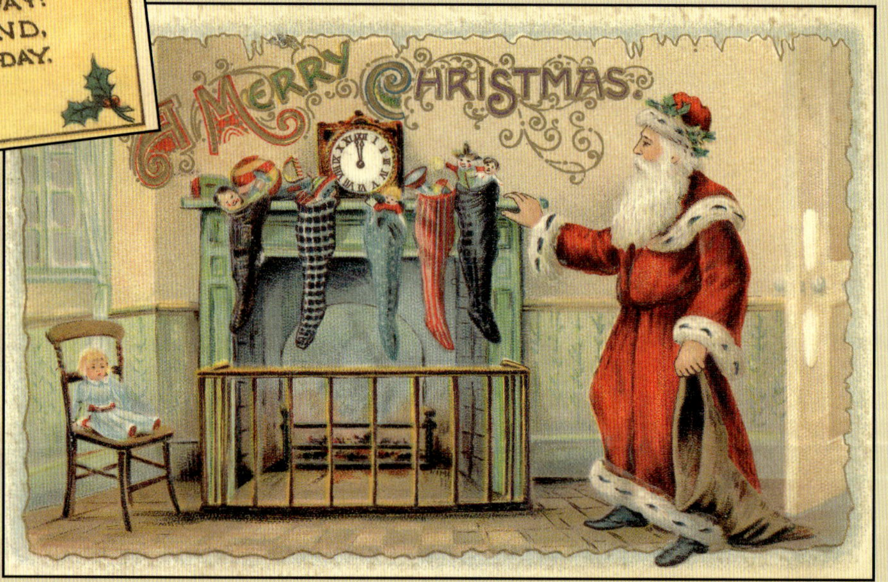
A Merry Christmas.

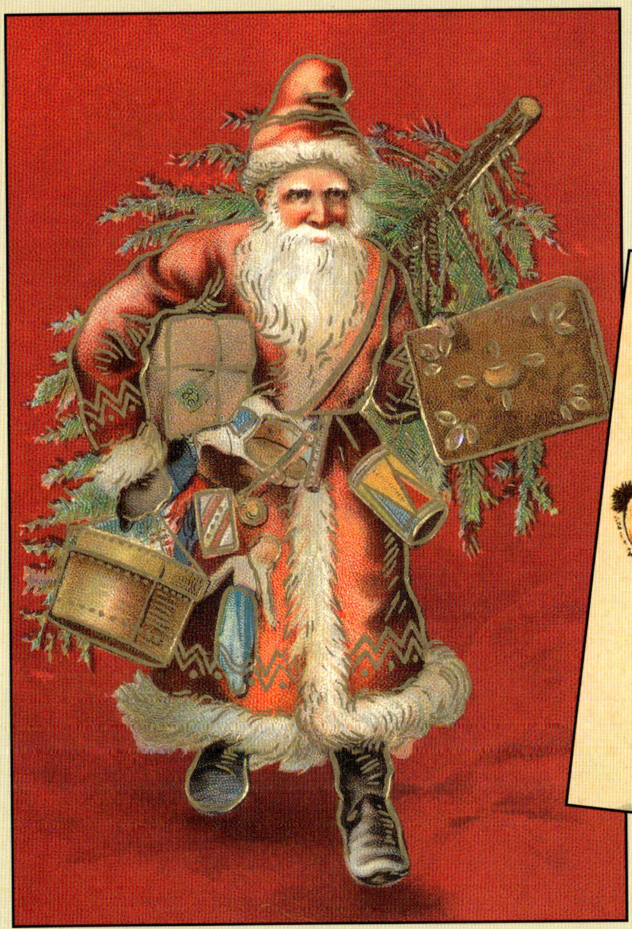

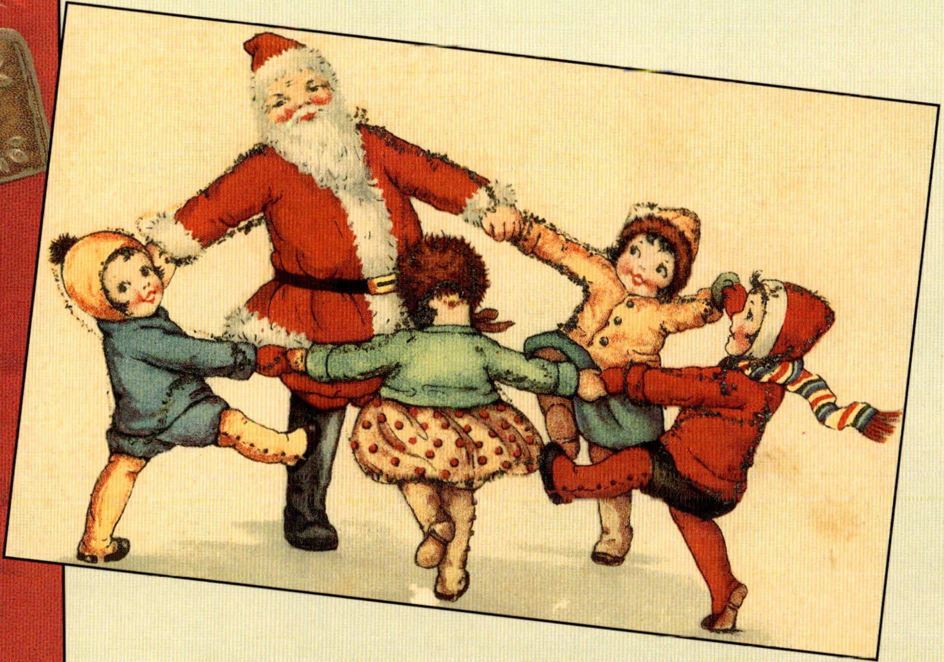

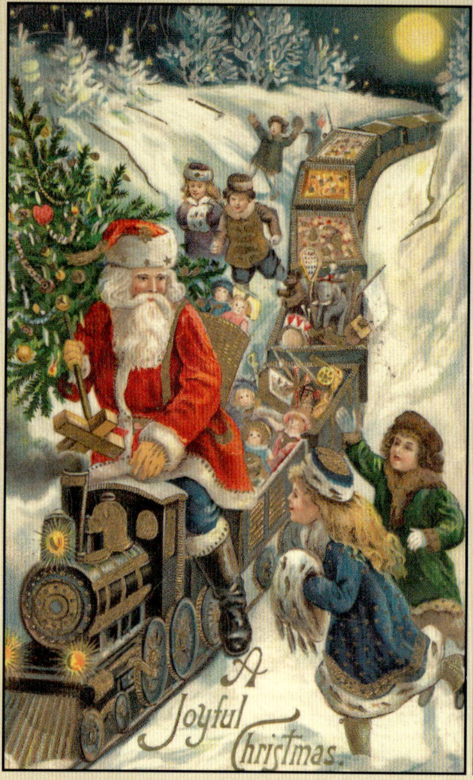
A Joyful Christmas.
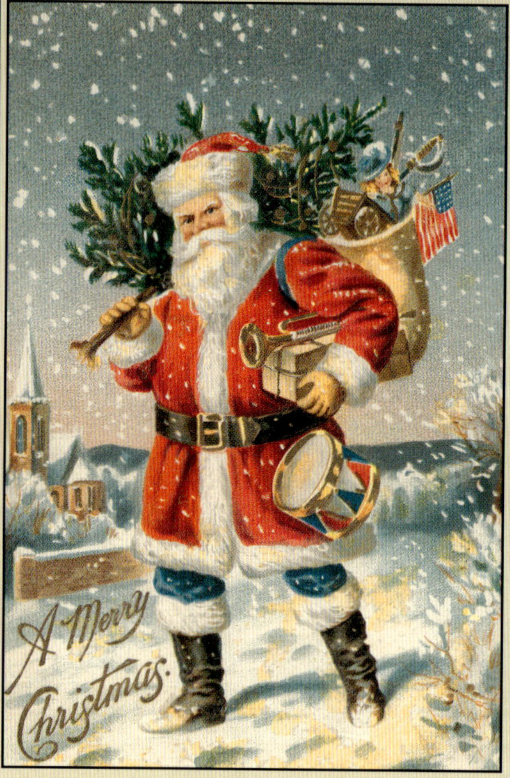
A Merry Christmas.
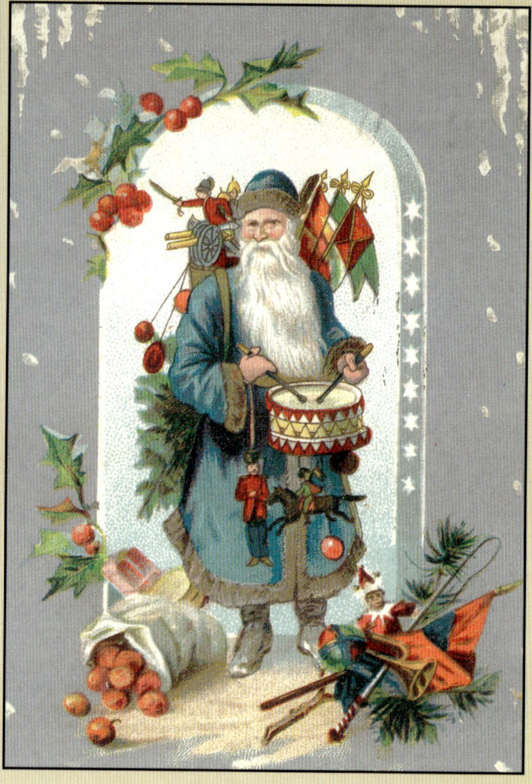

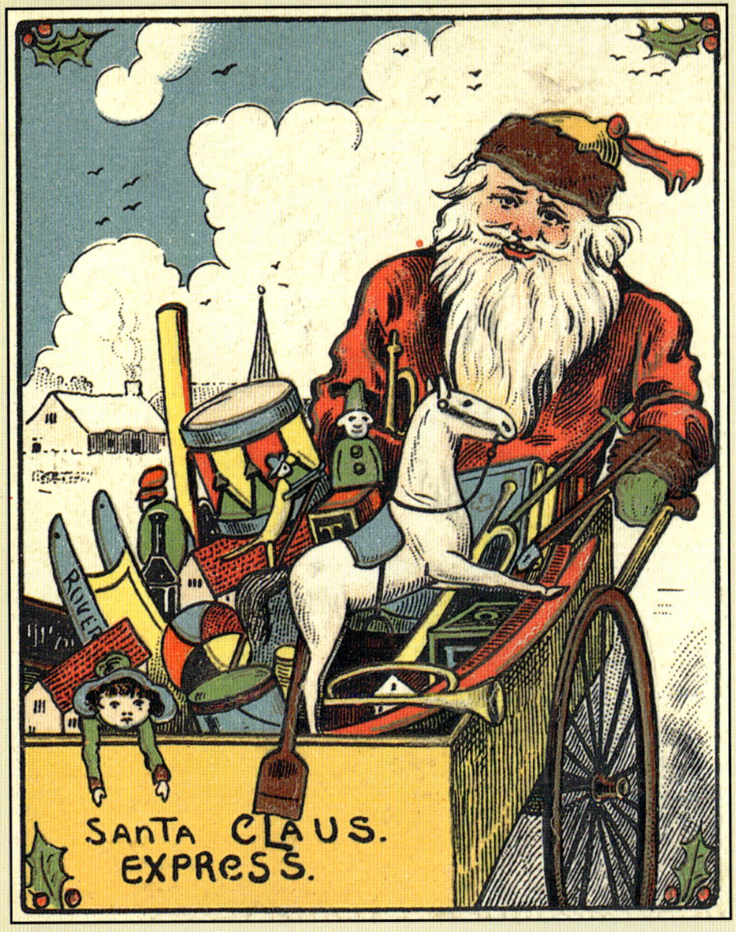
SANTA CLAUS.
EXPRESS.

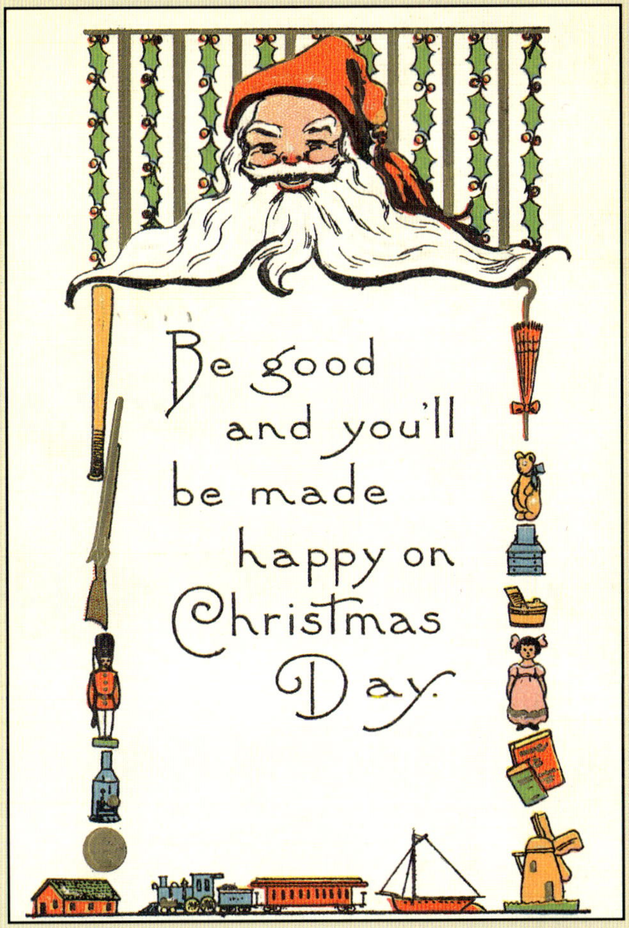
Be good and you'll be made happy on Christmas Day.

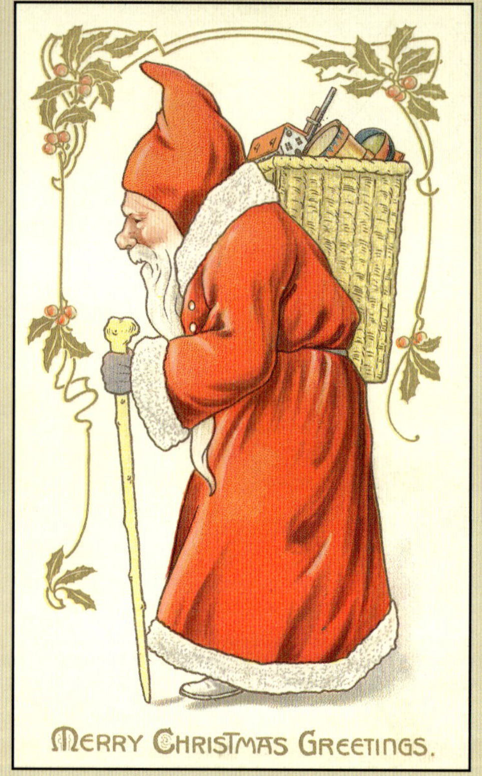
Merry Christmas Greetings.

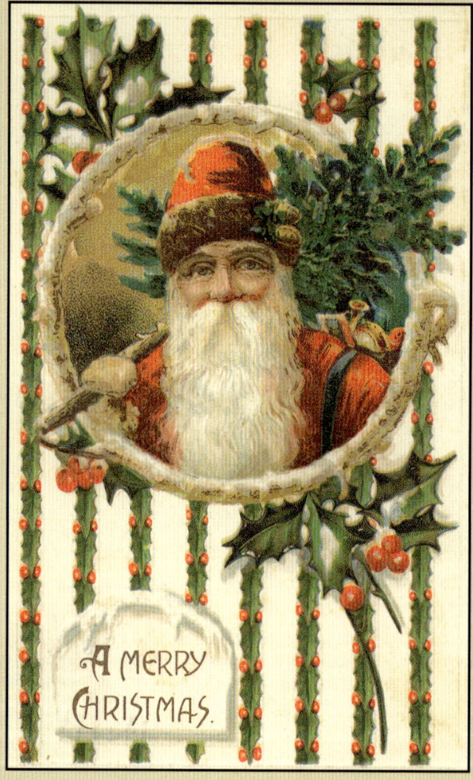
A Merry
Christmas.

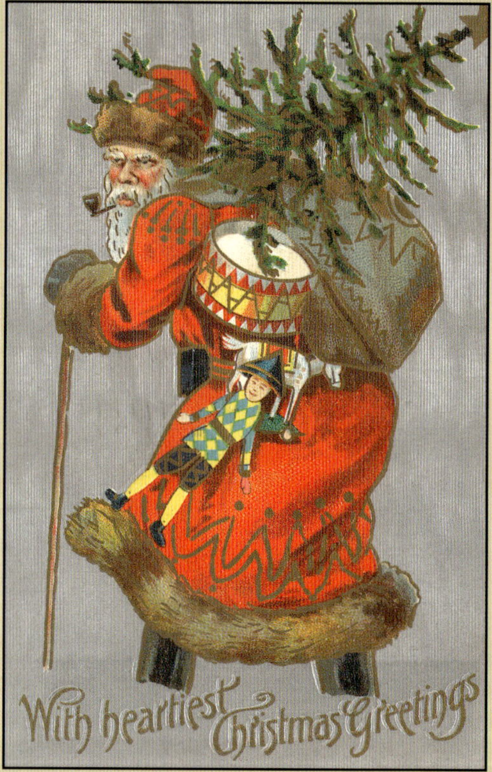
With heartiest Christmas Greetings

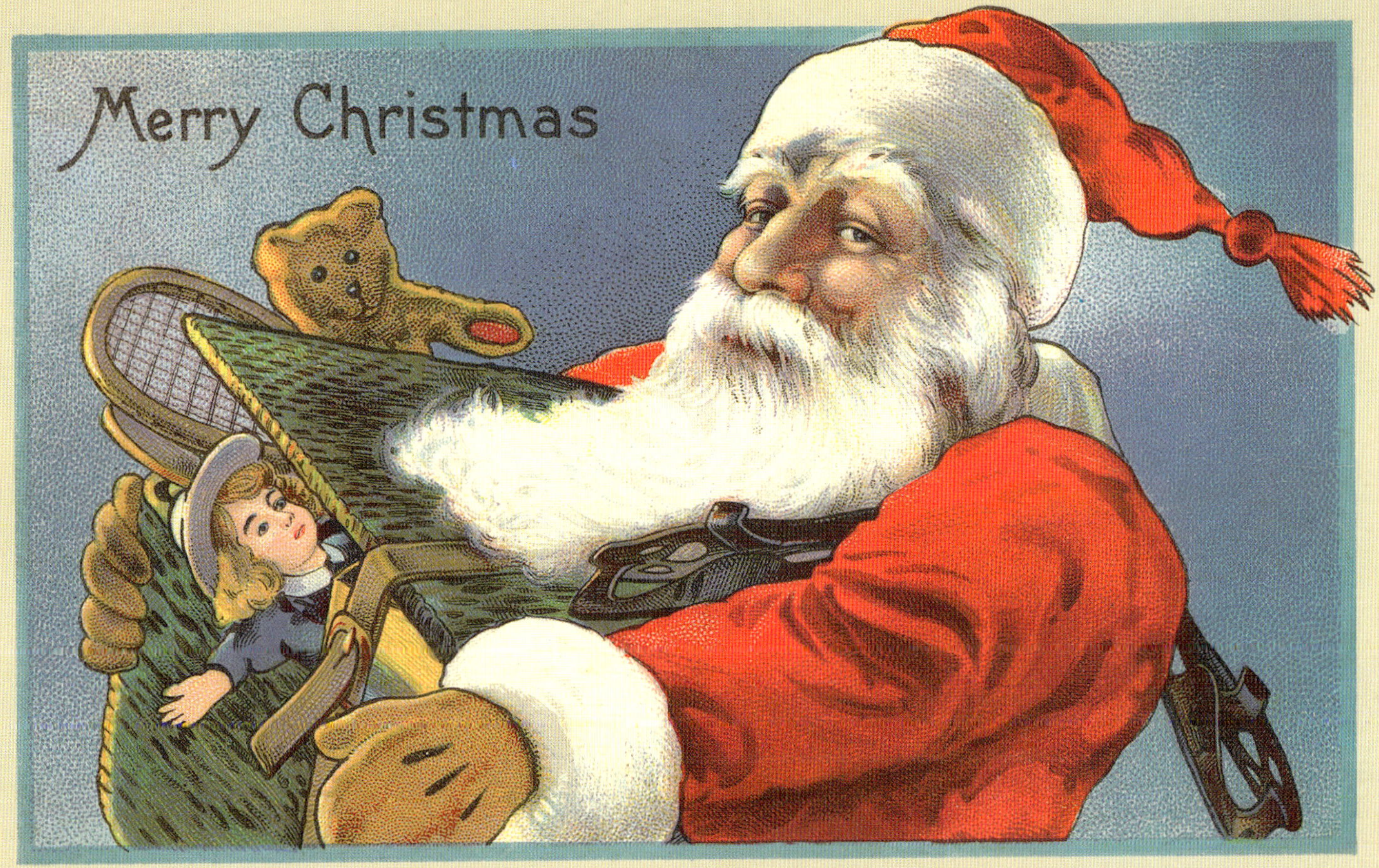
Merry Christmas

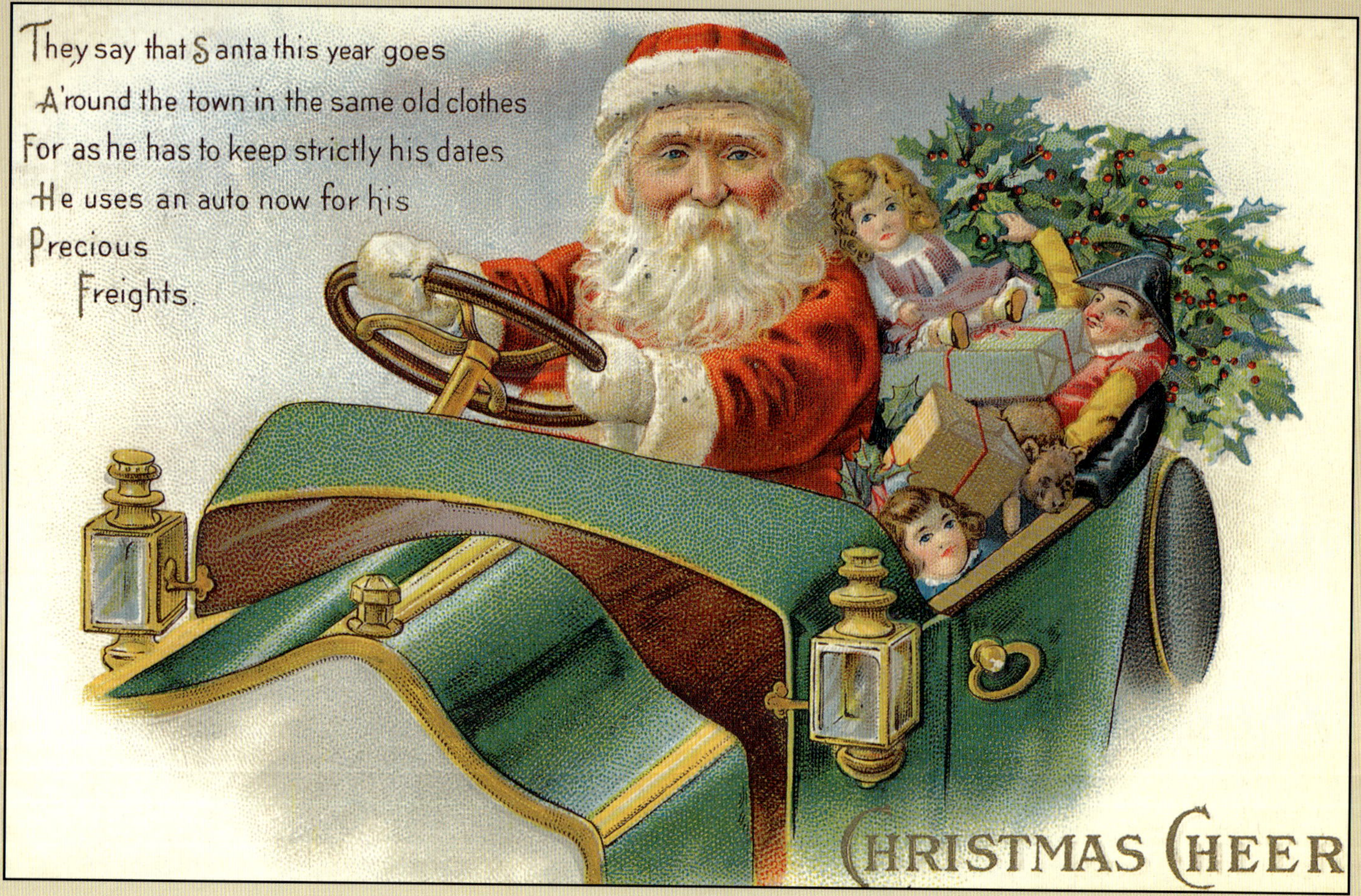
They say that Santa this year goes
A'round the town in the same old clothes
For as he has to keep strictly his dates
He uses an auto now for his
Precious
Freights.
CHRISTMAS CHEER

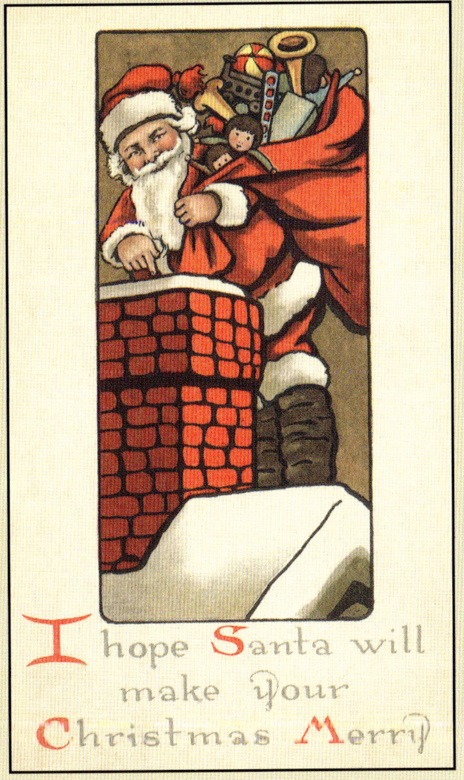
I hope Santa will
make your
Christmas Merry

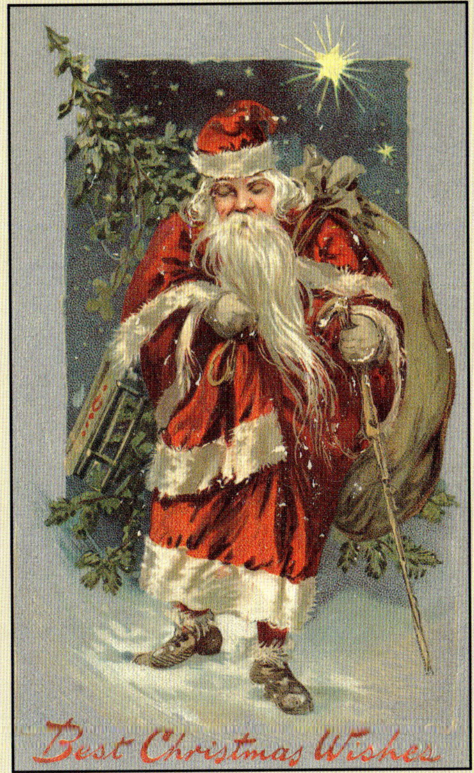
Best Christmas Wishes

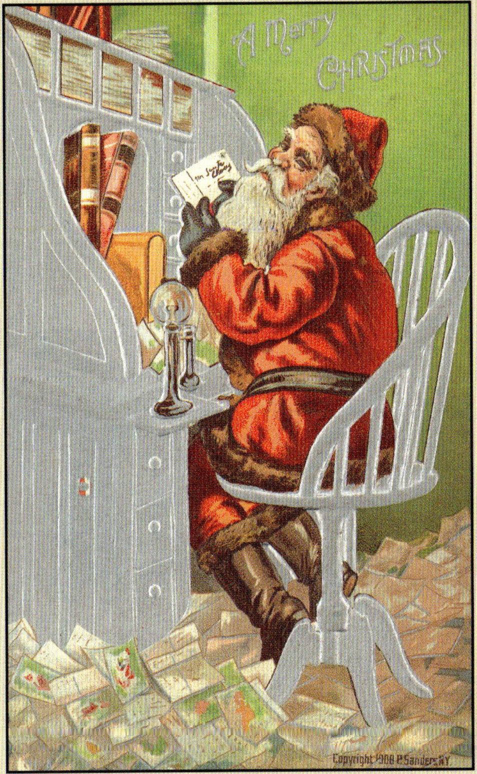
A Merry
Christmas
Copyright 1908 P. Sanders, N.Y.

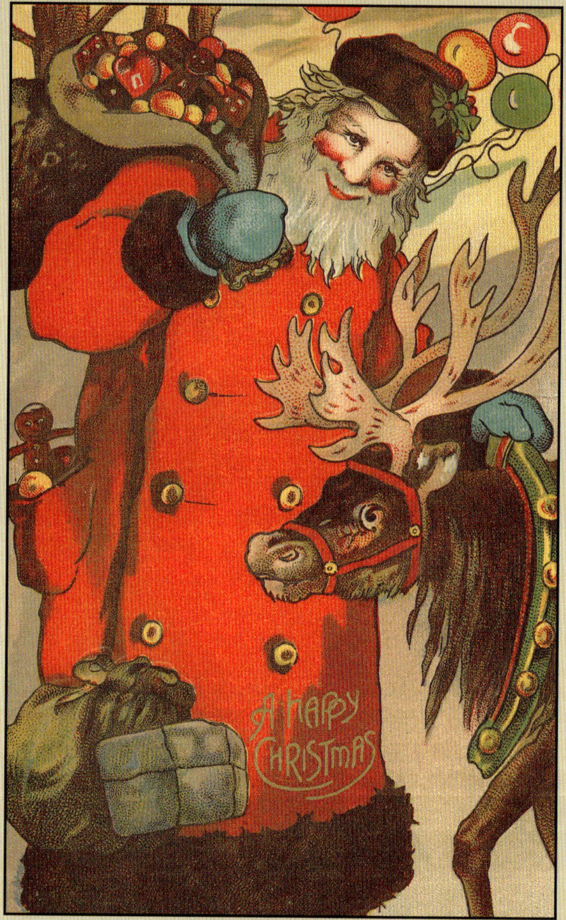
A Happy
Christmas

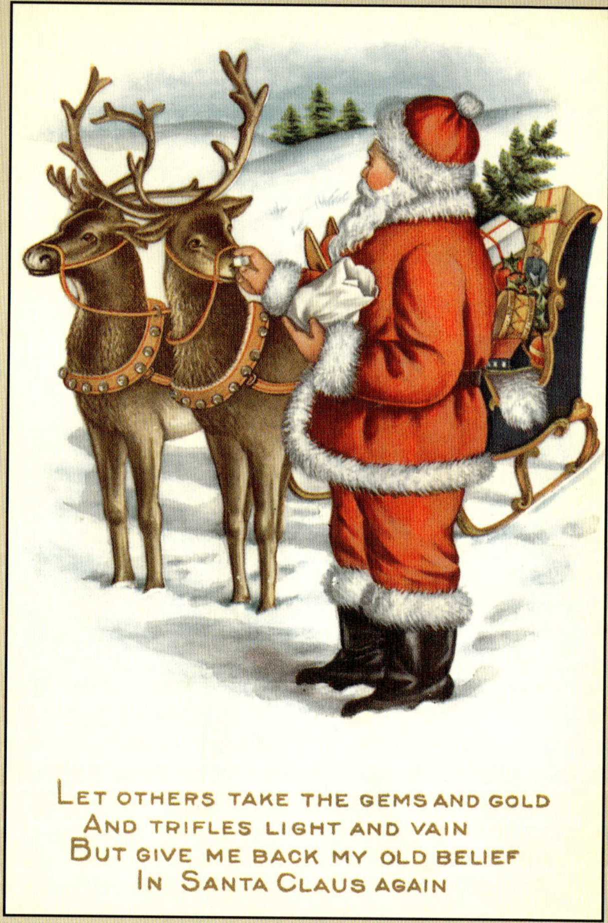
Let others take the gems and gold
And trifles light and vain
But give me back my old belief
In Santa Claus again

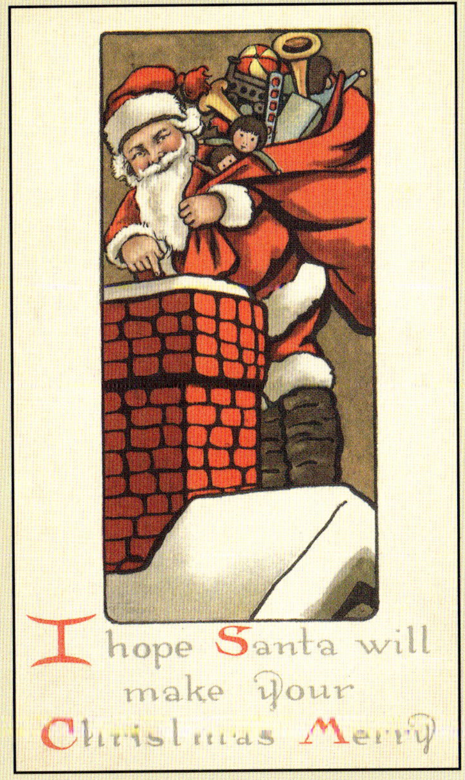
I hope Santa will
make your
Christmas Merry

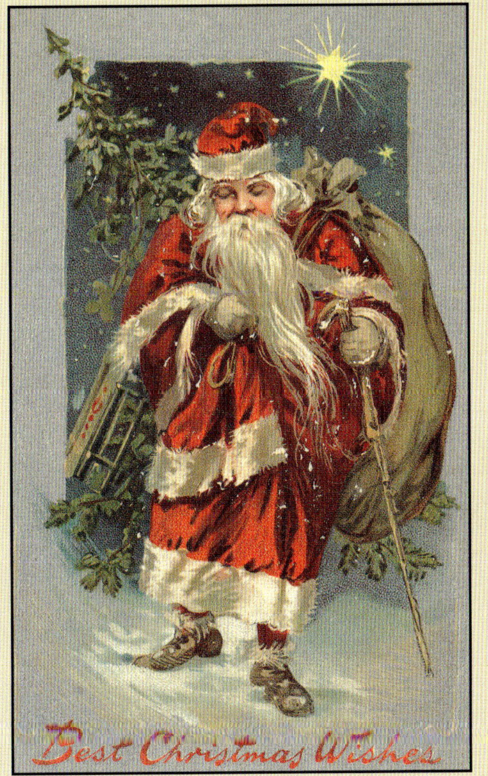
Best Christmas Wishes

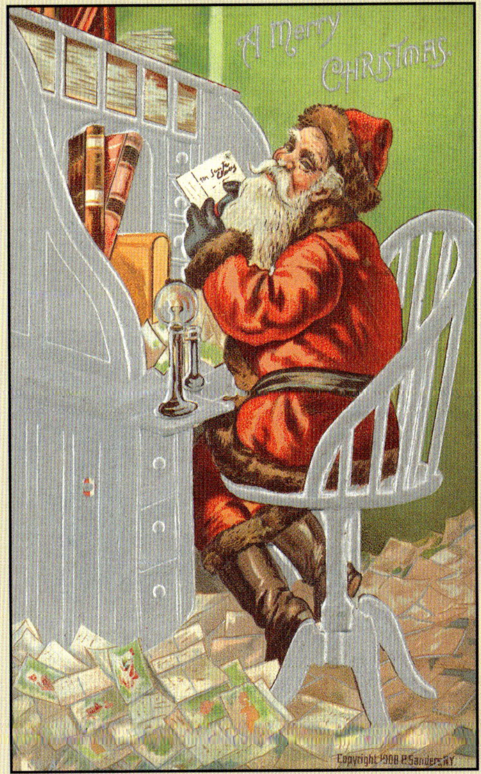
A Merry
CHRISTMAS
Copyright 1908 P. Sanders, N.Y.

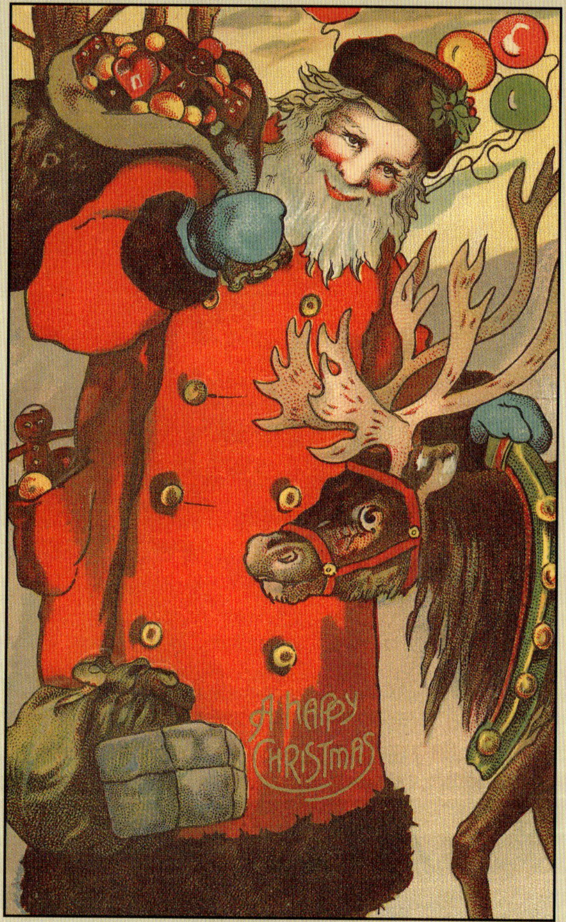
A Happy
CHRISTMAS

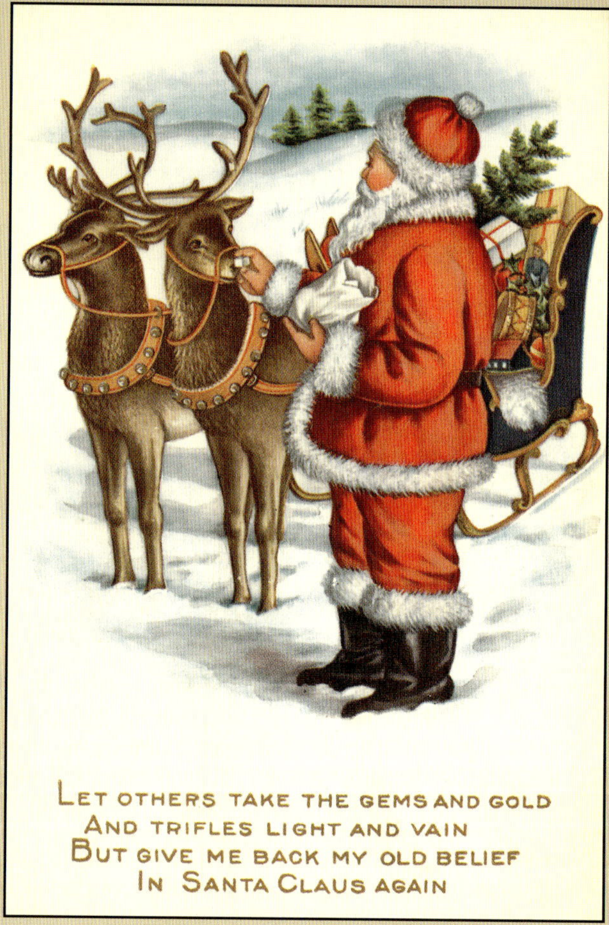
LET OTHERS TAKE THE GEMS AND GOLD
AND TRIFLES LIGHT AND VAIN
BUT GIVE ME BACK MY OLD BELIEF
IN SANTA CLAUS AGAIN

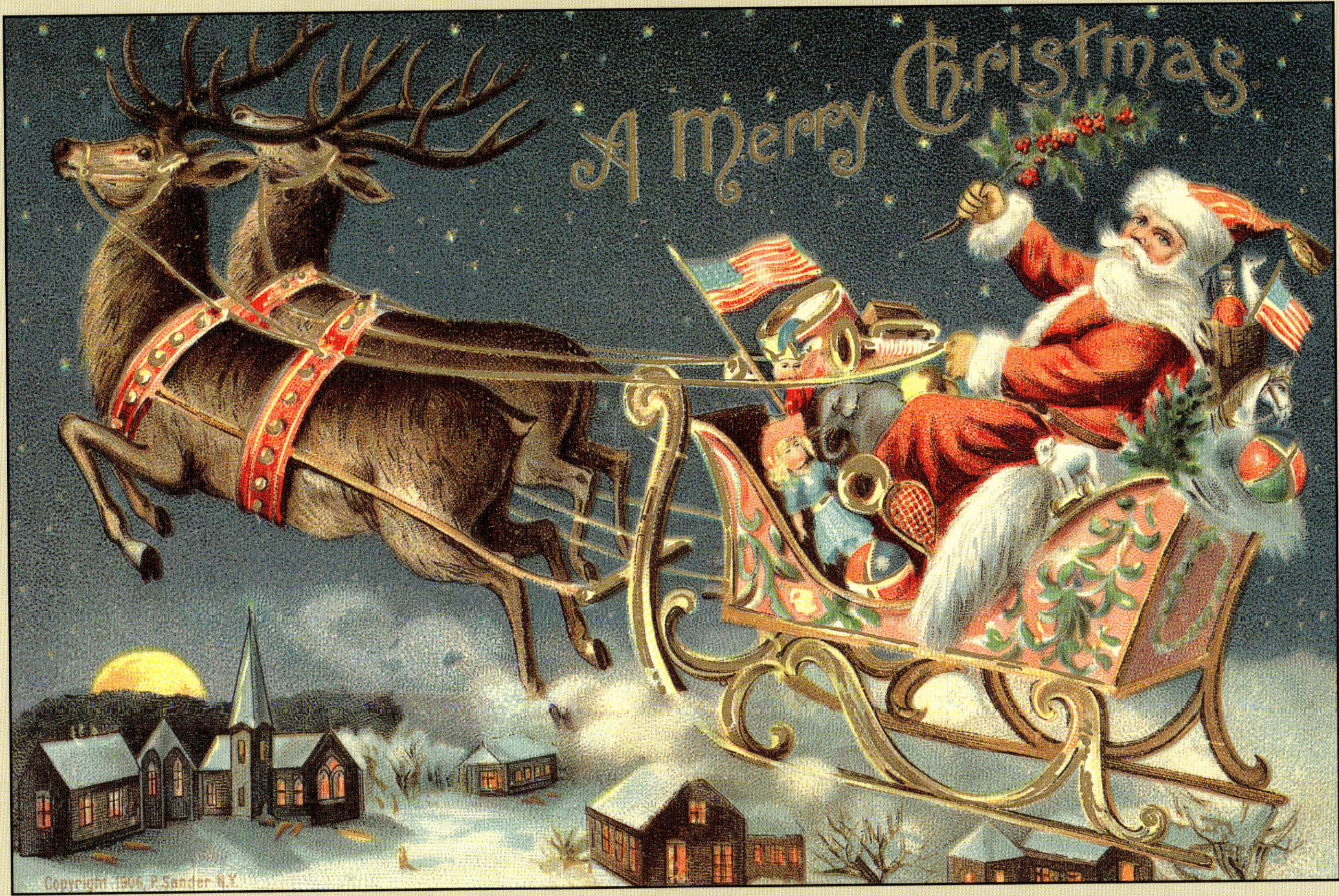
A Merry Christmas.
Copyright 1906, P. Sander N.Y.

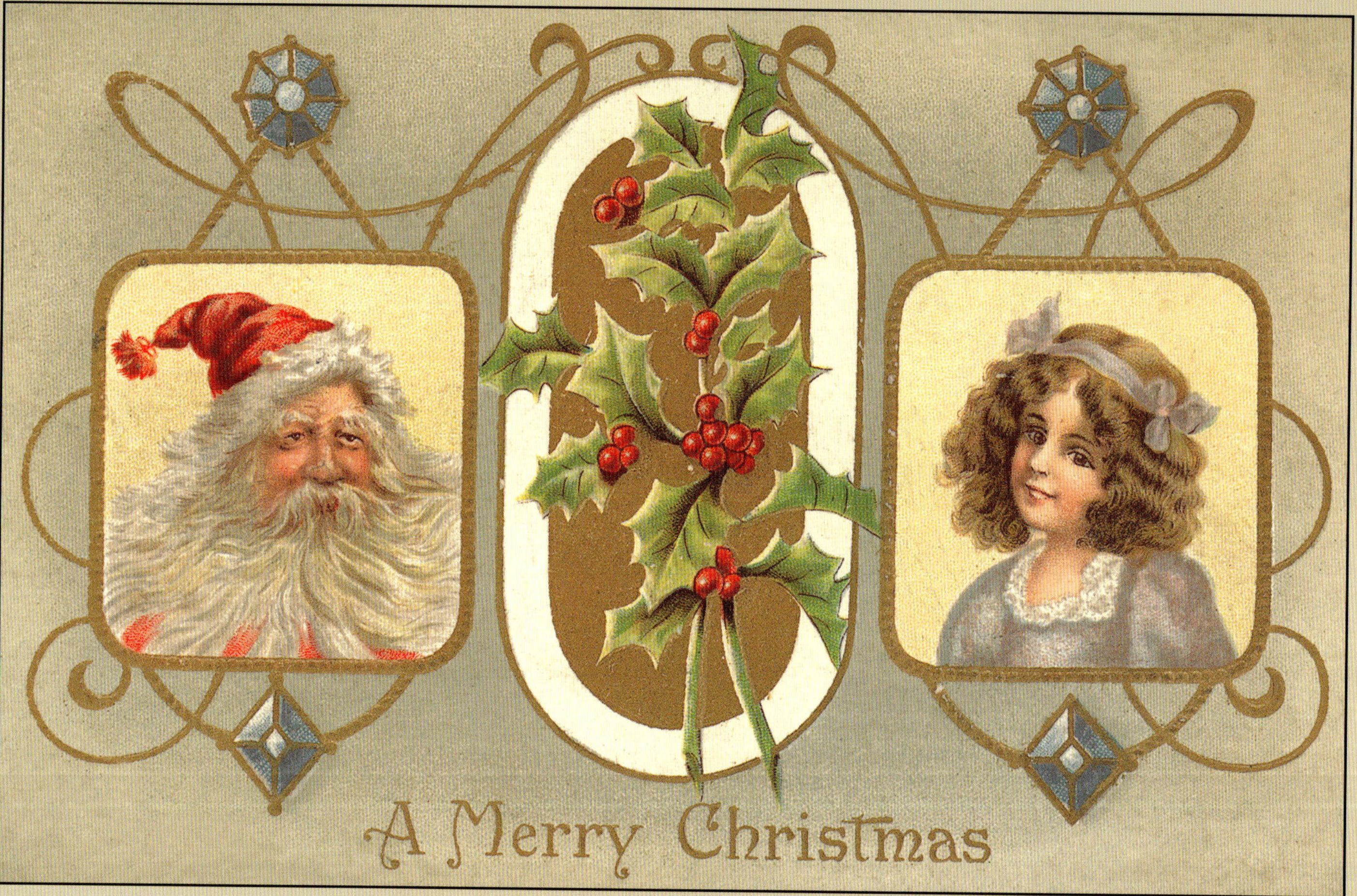
A Merry Christmas

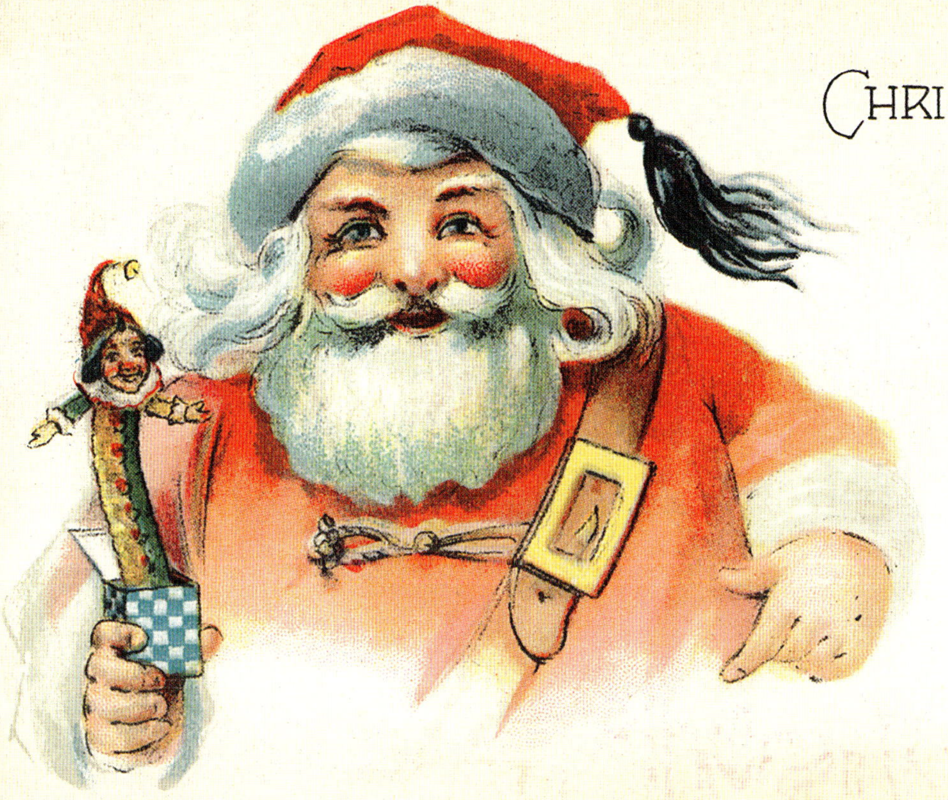

Christmas Greetings

No doubt you've
wishes, good
ones, too,
From Tom and
Dick and Andy,
But if it's what
I'm wishing
you,
Your Christmas
day's a dandy.

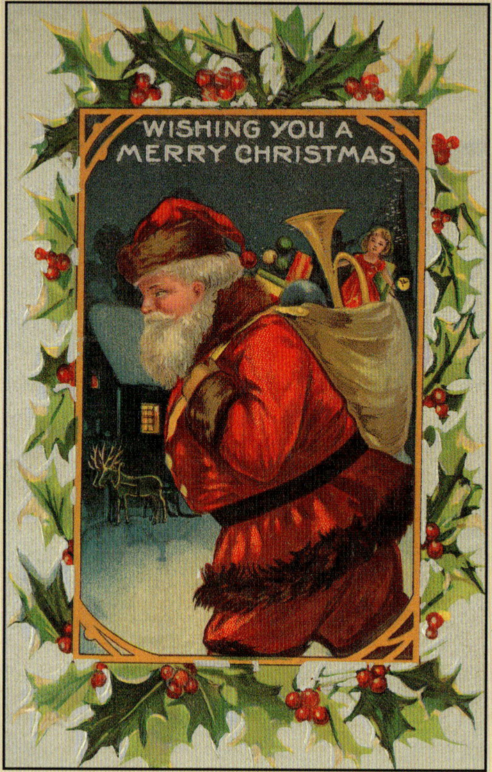
WISHING YOU A
MERRY CHRISTMAS

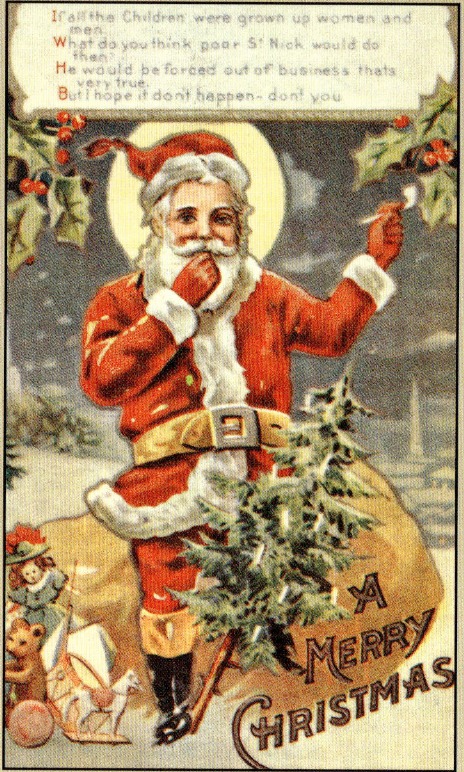
If all the Children were grown up women and men.
What do you think poor St Nick would do then?
He would be forced out of business thats very true.
But I hope it dont happen - dont you
A
MERRY
CHRISTMAS

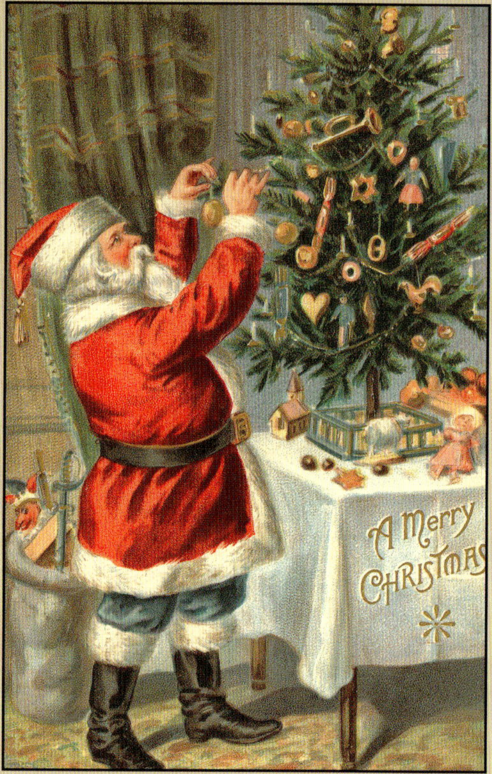
A Merry
CHRISTMAS

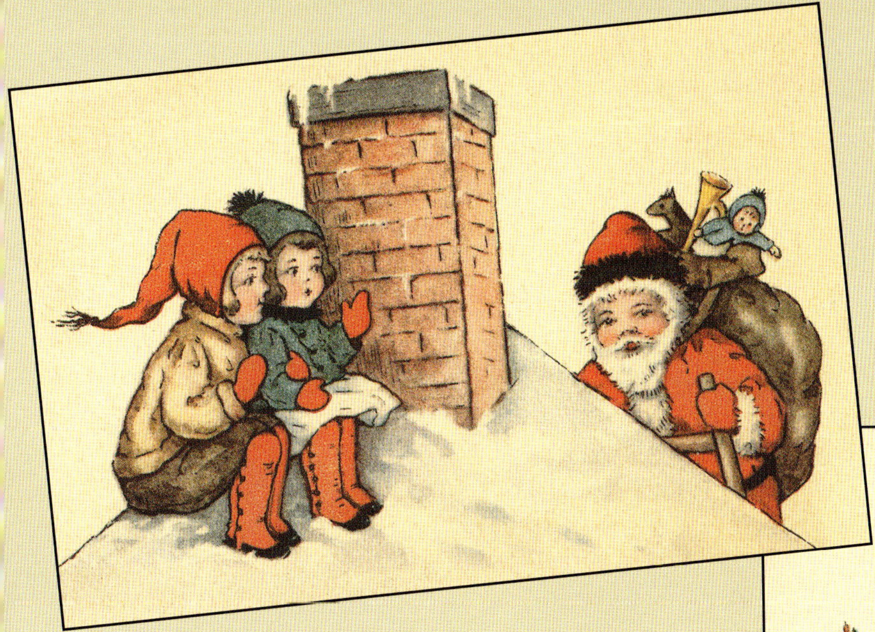

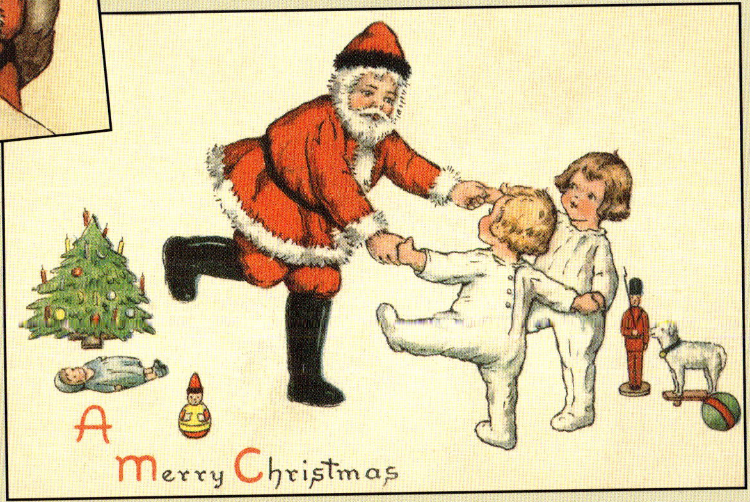
A
Merry Christmas

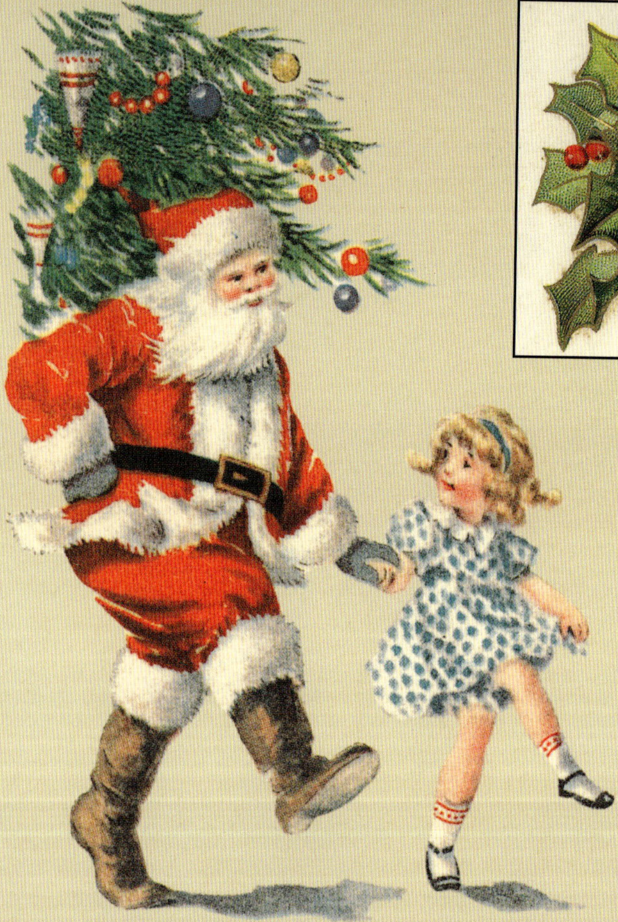

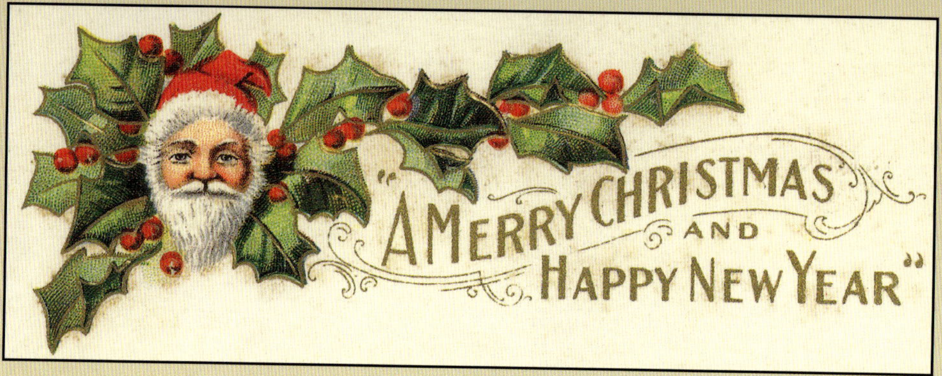
"A MERRY CHRISTMAS
AND
HAPPY NEW YEAR"

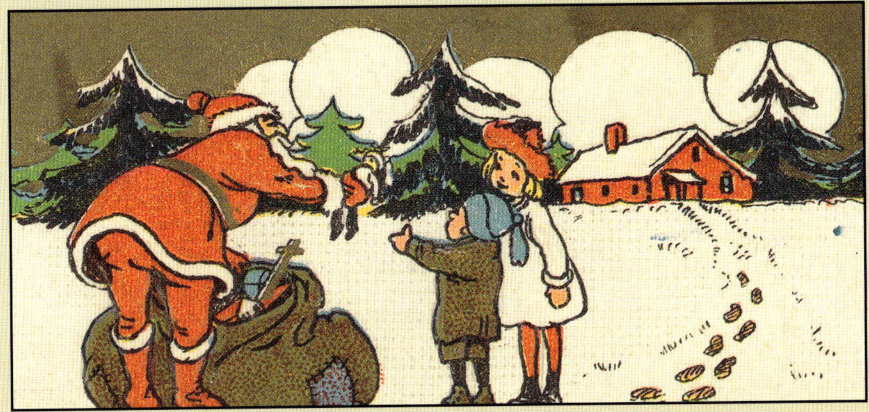

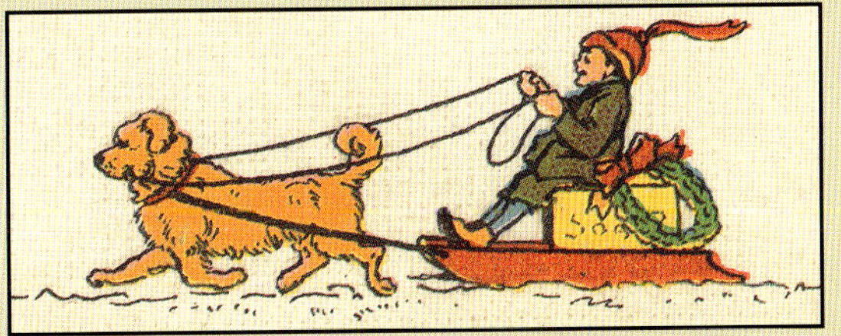

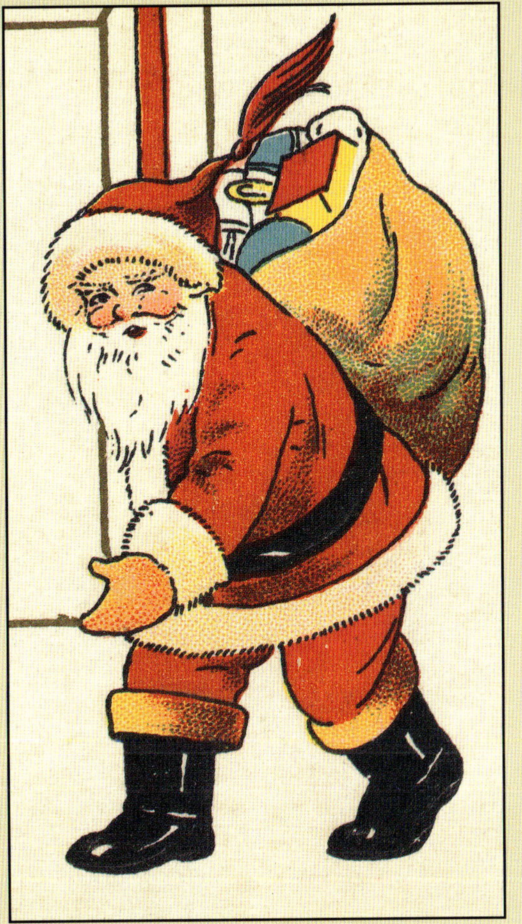

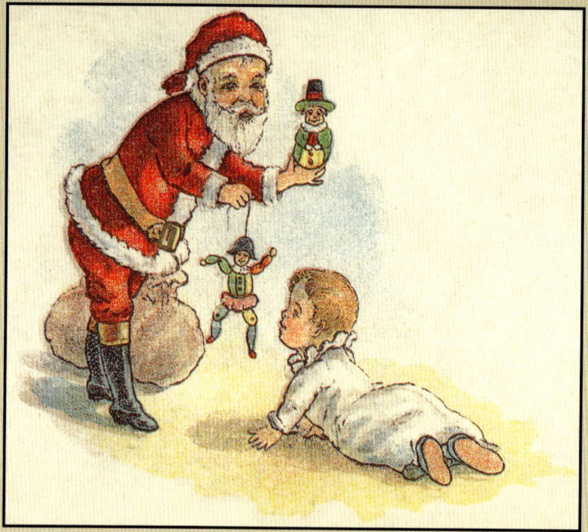

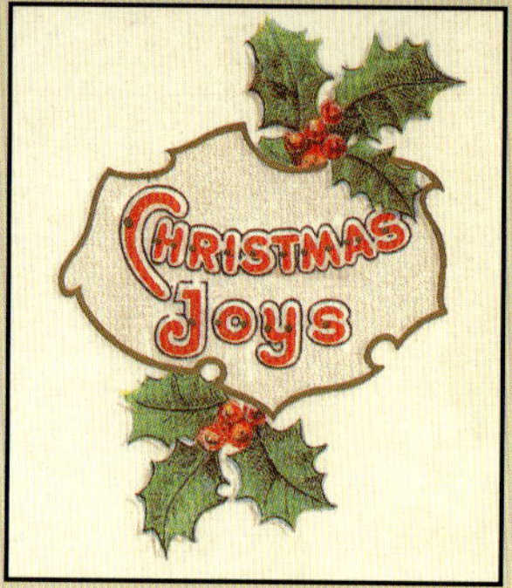
CHRISTMAS
JOYS

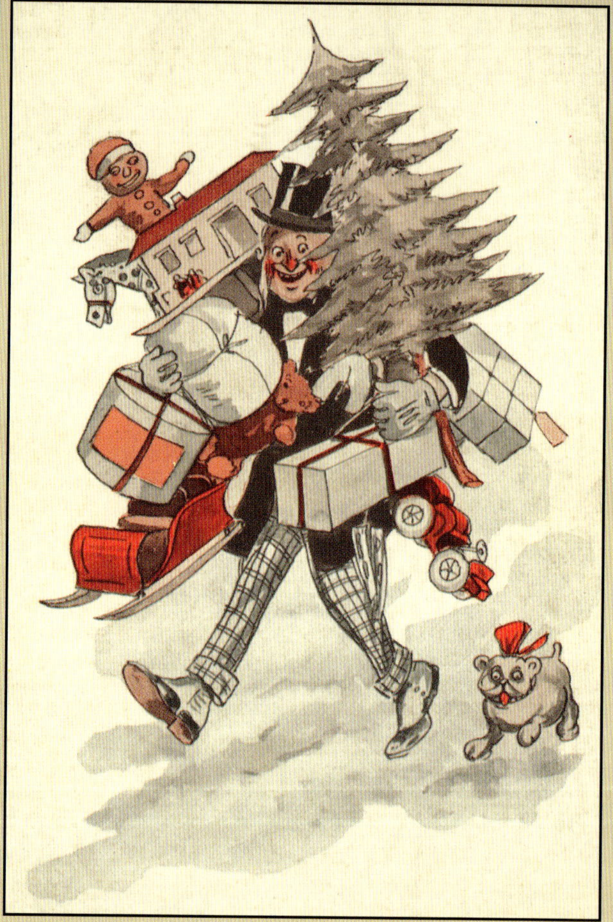

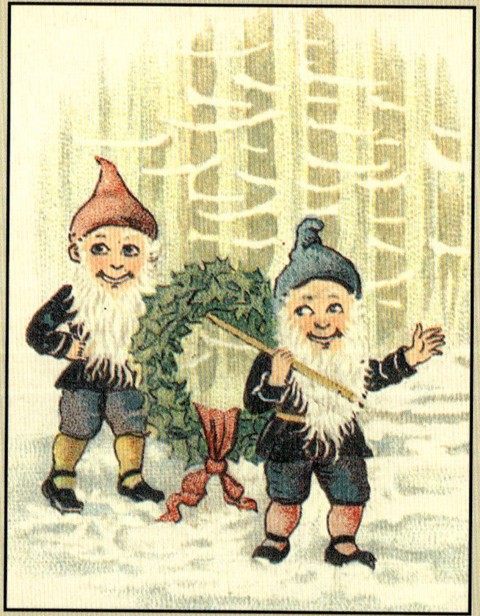

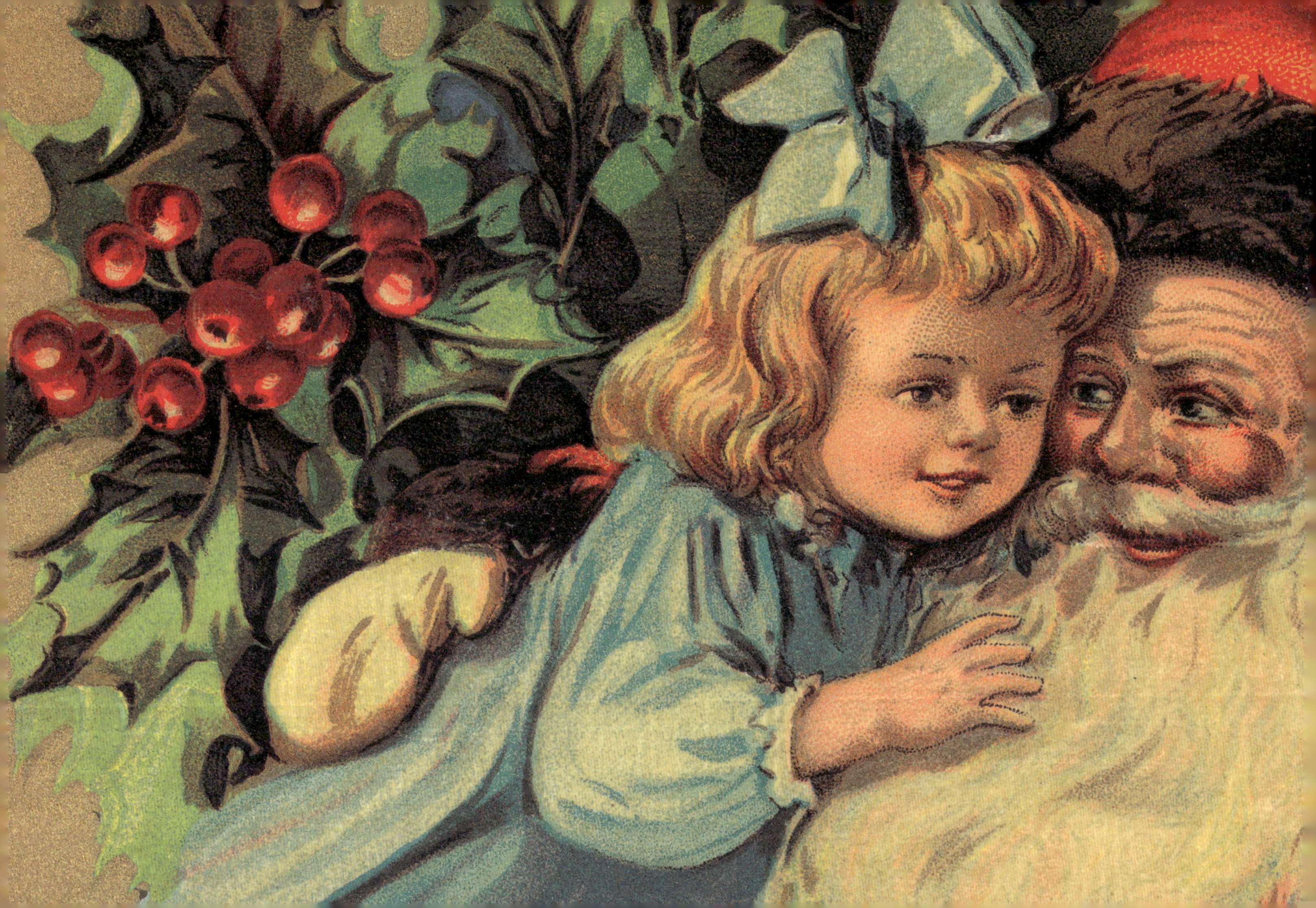